BEING HUMAN IN THE DIGITAL WORLD

Being Human in the Digital World is a collection of essays by prominent scholars from various disciplines exploring the impact of digitization on culture, politics, health, work, and relationships. The volume raises important questions about the future of human existence in a world where machine readability and algorithmic prediction are increasingly prevalent and offers new conceptual frameworks and vocabularies to help readers understand and challenge emerging paradigms of what it means to be human. *Being Human in the Digital World* is an invaluable resource for readers interested in the cultural, economic, political, philosophical, and social conditions that are necessary for a good digital life. This title is also available as Open Access on Cambridge Core.

Beate Roessler is a professor of philosophy at the University of Amsterdam. She is the author of *The Value of Privacy* (2004) and *Autonomy: An Essay on the Life Well-Lived* (2021). She is a member of the American Academy of Arts and Sciences.

Valerie Steeves is a professor in the Department of Criminology of the Faculty of Social Sciences at the University of Ottawa. She is the principal investigator of the eQuality Project, a multimillion-dollar project funded by the Social Sciences and Humanities Research Council of Canada researching young people's experiences online.

Being Human in the Digital World

INTERDISCIPLINARY PERSPECTIVES

Edited by

BEATE ROESSLER

University of Amsterdam

VALERIE STEEVES

University of Ottawa

CAMBRIDGE
UNIVERSITY PRESS

CAMBRIDGE
UNIVERSITY PRESS

Shaftesbury Road, Cambridge CB2 8EA, United Kingdom

One Liberty Plaza, 20th Floor, New York, NY 10006, USA

477 Williamstown Road, Port Melbourne, VIC 3207, Australia

314–321, 3rd Floor, Plot 3, Splendor Forum, Jasola District Centre, New Delhi – 110025, India

103 Penang Road, #05–06/07, Visioncrest Commercial, Singapore 238467

Cambridge University Press is part of Cambridge University Press & Assessment, a department of the University of Cambridge.

We share the University's mission to contribute to society through the pursuit of education, learning and research at the highest international levels of excellence.

www.cambridge.org
Information on this title: www.cambridge.org/9781009383875

DOI: 10.1017/9781009383851

First published 2025

A catalogue record for this publication is available from the British Library

A Cataloging-in-Publication data record for this book is available from the Library of Congress

ISBN 978-1-009-38387-5 Hardback

To Eli, Naomi, and Rebecca, who are the future

Contents

Acknowledgments

We are very grateful to a number of people who helped enormously during the various stages of putting this volume together. First, thanks to our authors, whose patience, cooperation, and commitment were invaluable throughout the process.

Helen Nissenbaum was especially helpful, as she cohosted the workshop we had at Cornell Tech in New York City where we met in person to discuss draft versions of each chapter. We are also grateful to Chloé S. Georas for the insightful and provocative photographs that grace the cover of the volume. To see more of Chloé's photo art, visit her unLine exhibition at www.equalityproject.ca/resources/unline-exhibition/.

Thanks as well to Matt Galloway at Cambridge, whose patience, professionalism, good will, and support were a tremendous help.

We also owe a debt of gratitude to the fantastic students who helped us with editing, citations, and formatting: Lukas H. Seidler, who has that rare combination of patience and perfectionism; and Franky Yousry, whose enthusiasm and creativity made our tasks much easier.

Lastly, we want to thank the Social Sciences and Humanities Research Council of Canada for their generous financial support.

Contributors

Azadeh Akbari University of Twente

Solon Barocas Cornell University/Microsoft Research

Julie E. Cohen Georgetown University

Chloé S. Georas University of Puerto Rico

Elizabeth Gray Intellectual property lawyer working in Ottawa, Canada

Margot Hanley Cornell Tech

David Lyon Queen's University

Jason Millar University of Ottawa

Helen Nissenbaum Cornell Tech

Frank Pasquale Cornell University Law School

Beate Roessler University of Amsterdam

Valerie Steeves University of Ottawa

Daniel Susser Cornell University

David Murakami Wood University of Ottawa

1

Introduction

Beate Roessler and Valerie Steeves

Over the past 20 years, digital technologies have been reshaping human activities: robots are reconfiguring work, personalized learning algorithms are changing education, social media are steering both private and public discourse, targeted advertising is driving consumption, and all in unanticipated and unprecedented ways. This digitization now permeates every fiber of our everyday lives, our relationships, and our self-understanding. As such, it not only reshapes how we communicate, learn, and do business, it also raises fundamental and as yet unanswered questions about what it means to be human in this new, emerging digitized world, particularly as we embed digital surveillance technologies into our bodies, our socio-political relationships, and our lived environments.

Until recently, the debates in the scholarly literature as well as in the more general public sphere about digital technologies have been dominated by the topics of privacy and surveillance, and specific utilizations of AI in industry, sciences, politics, culture, and social life. However, over the last dozen or so years, these debates have been enriched by a growing body of research that goes beyond specific areas or digitizable actions to address the more general, comprehensive questions about what datafication means for our lives and for our ideas of subjectivity and being human.

These debates about what is human obviously began long before the twentieth century. Since philosophy existed, philosophers have been thinking about the nature of human beings, the nature of the demarcation between humans and animals, the determination of (some, "real") humans based on specific characteristics (that often systematically exclude other humans), and the role of techniques for humans. The question of the human being had its peak in the enlightenment of the eighteenth century when the relevance of self-reference took its place at the centre of the debates: Kant claims in his anthropology: "The fact that the human being can have the 'I' in his representations raises him infinitely above all other living beings on earth." (Kant 2006 [1796], BA 3, 4). It is only in the late modernity of the twentieth and twenty-first century that the question is asked in a categorically new way: because the digitalization of society is so advanced and the tools of artificial intelligence are so efficient that one actually has to speak of a historical upheaval. The mode in which the questions about human nature are asked, about the finitude of the human being, about its vulnerability, about its ability to speak, and about its self-consciousness, has changed under the massive influence of recent technologies, notably AI. The change is manifest in all areas of life which have been digitized – language, communication in general, friendships and relationships in general, work, democracy. But the upheaval is maybe especially palpable in the economy: with digital or surveillance capitalism the market economy has taken on new forms thanks to categorically new technologies and the concentration of digital companies in the five or six biggest players (see Jasanoff 2016; Zuboff 2019). Since the digitized market has taken over all areas of human life, it has seemingly taken over what it means to be human as well.[1]

All these questions, against the background of the transformation of social life, will be addressed in our collection. On the one hand, we seek to explore fundamental issues, such as the extent to which the concept and idea of human beings (has to) change given the new socio-technical reality we are creating. On the other hand, we are also interested in more specific questions such as: What kinds of humans are expected to inhabit these new spaces? Will the machine learning that drives these spaces necessarily make us more predictable? What role, if any, is there for human agency in the emerging digital world?

To begin to address these questions, we gathered a group of leading scholars to reflect on how we – as individuals and as a society – change as digital technologies rewrite the fundamental conditions of our collective life and of our individual experiences of being human. We also asked these scholars to reflect on the kinds of vocabularies or conceptual frameworks that will give us the language we need to grapple with, understand and resist these conditions. We believe that this is an important conversation to initiate because how we as a society answer these questions will be among the defining issues of the coming years and decades.

In order to frame and delimit our conversations, we would first like to clarify how we will and will not engage with certain conceptual and normative approaches. Our goal in this introduction is accordingly to better situate ourselves in the current debates about the technological influence on and interaction with human beings. In the background – and sometimes in the foreground – of our discussions about the digital human are two theoretical trends that have attracted a great deal of attention over the last decades and have led to (at least) two central philosophical debates: posthumanism and transhumanism. We are briefly going to sketch each one in turn.

[1] This complete digitization of everyday life, the engineering of humans and the aim of perfect machine readability of everything we do (Frischmann and Selinger 2018; Selinger and Frischmann 2015; Stivers and DeHart-Davis 2022; see also Chapter 6) can also be read in the tradition of the Weberian theory of modernization as bureaucratization and therefore dehumanization of social relationships and society as a whole (see Slope 2022; on Weber, e.g. Brühlmeier 2024).

1.1 POSTHUMANISM

Posthumanism has two essential characteristics. First, it builds on critical genealogies of the concept of the human being: posthumanism argues that the concept in humanism only referred to the white male human being and as such legitimized exclusion and oppression of non-white people and women. Therefore, many post humanist philosophers and theorists of the humanities in the twentieth and twenty-first century have argued that the very conceptualization of a human being from the start is part of a practice – or at least collusive with practices – which justified the exclusion of women and all non-white people from the privileges of the moral community of human beings.

Such critical genealogies continue to be directed against universalist theorists such as Jürgen Habermas and his unambiguous opposition between pro-enlightenment modernity and counter-enlightenment postmodernity. Habermas (1996) clearly criticized the usage of an *exclusionary* concept of human being himself, and his critique of postmodernism goes hand in hand with his staunch defense of the normative content of modernity (see Allen 2017, 177; Habermas 1990; Wellmer 1991). From the post humanist perspective, this is synonymous with the pursuit of the traditional scientific justifications which lie at the heart of their efforts to delegitimize humanism, since all modern attempts to design a world based on these justifications point, or so they argue, toward humanity's deep-seated inhumanity (see Braidotti and Hlavajova 2018; Hayles 2008). One of the important post humanist voices, Rosi Braidotti, concludes that we should not clutch at the concept of human being, which is only an "outdated position" (Braidotti 2019, 3).

There is an obvious conflict between "modernists" like Habermas and some of the post humanists like Braidotti, but of course (as we will also see in this volume) many attempts have been made to find a way forward by holding on to a concept of the human and of accompanying normative convictions (such as human autonomy and human rights) without accepting the exclusionary and oppressive implications of traditional humanist concepts of human nature (see for instance Chapter 5 by Lyon and Chapter 3 by Roessler). Among these, Habermas himself is also critical of the exclusionary and racist consequences of the concept of human beings and argues that a more correctly understood concept is emancipatory for everyone.

The second essential characteristic of post humanist theories is their strong critique of all dichotomies. Posthumanism even aims at the *general* overcoming of common scientific dichotomies and many postmodern theories pin their hopes for this on technology. Therefore, from this perspective, the dichotomy between humans and technology clearly must be overcome to correct the fundamental misconceptualization of this relationship that has troubled philosophy.

This is why Donna Haraway occupies a prominent place in this debate. Haraway (2016) takes the cyborg as a paradigm and aims to achieve not only a postmodernist, non-naturalist mode but also a socialist–feminist culture rooted in the utopian tradition of imagining a world without gender. It is the dichotomy between human and animal, between animal–human and machine, and between physical and nonphysical which lies at the centre of her critique in her Cyborg Manifesto. The cyborg is, according to Haraway, a combination of machine and organism, of technology and human being, and she develops a new ontology based on the hybridization of nature and culture. Her Manifesto has been especially influential in feminist debates since she conceptualized the cyborg as a powerful woman. She writes: "By the late twentieth century, our time, a mythic time, we are all chimeras, theorized and fabricated hybrids of machine and organism – in short, cyborgs. The cyborg is our ontology; it gives us our politics" (Haraway 2016, 44).

Haraway and others place themselves in opposition to philosophical positions like Habermas', but also taken up by Joseph Weizenbaum. Weizenbaum (1976) is an especially suitable example because he is one of the revolutionary computer technologists of the twentieth century and at the same time wants to hold on to the so-called traditional and modernist human values and concepts like autonomy and human rights. Hayles, for example, writes:

> Hence there is an urgency, even panic, in Weizenbaum's insistence that judgment is a uniquely human function. At stake for him is nothing less than what it means to be human. In the posthuman view, by contrast, conscious agency has never been "in control". In fact, the very illusion of control bespeaks a fundamental ignorance about the nature of the emergent processes through which consciousness, the organism, and the environment are constituted. Mastery through the exercise of autonomous will is merely the story consciousness tells itself to explain results that actually come about through chaotic dynamics and emergent structures. (Hayles 2020, 288)

This brief look at the post humanist discourse shows various questions that will continue to play a role in the following chapters: the compatibility of human nature and technology; its ideological roots; the finality of human existence; and whether (or how) this existence can be overcome or surmounted. Hayles and Ferrando, to name but two, seem to be keeping some elements of the traditional idea of human nature as they seek to go beyond how Weizenbaum and others conceptualize the human in a liberal humanism. Returning to classical theories of human nature or even insisting on these theories fundamentally because of their normative content (as Habermas and many other defenders of human rights do) remains controversial. The critical attempts, however, do not entail abandoning the idea that there is something worth preserving in human beings' vulnerable nature.

One position within the post humanist discourse deserves particular attention, namely that of the post-phenomenologists. Why might it be a problem that humans are striving to become more open to being "technologized"? In a first step, following the post-phenomenologists, this concerns the more general question of the relation between human beings and technology. It is helpful to turn to Don Ihde (1990) because he is one of the most influential contemporary thinkers in post-phenomenological discourses on humans and technology. Ihde connects to phenomenology's fundamental critique (in the tradition of Heidegger and Merleau-Ponty) of the Cartesian and Kantian dichotomies between subject and object and, thus, their epistemological primacy or precedence over what Ihde calls the "praxical orientations for philosophy" (Heidegger 2010; Ihde 1990, 31).[2] This traditional dichotomy obscures the fact, according to Ihde, that our perceptions and experiences are always already mediated by technology – from Heidegger's hammer to, for instance, the smartphone (see Jasanoff 2016). This mediation co-shapes our concepts as well as our experiences of subjectivity and objectivity. Furthermore, we must assume that we get used to technologies to such a degree that they become unnoticeable and grow to be part of us, and yet mediate our relation to the world. Ihde (1990) coined the image of technologies functioning like spectacles: when we use such technologies, they recede from view. We attend not to the spectacles themselves, but to what we can see *through* them (see Verbeek 2011). Verbeek, one of Don Ihde's students, clarifies this idea and process of shaping and mediating by explaining the way a "personal digital assistant" (e.g. the mobile phone) works:

> A PDA helps to shape its user's existence and experience; it shapes specific aspects of its user's subjectivity and the objectivity of that user's world. It is more than a functional instrument and far more than a mere product of "calculative thinking." It mediates the relation between humans and world, and thus co-shapes their experience and existence. (Verbeek 2011, 198–199)

In one sense, this certainly must be right: we shape and form technologies and thereby shape our world, whereas at the same time we are being formed and shaped by these technologies and their "affordances." However, will it still be possible to demarcate, to delimit humans and technologies? This is not completely clear in the post-phenomenological approach, and Ihde (1990), for one, seems to avoid taking a critical look at the way in which technologies determine our lives. Since human beings are always already mired in technologies, a critical perspective that focuses precisely on the influence of technologies on our life and social practices is here seemingly impossible.

1.2 TRANSHUMANISM

Transhumanism, in stark opposition to posthumanism, begins its criticism from the opposite side and seeks its origins in the Enlightenment, and therefore does not expropriate humanism; on the contrary, it can be defined as an "ultra-humanism" (Onishi 2011). In order to greatly enhance human abilities, transhumanism opts for a

[2] See the debate about the "neutrality" of technology, on the question whether technologies are the *Gestell* (the enframing) or the *Bestand* (the standing reserve) which place us in the world at the same time as in technologies (or the *Technik*) (for instance Borgmann 1984; Ihde 1990; Verbeek 2011; Winner 2020).

radical transformation of the human condition through existing, emerging, and speculative technologies, such as regenerative medicine, radical life extension, mind uploading, and cryonics (see Ferrando 2019). The post-phenomenologists, like Ihde (1990), as we have seen would not want to take part in that, since for them the question is not one of exceeding human abilities, but only of successfully cooperating with technologies. Ihde's perspective acknowledges that in our lived experiences we seem to understand every day anew that we do not have complete control over our bodies and its vulnerabilities – something the transhumanists want to change or, better, to supersede. It is precisely the idea of striving to have complete control over our bodies that inspires the transhumanist fantasy and imagination and feeds transhumanist theories. The overcoming of corporeality and the attempt to turn the body into trans-humans is, for Nick Bostrom, probably the best known and most influential of the transhumanists, the explicit aim. According to him, transcending the human body is a human desire present in all times and all cultures. This desire is now no longer a childish dream but, for the first time in history, has been turned into a proper scientific project. What these transhumanist philosophical approaches share is the idea that we should as far as possible get rid of our "wetware" (see Lovink 1997) and of all malaises connected to it. The body is mostly seen as an obstacle to freedom. Note that, not only but especially in the transhuman variant, these theories are all individualistic: although relationships are possible, they are not necessary for human thriving, and intersubjectivity is not the fundamental and genuine characteristic of a life well lived.

Clearly, transhumanists are not interested in the critique of concepts such as reason or autonomy, a critique which is, as we have seen, the fundamental interest of posthumanism (see again Ferrando 2019; Hayles 2008, 288). Rather, transhumanism is concerned with getting a technological grip on finiteness, on limited cognitive capacities, and on vulnerability, and aiming to technologically eradicate – or at least reduce as far as possible – these human weaknesses. From this perspective, science and technology are extremely helpful because they are the instruments that will enhance and transform human nature.

Unlike posthumanism, then, transhumanism explicitly builds on the concept of the human being, but the human being in its ideal version (see Anthony 2024; Bostrom 2005; also Kurzweil 2006). Julian Huxley, one of the first eponymous transhumanists, strove to use technology to transcend human nature in this way. From the start, though, one of the central themes was that it is not only important and desirable but also possible at some point in the future to overcome illness, aging, and even death.[3] Of course, *prima facie* this is not completely implausible:

[3] Max More (2013, 13); See Sorgner (2022) on the pluralistic forms of transhumanist theories. Philosophically one of the difficult problems in these debates is how to get from the structural biological or empirical level to the normative one. Why should we treat humans (in a natural sense) in a respectful way, why should we not try to transcend them, and where does the normativity come from? (see Korsgaard 1996; Chapter 4 by Pasquale; Chapter 3 by Roessler).

medicine is nothing other than making people better with the help of the cognitive capacities of humans and, if necessary, technologies. However, how far we should go with the possibilities that technologies make available to us remains a contested question.

Maybe we could say that, if we were as human as we can be in our *best* moments, there would be no reason for the transhumanist to transcend us. This question of *how we could best be human* seems to be essential because, in all criticisms of transforming human nature (in posthumanism as well as in transhumanism), we have to be conscious of a rather fundamental question: what's so good about being human that we want to hold on to it?

1.3 OVERVIEW OF THE CHAPTERS

This question is also what the following chapters have in common. In various contributions, human intersubjectivity is of decisive concern (see for instance Chapter 8, by Steeves), an aspect of the human being that is, as we have already seen, perceptibly absent from the postmodernist as well as the transhumanist theories. Others examine the messy social practices in which people are always already anchored and which, for traditional theories of human nature, constitute a substantial and fundamental aspect of being human (see for instance Chapter 4, by Pasquale) or demonstrate that these practices do not seem to be a relevant element in the pursuit of the perfect transhuman being (see Chapter 2, by Murakami Wood). All the following contributions assume that it is possible to hold on to the concept of the human being and still conceptualize the changes – possibly also conceptual changes – that accompany the digitization of our societies. Accordingly, our collection aims at presenting new conceptual frameworks and vocabularies to help us understand and challenge emerging paradigms of what should be human and humanly possible for the digitized person, and to elucidate the economic, political, or social conditions that are necessary for a good digital life. The collection, as we understand it, is accordingly a further step toward thinking about and discussing the grounds for the possible and ongoing transformations of being human.

Part I begins by examining the types of people and social spaces anticipated by the technology companies building the platforms that undergird the digital world and offers conceptual means to evaluate the ways that this technical vision supports and at the same time constrains human striving for autonomy and meaningful relationships.

David Murakami Wood (Chapter 2) starts the section off by analyzing smart city marketing materials to create a detailed description of the kind of human who is expected to reside in these cities. He offers a fascinating portrait of the "platform human," a being whose entrepreneurial and libertarian needs are seamlessly enabled by technology built into the lived environment in ways that resonate strongly with the transhumanist imaginary. In sharp contrast, Beate Roessler's contribution (Chapter 3) explores the centrality that self-consciousness, vulnerability, and finiteness play in being human, and uses Ian McEwan's novel, *Machines Like Me* to explore the unprogrammability that defines humanness. Frank Pasquale (Chapter 4) also draws from the world of literature and film to explore the role of emotions in being human and the ways that affective computing both seeks to duplicate and constrain caring as a fundamental human quality. In the final chapter in this section (Chapter 5), David Lyon reflects on the COVID epidemic to think about the instrumentalizing role of surveillance capitalism in digital society. He offers Eric Stoddart's notion of the "common gaze" as a counterpoint to begin to articulate what it might mean to flourish in the digital world.

Part II examines central aspects of living within these digitized platforms, specifically those concerned with how the demands of machine readability and algorithmic prediction shape the possibilities of human existence.

Margot Hanely, Solon Barocas, and Helen Nissenbaum (Chapter 6) argue that we have moved beyond being legible to systems of assessment to being remade as machine readable humans who are more vulnerable to systems of control. They review and discuss a variety of apps to explore when this machine readability may or may not be ethical. In Chapter 7, Chloé S. Georas does a deep dive into carebots to unpack how care technologies rewrite the material and discursive underpinnings of caring as a central part of humanness. Valerie Steeves (Chapter 8) provides an empirical snapshot of the networked "community" and draws on understandings of intersubjective communication developed by G. H. Mead to better understand emerging notions of self and other in order to reclaim normative space for any sense of agency. Azadeh Akbari (Chapter 9) focuses on digital embodiment and the experiences of the most marginal as they move through borders, using poetry to help relieve "the linguistic distress for finding the right words to describe embodied feelings" in digitalized geographies.

Part III focuses attention on new approaches to technology policy that can better grapple with the human issues raised by digitization. In Chapter 10, Daniel Susser provides a thoughtful examination of what we mean by (digital) exploitation and suggests that regulation should constrain platform activities that instrumentalize people or treat them unfairly. Jason Millar and Elizabeth Gray (Chapter 11) detail emerging uses of mobility tracking and draw an analogy to net neutrality to think through potential regulatory approaches. Finally, in Chapter 12, Julie E. Cohen adapts the doughnut model of sustainable economic development to suggest ways for policymakers to identify regulatory policies that can better serve the humans who live in digital spaces.

We hope to have put together a volume with interestingly different perspectives and stimulating new insights which can open up new ways for us to think about what it means to be human in the digital world.

REFERENCES

Allen, Amy. "Poststructuralism." In *The Habermas Handbook*, edited by Hauke Brunkhorst, Regina Kreide, and Cristina Lafont, 177–183. New York: Columbia University Press, 2017.

Anthony, Andrew. "'Eugenics on Steroids': The Toxic and Contested Legacy of Oxford's Future of Humanity Institute." *The Guardian*, April 28, 2024.

Borgmann, Albert. *Technology and the Character of Contemporary Life. A Philosophical Inquiry*. Chicago: University of Chicago Press, 1984.

Bostrom, Nick. "A History of Transhumanist Thought." *Journal of Evolution and Technology* 14, no. 1 (2005): 1–25.

Braidotti, Rosi. *Posthuman Knowledge*, 1st ed. Cambridge: Polity Press, 2019.

Braidotti, Rosi, and Maria Hlavajova, eds. *The Posthuman Glossary*. London: Bloomsbury, 2018.

Brühlmeier, Daniel. "Das 'stahlharte Gehäuse': Zwei Beobachtungen zu Max Webers berühmter Metapher." *Berliner Journal für Soziologie* 34 (2024): 129–144. https://doi.org/10.1007/s11609-024-00518-3.

Ferrando, Francesca. *Philosophical Posthumanism*. Kindle ed. London: Bloomsbury Publishing, 2019.

Frischmann, Brett, and Evan Selinger. *Re-Engineering Humanity*. Cambridge: Cambridge University Press, 2018.

Habermas, Jürgen. *Between Facts and Norms. Contributions to a Discourse Theory of Law and Democracy*, translated by William Rehg. Cambridge, MA: MIT Press, 1996.

The Philosophical Discourse of Modernity: Twelve Lectures, translated by Frederick G. Lawrence. Cambridge, MA: MIT Press, 1990.

Haraway, Donna J. "A Cyborg Manifesto: Science, Technology, and Socialist-Feminism in the Late Twentieth Century." In *Manifestly Haraway*, edited by Donna J. Haraway and Cary Wolfe, 3–90. Minneapolis: University of Minnesota Press, 2016. www.jstor.org/stable/10.5749/j.ctt1b7x5f6.

Hayles, N. Katherine. *How We Became Posthuman*. Chicago: University of Chicago Press, 2020.

How We Became Posthuman: Virtual Bodies in Cybernetics, Literature, and Informatics. Kindle ed. Chicago: University of Chicago Press, 2008.

Heidegger, Martin. *Being and Time: A Revised Edition of the Stambaugh Translation*. SUNY series in Contemporary Continental Philosophy. New York: State University of New York Press, 2010.

Ihde, Don. *Technology and the Lifeworld: From Garden to Earth*. Bloomington, IN: Indiana University Press, 1990. https://philarchive.org/rec/IHDTAT-3.

Jasanoff, Sheila. *The Ethics of Invention: Technology and the Human Future*. New York: Norton, 2016.

Kant, Immanuel. *Anthropology from a Pragmatic Point of View*, edited and translated by Robert B. Louden. Annotated ed. 1796. Reprint. Cambridge: Cambridge University Press, 2006.

Korsgaard, Christine. *The Sources of Normativity*. Cambridge: Cambridge University Press, 1996.

Kurzweil, Ray. *The Singularity Is Near: When Humans Transcend Biology*. London: Penguin Books, 2006.

Lovink, Geert. *Hardware, Software, Wetware, Adilkno* (The Foundation for the Advancement of Illegal Knowledge). 1997. www.nettime.org/Lists-Archives/nettime-l-9606/msg00026.html.

More, Max. "The Philosophy of Transhumanism." In *The Transhumanist Reader*, edited by Max More and Natasha Vita-More, 3–17. Chichester: John Wiley & Sons, Ltd., 2013. https://doi.org/10.1002/9781118555927.ch1.

Onishi, Brian B. "Information, Bodies, and Heidegger: Tracing Visions of the Posthuman." *Sophia* 50, no. 1 (2011): 101–112. https://doi.org/10.1007/s11841-010-0214-4.

Selinger, Evan, and Brett Frischmann. "Will the Internet of Things Result in Predictable People?" *The Guardian*, August 10, 2015. www.theguardian.com/technology/2015/aug/10/internet-of-things-predictable-people.

Slope, Rowena. *Care in the Iron Cage. A Weberian Analysis of Failings in Care*. London: Routledge, 2022.

Sorgner, Stefan Lorenz. *On Transhumanism*. Pennsylvania: Pennsylvania State University, 2022.

Stivers, Camilla, and Leisha DeHart-Davis, eds. Symposion Issue on Reappraising Burocracy in the 21st Century. *Perspectives on Public Management and Governance* 5, no. 2 (June 2022).

Verbeek, Peter-Paul. *Moralizing Technology: Understanding and Designing the Morality of Things*. Chicago: University of Chicago Press, 2011.

Weizenbaum, Joseph. *Computer Power and Human Reason: From Judgement to Calculation*. New York: W. H. Freeman Ltd, 1976.

Wellmer, Albrecht. *The Persistence of Modernity: Aesthetics, Ethics, and Postmodernism*. Cambridge: Polity Press, 1991.

Winner, Langdon. *The Whale and the Reactor: A Search for Limits in an Age of High Technology*. Chicago: University of Chicago Press, 2020.

Zuboff, Shoshana. *The Age of Surveillance Capitalism: The Fight for a Human Future at the New Frontier of Power*. New York: Public Affairs, 2019.

PART I

Conceptualizing the Digital Human

2

Platform City People

David Murakami Wood

In the course of my research on what I am now thinking about as the transition from smart cities to platform cities, I almost immediately began to ask what the characteristics of the proposed *platform citizens*, the humans who will live in these places, were. There has been writing on "smart citizens" and much of this takes a normative stance, even when critical. On the one hand, many such pieces argue for the displacement or supplementing of the concept of the "smart city" with that of the "smart citizen," in other words as a form of empowerment or bottom-up development or even as a way of ameliorating the potential negative and technocentric effects of smart city development (see e.g. Cardullo and Kitchin 2019; Powell 2021, for critical takes on this genre). On the other hand, some approaches to smart citizenship have taken an integrative approach, considering what people, suitably educated, can add to the smart city, in other words how they can become part of this vision of smart urbanism or smart governance more broadly (e.g. Noveck 2015).

However, the aim of this preliminary and somewhat experimental intervention is not a normative one but is at once empirical and theoretical. I want to concentrate on the way in which the proposed inhabitants of platform cities are imagined by the developers and promotors of these cities, in other words how the developers understand the "nature" of the inhabitants of their specific kind of these neoliberal smart urban developments. I show that the envisaged inhabitants of such platform cities are a specific kind of human being, not humanity in general but platform city people who combine a technologically enabled class and political identity (property owning, entrepreneurial, libertarian) with generic environmental "goodness," that verges on an imagination of transhumanist speciation (data-driven, surveillant, robotic).

2.1 THE PLATFORM CITY

The concept of the platform city is my own and is not (yet) a general one. It is not the primary purpose of this chapter to describe platform cities in general; however, I do need to provide a brief outline of the concept and of the broader argument here.

In the planetary age, emerging conjunctions of technology, surveillance, security, and urbanism are networking ordinary objects and infrastructures via the "Internet of Things," "... a global infrastructure for the Information Society ... interconnecting things based on ... interoperable information and communication technologies" (ITU 2012). Up until this point, the primary urban instantiation has been termed the "smart city" (Coletta et al. 2018; Hall et al. 2000; Marvin et al. 2015). The smart city is an "urban assemblage" (Venn 2006), characterized by "sociotechnical imaginaries" (Jasanoff and Kim 2015) of pervasive and seamless wireless networks and distributed sensor platforms from video surveillance to meteorological stations, monitoring flows from sewerage to traffic to criminal activities and providing information in real-time or in anticipation of risks. Surveillance and security are uneasy components of these visions, but smart cities are inevitably disciplinary structures (Vanolo 2014) or surveillance cities (Murakami Wood 2015), because technocentric management of urban flows structurally requires data *about* everything, including people, and simultaneously requires everything, including people, to also *be* data (Mattern 2021; cf. Kitchin 2014).

"Actually existing smart cities" (Shelton et al. 2015) have often been unimpressive and radically incomplete (Murakami Wood and Mackinnon 2019). An early project, Rio de Janeiro's IBM-sponsored Smart City control room, was lauded by then Mayor Eduardo Paes as giving him the ability to manage the city from anywhere (Murakami Wood 2013), but it has had little long-term impact on urban security in Rio. Studies of India's "hundred smart cities" policy have shown that the ambitious scheme is creating very different and not necessarily compatible official and subaltern imaginations of urban futures and concepts of citizenship. In other words, while the official aims may always have been overpromised, citizens themselves have attempted to harness the opportunities offered to generate their own realities (Datta 2018, 2019).

However, before and during the now almost 20-year history of smart cities, there have been pre-existing and parallel histories of other urban forms like Freeports, Charter Cities, Special Investment Zones or Enterprise Zones, leisure/tourist cities like Las Vegas or Dubai, exclusive cities from gated communities to massive projects like Brazil's Alphavilles (see e.g. Caldeira 2001; Davis and Monk 2008; Graham and Marvin 2001), to the whole recent history of police and military urbanism (Graham 2011). For precursors, one can look to Malaysia's 1990s-in-origin Multimedia Super Corridor (Bunnell 2002) consisting of the twin cities of Putraya (administration) and Cyberjaya (business), or the much cited South Korean business district of Songdo (Halpern et al. 2013), and, of course, Singapore, a city-state that has come to stand for a great deal in this new model (Calder 2016; Mahizhnan 1999), probably much more than its actual history can bear (Walton 2019). The more educated designers also look to the modernist *tabula rasa* ideology of Le Corbusier's Plan Voisin or Ville Radieuse, or Costa and Niemeyer's Brasilia, but stripped of the latter's mid-century socialism, which is portrayed now as a naïve post-war dream of a common humanity, lost following the neoliberal turn of the 1970s which admitted no other options but free-market capitalism (see Slobodian 2018).

In various ways these other histories have intersected with smart cities and are often considered as simply another aspect of the same phenomenon. What I am examining is one such convergence: billion-dollar projects for new cities or urban neighbourhoods that demonstrate characteristics of several of these ideal urban forms. These hybrids are corporate-oriented and neoliberal whether or not they are created or managed by corporations directly. These are what I term *platform cities* because they exist on a foundation with a specific kind of neoliberal capitalism, which has important implications for the place of democracy in relation to the economy, and to which I shall return later.

There are significant differences between these new platform cities, which I explore in other pieces, but what is equally striking are the shared material and ideological elements. Briefly, the first of these is a noticeable, sometimes advertised, degree of separation from the surrounding polity, varying from at least some kind of local economic, social, cultural, or political autonomy through to a full-blown city-state model. Singapore's "smart nation" or the leisure/investment metropolis of Dubai are of course the inspirations here, but there are many older examples or even those to be found in fiction that are cited by proponents. Singapore is a particular example to this latest wave of platform city developers, mainly for its politics rather than its technological aspects: the concept of an independent city-state appeals partly at least because it is free from the supposedly constrictive embrace of the extended territorial nation-state. However, it is also an example of the second shared element: a highly neoliberal conception of governance in which democracy is de-emphasized or even abandoned versus financial freedom and property rights, while remaining visibly multicultural. The third is the dependence upon almost total data extractivism and ubiquitous surveillance, underpinned by some kind of Artificial Intelligence (AI). The fourth and final shared element is a bland neoliberal globalist aesthetics, which at its most extreme verges on a neo-colonial presentation. This consists of smooth computer-generated visualizations, smiling putative, often white or racially ambiguous residents, starchitect master planners, and advisory boards consisting of the "usual suspects" from the transnational ruling class in law, urban planning, finance, and consultancy.

2.2 WHO ARE THE PLATFORM CITY PEOPLE?

That final shared element leads to an obvious question around the implied "nature" of the inhabitants, in other words the identity and subjectivity not of "actually existing smart citizens" (Shelton and Lodato 2019) but of the proposed platform city people. For the remainder of this chapter, I will concentrate on the shared characteristics of the envisaged new inhabitants of these platform cities, platform city people, based on five cases, a corpus whose publicity documents, plans, and charters or constitutions (where appropriate) I have examined and analysed as part of a preliminary study for a much larger project examining platform cities in an age of planetary crisis and surveillance. I have not given specific references to each of these quotations or paraphrases here. These projects are at differing stages: some of these remain on the drawing board, some are in development or being built, some have experienced setbacks, some have failed but nevertheless remain as inspirations for further smart cities development.

1. Sidewalk Labs' failed Toronto Quayside development;
2. Nevada's at least temporarily derailed "Innovation Zones" plan;
3. The Próspera Platform, still proposed for development, in Honduras;
4. Saudi Arabia's massive in-construction NEOM project; and
5. Japan's Super City policy, which plans multiple new AI-driven urban developments.

In this chapter, I deployed a simple thematic analysis to uncover the power relations behind talk and text, and the genealogical roots of clusters of meaning and how they have developed over time. This section is framed around declarative sentences that begin, "Platform city people are . . .," each of which quotes a term or more that are used by at least one of the documents produced by the proposed cities or policies that I have been examining. These declarative sentences are followed by explanation that develops, in brief, some aspects of the broader discursive formation of which the particular discourse is part.

2.2.1 *Platform City People Are Entrepreneurs*

Within a context of "test-bed urbanism" (Halpern et al. 2013), platform city people are portrayed as innovative risk-takers. Developing Adam Smith, Michel Foucault (2008) described the subjectivity produced by neoliberalism as *homo oeconomicus*, a humanness not characterized by intelligence or wisdom but by their market relationships. The platform human is the cybernetic upgrade of *homo oeconomicus*, perfectly adapted for the intensified neoliberal capitalist mode of production filtered through technology based innovation or disruption. NEOM is explicit that "[r]esidents of NEOM will . . . embrace a culture of exploration [and] risk-taking . . ." (NEOM 2020). The platform human is not a fixed subject, but a relentless innovator and experimenter: as Eric Schmidt, former CEO of Alphabet, asked us to imagine prior to the Sidewalk Toronto experiment, "all the things you could do if someone would just give us a city and put us in charge" (Williams 2017). But the city and its inhabitants are also themselves the subjects of continuous experiment – part of what it means to be a risk-taker in this context is to take on the risk to oneself and to absorb risk *for* the platform. And, as we have seen with Sam Bankman-Fried and FTX (Roth 2022), large-scale financial failure is always imminent and precipitous in platform capitalist culture.

2.2.2 *Platform City People Are Free*

As Slobodian (2018) shows, in the dominant "Geneva school" of neoliberalism, nation-states have always been seen as a hinderance to the creation of a true world economy, and high (or even any) taxation and regulation were presented as preventing innovation. The platform city has adopted this idea that the most innovative spaces have always been cities, and free and independent cities are the best. While none of the examples I have examined makes explicit reference to Paul Romer's "Charter City" model (Romer 2010), most do have some kind of charter or principles that set out their independence from the surrounding polity, particularly Próspera and the proposed Nevada Innovation Zones policy, but also NEOM, which claims that it will have "a progressive law compatible with international norms and conducive to economic growth". (NEOM 2020). It is a particular and peculiar Randian "freedom from" which enables the platform human to remove themselves from responsibility and consequences for those unnamed others outside, who are clearly seen as lesser humans, and indeed "freedom from government." It is notable in this context that the Próspera Platform also includes, on its "advisory team," Oliver Porter, the founder of Sandy Springs, in Georgia, USA, a city notable for being the first to incorporate a public–private partnership model and the closest extant US city to being a charter city (Klein 2007).

2.2.3 *Platform City People Are Leaders*

NEOM's (2020) website claims that "[a]s a hub for innovation, entrepreneurs, business leaders and companies will come to research, incubate and commercialize new technologies and enterprises in ground-breaking ways." The Próspera website (2022) claims that the city "enables entrepreneurs to solve problems structurally and responsibly" and, according to its charter, in the first place only people with "significant business, management or leadership experience" are eligible to stand for selection to the Council that will run the city. The fact that this conception of leadership serves to embed existing power, prejudices, and inequalities is not a bug, it is a feature. It replaces Plato's elitist utopian model of *The Republic*, of philosopher-kings with entrepreneur-kings or, as we shall see, proprietor-kings.

2.2.4 *Platform City People Are Tech Bros*

Platform cities are founded in techno-determinism: whatever is wrong now, there is a clear path to a better, more prosperous future through technology. While, in many cases, there is no specific reference of any requirement as to the profession of platform city people, technology is almost always clearly implied. When Dan

Doctoroff, CEO of Sidewalk Toronto, the development that would be built "from the Internet, up," addressed the question of who would live in the new neighbourhood, and said with a smirk that "they won't all be tech bros," his implication was clearly the opposite, that the target of this development was indeed young men in the tech sector (Murakami Wood 2020, 96). Nevada's Innovation Zones policy attempted no such deception: the failed bill specified the exact kinds of corporations that would be allowed to create an Innovation Zone, those working in blockchain, autonomous technology, IoT, robotics, AI, wireless, biometrics, and renewables. The last area seems to have been added on to claim some small amount of eco-credibility faced with the mounting reports of the unsustainability of blockchain and cryptocurrencies, but the important thing is that it was clearly still a technology driven sector.

2.2.5 *Platform City People Are Data-driven*

Platform city people will find strength through data. Their bodies will be maintained with vigorous and carefully calibrated exercise, assessed through wearable technologies. They will sleep exactly the recommended amount and will wake at precisely the optimal time every day. In Japan's Super City proposals, all of this data from multiple bodily and environmental sensors will be collected for medical and unspecified "improvement" purposes. NEOM's Head of Technology and Digital, Joseph Bradley, argues that the city will collect and use "90% of available data" for the benefit of its inhabitants. This benefit will come, as we shall see, from the analysis of all that data by AI.

2.2.6 *Platform City People Are Frictionless*

As if Giles Deleuze's "Postscript on the societies of control" (1992) was an instruction manual, platform humans will operate in all ways as smoothed, modulated, and unhindered. Nothing will slow down their movements or transactions. Nothing will impede the flow of goods, ideas, or finance. Japan's Super Cities are envisaged as entirely cashless, running on some kind of blockchain-based virtual currency – although it is unclear exactly what or how. But the spice must flow. Próspera offers virtual citizenship and the ability to access the platform from anywhere in the world: one need not be in Próspera to be part of Próspera. Sidewalk Toronto tried to recombine this virtual friction-free flow with material seamlessness: promising total convenience and integration of transaction and delivery with all services as literal infrastructure: in a network of underground tunnels, where a ceaseless traffic of AI-driven autonomous delivery vehicles would ensure the inhabitants of the rabbit hutch-like, reduced-size apartments would always get what they wanted ideally – once the Google predictive marketing analytics were functioning perfectly – before they even knew they needed it.

2.2.7 *Platform City People Are Private*

Ironically, the platform human is both totally known to the AI-driven systems that harvest and sort and sift their data and to those others they chose to be known to, but private and indeed unknowable to the vast majority of ordinary humanity and the authorities and governments who would wish to tax them or regulate them. Their dealings are closed, their tax records sealed, their transactions in offshore banks – indeed, the entire geopolitical point of any of these developments is for them to be "offshore." That kind of privacy is very important to the platform city person. In other words, drawing on Foucault (2007), this is an inclusive, enfolding biopolitical governmentality – for those inside.

2.2.8 *Platform City People Are Safe*

In ways that are both implicit and explicit, total safety is promised by all these platform cities. Clearly the "risk-taking" that is considered so essential to the personality of the platform human does not extend to their own lives and well-being. Platform city people are happy to be checked out, examined, identified, evaluated, and cleared. Platform city people are happy to be under surveillance "for their own good," and suspicious of those who resist surveillance. The platform city person is not a threat, a terrorist, a criminal, or even anti-social. Platform city people raise no flags, they have no suspicious data-points. Their internet search history is impeccable. Platform city people are smooth, bland, and unthreatening. Their friends and family are just like them. And, despite the libertarian rhetoric, "social credit" style "assessment with consequences" is hinted at in several schemes and is overt in Japan's Super City proposals where good deeds will be rewarded with payment in an internal blockchain-based currency. This is what Chris Gilliard and David Golumbia (2021) call "luxury surveillance" – inside there are only carrots, no sticks.

2.2.9 *Platform City People Are Secure*

In most of the plans, security is not usually overt: you will not find the multiple control rooms, drone swarms, and a special new private security force that NEOM will have in its promotional literature, rather in security industry publications, one can find references to Mohammed Bin Salman's billion-dollar investment in security for the linear city (Murakami Wood 2024). It was only implied that Nevada's Innovation Zones would have had a Sheriff's department since it is by virtue of being politically a "county," that an Innovation Zone has control over local police (Blockchain LLC 2021) – a Sheriff's Department in Nevada is the entirety of municipal police, not some lesser rural form.

But, in some cases, particularly in the case of Próspera, security is a named function of the city in Article X of its charter, and here there appear to be no limits in the charter to the defensive rights of the platform city. It can have police, security, and intelligence services and perhaps even an army; and, despite being inside Honduras, it can even request security assistance from other external nation-states. This is unusual not in the depth of the possible security that platform city people will enjoy but in the fact that it is so overt. Ostensibly "small government" platform cities mask increasingly distributed and networked technologies of security and governance. All platform cities are highly securitized in their conception, financially and socially exclusionary, implicitly racialized/eugenic in some cases, metaphorically and legally, if not physically, walled and gated. This is the other side of the interior biopolitical governmentality. For those people outside, platform city governmentality is pure necropolitics (Mbembe 2020): their security/policing objects are not the safe platform humans but those risky external and excluded others.

2.2.10 *Platform City People Are Colonists*

The platform city is portrayed as an explicit island of safety in an implicit world of chaos. Platform city people are portrayed like brave explorers in a twenty-first century version of European expansion. In the case of Próspera, the literal island of Roatan exists in one of the most violent nations in the world, Honduras. However, the natives are friendly! In fact, the local inhabitants will be "integrated," guaranteed jobs at 25 per cent above the local minimum wage, but they will not be residents, even as the city is built on their lands. It is clear that they are not happy about this, but not being platform city people, their views are discounted (MacDougall and Simpson 2021). This builds in the model operated by Singapore with its thousands of Malay and other day-labourers who cross the international border morning and night to support this marvel of smart capitalism but who are not allowed to live there; or the armies of temporary workers who constitute 90 per cent of the population of Dubai or Qatar but are entirely outwith its polity.

2.2.11 *Platform City People Are Property Owners*

A key element of the contract is what makes a platform human is their investment in the platform city. The platform human owns property and, given the Lockean worldview that underlies this system, it is this ownership that grants them rights. In contrast, the "locals" will be "willingly" incorporated (Próspera) or removed like nomadic desert people who currently inhabit the area proposed to become NEOM (Whitson and Alaoudh 2020) to be imprisoned or simply executed (AFP 2023). It is a return of the colonial doctrine of *terra nullius* (Fitzmaurice 2007) and the *tabula rasa*, or where this doctrine has already been applied with extreme prejudice, as in Nevada, US, the land owned by corporations seeking to become Innovation Zones was simply assumed to be "uninhabited" and owned entirely by the corporation. Indigenous people are already assumed to be extinct (cf. King 2013).

2.2.12 *Platform City People Are Multicultural*

The language of "multiculturalism" and "diversity" is ubiquitous in the brochures and websites of platform cities. But, like the swordsman, Inigo Montoya's much-memed remark from *The Princess Bride*, it does not mean what they think it means. Multiculturalism in platform cities is coded language. It means whiter, less brown, less black, less of whatever the local surrounding population consists of, and safely, blandly, international, educated, schooled in, aspiring to, and representing whiteness. It is not so much that platform city people are necessarily visibly white, but rather that the platform human strives toward whiteness as a "habit" of existence or a normative condition of being (c.f. Ahmed 2007). They are Kees van der Pijl's new "transnational ruling class" (Van der Pijl 2005) and they "embody an international ethos" (NEOM 2020): educated, mobile, groomed, comfortably multilingual, and expecting the world they inhabit to conform to their expectations.

2.2.13 *Platform City People Are Designed*

In the brochure-websites of Próspera and NEOM, the future platform human lives in spaces that conjure the images of the technologies they develop: their preferred environments are created by the best architects, *Starchitects* (Knox 2011), like Norman Foster (one of the original advisors to NEOM) and Zaha Hadid Associates (the official architects for Próspera), who will generate sleek, minimal, and weightless living spaces, composed of glass, bamboo, and natural wood in neutral and calming colours, materializing the promise of 1990s techno-utopian hype, like *Living on Thin Air* (Leadbeater 2000). It should also be noted that clutter and visual noise confuse surveillance cameras and biometric recognition technologies (for more on the affordances of modern architecture for surveillance, see Steiner and Veel 2011).

2.2.14 *Platform City People Are Sustainable*

Platform city people are carbon-neutral and live in communities designed to maximize technological innovation to work seamlessly and sustainably. They like John Kerry's May 2021 statement that 50% of reductions in greenhouse gasses will come from future technologies, because these are the technologies they are building, and they trust that they are the people who Kerry argued would not have to give up their quality of life to stop the climate crisis (see Murray 2021). They know they are not responsible for the unsustainable practices of lesser people. However, like multiculturalism, sustainability is another code and part of an aesthetic politics of marketing. Platform cities can be seen as a form "becoming war" (Bousquet et al. 2020): a mode of geopolitics and of emerging conflict. There is unshakeable belief that the platform economy is a clean economy, but its environmental effects are externalized to distant places and to the future, as the research on energy use of server farms and bitcoin mines has shown. Thus, "sustainability" is another marker of inclusion and exclusion between the clean, sustainable inside and the environmentally degraded, unliveable outside, and this division between islands of clean perfect cities with clean perfect humans and the "dumb, rude and dirty" old cities (SAP 2013) outside will become a key characteristic of the politics of the Anthropocene, if platform cities are allowed to proliferate.

2.2.15 *Platform City People Are "All Watched over by Machines of Loving Grace"*

Artificial Intelligence (AI) is a constant in platform city proposals. It was at the heart of what Google was proposing to do with all that data in Sidewalk Toronto, and the bet on which Google is staking its entire future (Eliot and Murakami Wood 2022). NEOM will be a "cognitive city" that will make "everyday life seamless through invisible AI-enabled infrastructure that continuously learns and predicts ways to make life easier for residents and businesses." Japan's Super Cities will be where "artificial intelligence, big data and other technologies are utilized to resolve social problems" (National Strategic Special Zones 2020). The language of "social physics" and the idea highly amenable to technocracy that social issues will be solved simply by collecting and analysing data rather than through qualitative, participatory democratic deliberation, is everywhere here – and Carlo Ratti, one of the key proponents of such thinking in quantified urbanism, was a member of the original advisory board of NEOM.

2.2.16 *Platform City People Are a New Species*

With their technologically integrated body and life, platform city people are almost the beginning of the transhumanist speciation of humanity, as was argued could be the result of current trajectories in tech development a decade ago (Stephan et al. 2012). They will separate themselves from less human beings; they are better than other human beings. They feel compassion for those that are being left behind, but evolution is inevitable. It was easy to be sceptical of such claims in 2012, despite the longstanding warnings from science-fictional portrayals of the same outcome from H. G. Wells' "Morlocks" and "Eloi" in *The Time Machine* (1895) to Paul J. McAuley's "Golden" in *Four Hundred Billion Stars* (1988) and its sequels. These basic building blocks for transhumanism should remind us of the longstanding connection between fascism and the celebration of the machine, and the speed of technological transformation that caused many Italian Futurists to join Mussolini in the 1920s (Berghaus 1996). Thus it was striking how, just a few years after 2012, one could see the juxtaposition of Israel rebranding itself as the "Start-up Nation"[1] while its Prime Minister, Netanyahu, was almost simultaneously arguing that the strong and adaptable survive and the weak are destined to be erased.[2] David Golumbia (2009; 2016) has made similar convincing observations about the right-wing politics of Bitcoin, indeed that such is the ultimate "cultural logic of computation" more generally. With the emergence of the so-called TESCREAL[3] cluster, an increasingly coherent ideological constellation embraced by platform capitalist CEOs like Elon Musk, we see neo-eugenicism with technological determinism, neoliberal economics and right-libertarian social policy would seem to provide the up-front or retrospective justification for many more authoritarian platform city initiatives.

2.2.17 *Platform City People Could Be Robots*

For platform city people, it is easier to imagine robot rights than the acknowledgment of human rights for the workers who support their exclusive lifestyle or for the rights of other living beings. The consultants' report for the NEOM plan included the idea that 50 per cent of the population of the proposed city would be robots (Scheck et al. 2019), building on a rather curious fascination with robots evidenced by the granting of Saudi citizenship to "Sophie," a rather limited conversation bot, when neither Saudi women nor immigrants have full citizenship rights in the kingdom (Hart 2018). Again, this links into the TESCREAL constellation, with philosopher, Nick Bostrom's "long termism" specifically advocating policy directions based on the alleged ethical imperative of maximizing the supposed future trillions of "humans" living as uploaded consciousnesses in machines far beyond our solar system.

2.3 CONCLUSION

Platform city people are the proposed inhabitants of a new world: a clean, safe, sustainable, technologically advanced, and inventive world of minimal government and maximum empowerment and support for entrepreneurialism and the enjoyment of ownership. The problem is that it is a niche world, an archipelago of enclaves that constitutes only a tiny proportion of a planet in crisis, and its biopolitical exclusivity and violently exclusionary necropolitical character are evidence

1 Start-Up Nation Central, https://startupnationcentral.org/

2 Prime Minister of Israel official Twitter account @IsraeliPM, August 29, 2018: https://twitter.com/IsraeliPM/status/1034849460344573952

3 "TESCREAL" stands for Transhumanism, Extropianism, Singularitarianism, Cosmism, Realism, Effective Altruism, and Longtermism, and was coined by Timnit Gebru (c.f. Gebru and Torres 2024).

not of a desire to deal with the crisis itself but rather to engage in what Mike Davis memorably described as "padding the bunker" (Davis 1999) – retreating to the childish denial of an unreal security enabled fantasy. This is the California ideology (Barbrook and Cameron 1996; Turner 2010) taken to even greater extremes. This new California ideology (Murakami Wood 2024) is most clearly expressed in the eugenic TESCREALity of Nick Bostrom, and Elon Musk would see such developments as a form of lifeboat for those most worth saving, who would be the basis for what they regard as the ultimate future of humanity. Their stance is that we should abandon any hopes for real material developments that would benefit the vast majority of actually existing human beings and those in the foreseeable future, like social and environmental justice, if they imperil their imaginary science-fictional future universe. The point here is not even to consider what "we" might lose in this transition, rather to draw attention to this fracturing of any possibility of a collective "we" as it relates to humanity in the present and the concentration on a winnowed, broadly white, supreme, selective "elite." Platform city people are, therefore, emblematic of a kind of imaginary of human eco-socio-technological future that anyone interested in an equitable and just world should oppose as vigorously as possible.

REFERENCES

Agence France Presse (AFP). "UN Rights Experts Denounce Planned Saudi Executions of Megacity Opponents." *The Guardian*, May 3, 2023. www.theguardian.com/world/2023/may/03/un-rights-experts-denounce-planned-saudi-executions

Ahmed, Sara. "A Phenomenology of Whiteness." *Feminist Theory* 8, no. 2 (2007): 149–168. https://journals.sagepub.com/doi/10.1177/1464700107078139

Barbrook, Richard, and Andy Cameron. "The Californian Ideology." *Science as Culture* 6, no. 1 (1996): 44–72. www.researchgate.net/publication/249004663_The_Californian_Ideology.

Berghaus, Günter. *Futurism and Politics: Between Anarchist Rebellion and Fascist Reaction, 1909–1944*. New York: Berghahn Books, 1996.

Blockchain LLC. "Nevada Innovation Zone Facts." June 19, 2021. https://innovationzonefacts.com/. [archived at: https://web.archive.org/web/20210619211748/https://innovationzonefacts.com/]

Bousquet, Antoine, Jairus Grove, and Nisha Shah. "Becoming War: Towards a Martial Empiricism." *Security Dialogue* 51, no. 2–3 (2020): 99–118. https://journals.sagepub.com/doi/full/10.1177/0967010619895660.

Bunnell, Tim. "Multimedia Utopia? A Geographical Critique of High-tech Development in Malaysia's Multimedia Super Corridor." *Antipode* 34, no. 2 (2002): 265–295. https://ap5.fas.nus.edu.sg/fass/geotgb/Final%20Paper.pdf.

Caldeira, Teresa P. R. *City of Walls: Crime, Segregation, and Citizenship in São Paulo*. Oakland, CA: University of California Press, 2001.

Calder, Kent E. *Singapore: Smart City, Smart State*. Washington, DC: Brookings Institution Press, 2016.

Cardullo, Paolo, and Rob Kitchin. "Smart Urbanism and Smart Citizenship: The Neoliberal Logic of 'Citizen-focused' Smart Cities in Europe." *Environment and Planning C:*

Politics and Space 37, no. 5 (2019): 813–830. https://journals.sagepub.com/doi/abs/10.1177/0263774X18806508.
Coletta, Claudio, Leighton Evans, Liam Heaphy, and Rob Kitchin, eds. *Creating Smart Cities*. New York: Routledge, 2018.
Datta, Ayona. "The Digital Turn in Postcolonial Urbanism: Smart Citizenship in the Making of India's 100 Smart Cities." *Transactions of the Institute of British Geographers* 43, no. 3 (2018): 405–419. https://rgs-ibg.onlinelibrary.wiley.com/doi/full/10.1111/tran.12225.
"Postcolonial Urban Futures: Imagining and Governing India's Smart Urban Age." *Environment and Planning D: Society and Space* 37, no. 3 (2019): 393–410. https://journals.sagepub.com/doi/10.1177/0263775818800721?icid = int.sj-abstract.citing-articles.89.
Davis, Mike. *Ecology of Fear: Los Angeles and the Imagination of Disaster*. New York: Vintage, 1999.
Davis, Mike, and Daniel Bertrand Monk. *Evil Paradises: Dreamworlds of Neoliberalism*. New York: The New Press, 2008.
Deleuze, Gilles. "Postscript on the Societies of Control." *October* 59 (1992): 3–7. www.jstor.org/stable/778828.
Eliot, David, and David Murakami Wood. "Culling the FLoC: Market Forces, Regulatory Regimes and Google's (mis)Steps on the Path Away from Targeted Advertising." *Information Polity* 27, no. 2 (2022): 259–274. https://content.iospress.com/articles/information-polity/ip211535.
Fitzmaurice, Andrew. "The Genealogy of Terra Nullius." *Australian Historical Studies* 38, no. 129 (2007): 1–15. www.tandfonline.com/doi/abs/10.1080/10314610708601228.
Foucault, Michel. *The Birth of Biopolitics: Lectures at the Collège de France, 1978–1979*. New York: Palgrave, 2008.
Security, Territory, Population: Lectures at the Collège de France 1977–1978. London: Picador, 2007.
Gebru, Timnit and Émile P. Torres. "The TESCREAL Bundle: Eugenics and the Promise of Utopia through Artificial General Intelligence." *First Monday*, 29, no. 4 (2024). https://doi.org/10.5210/fm.v29i4.13636.
Gilliard, Chris, and David Golumbia. "Luxury Surveillance." *Real Life Magazine*, July 6, 2021. https://reallifemag.com/luxury-surveillance/.
Golumbia, David. *The Cultural Logic of Computation*. Cambridge, MA: Harvard University Press, 2009.
The Politics of Bitcoin: Software as Right-wing Extremism. Minneapolis: University of Minnesota Press, 2016.
Graham, Stephen. *Cities under Siege: The New Military Urbanism*. New York: Verso Books, 2011.
Graham, Stephen, and Simon Marvin. *Splintering Urbanism*. New York: Routledge, 2001.
Hall, Robert. E., B. Bowerman, J. Braverman, J. Taylor, H. Todosow, and U. von Wimmersperg. "The Vision of a Smart City." *Presented at the 2nd International Life Extension Technology Workshop*, Paris, France, September 28, 2000. https://digital.library.unt.edu/ark:/67531/metadc717101/.
Halpern, Orit, Jesse LeCavalier, Nerea Calvillo, and Wolfgang Pietsch. "Test-Bed Urbanism." *Public Culture* 25, no. 2 (2013): 272–306. www.researchgate.net/publication/270637741_Test-Bed_Urbanism.
Hart, Robert David. "Saudi Arabia's Robot Citizen Is Eroding Human Rights." *Quartz*, February 14, 2018. https://qz.com/1205017/saudi-arabias-robot-citizen-is-eroding-human-rights/.
ITU. "Internet of Things Global Standards Initiative." ITU. 2012. www.itu.int/en/ITU-T/gsi/iot/Pages/default.aspx.

Jasanoff, Sheila, and Sang-Hyun Kim, eds. *Dreamscapes of Modernity. Sociotechnical Imaginaries and the Fabrication of Power*. Chicago: Chicago University Press, 2015.

King, Thomas. *The Inconvenient Indian: A Curious Account of Native People in North America*. Minneapolis: University of Minnesota Press, 2013.

Kitchin, Rob. *The Data Revolution: Big Data, Open Data, Data Infrastructures and their Consequences*. New York: Sage, 2014.

Klein, Naomi. "Disaster Capitalism." *Harper's Magazine*, 2007. https://harpers.org/archive/2007/10/disaster-capitalism/.

Knox, Paul. "Starchitects, Starchitecture and the Symbolic Capital of World Cities." In *International Handbook of Globalization and World Cities*, edited by Ben Derudder, Michael Hoyler, Peter J. Taylor, and Frank Witlox, 275–283. New York: Edward Elgar Publishing, 2011.

Leadbeater, Charles. *Living on Thin Air: The New Economy*. London: Penguin, 2000.

MacDougall, Ian, and Isabelle Simpson. "A Libertarian 'Startup City' in Honduras Faces Its Biggest Hurdle: The Locals." *Rest of World*, October 5, 2021. https://restofworld.org/2021/honduran-islanders-push-back-libertarian-startup/.

Mahizhnan, Arun. "Smart Cities: The Singapore Case." *Cities* 16, no. 1 (1999): 13–18. www.sciencedirect.com/science/article/abs/pii/S026427519900050X.

Marvin, Simon, Andrés Luque-Ayala, and Colin McFarlane, eds. *Smart Urbanism: Utopian Vision or False Dawn?* New York: Routledge, 2015.

Mattern, Shannon. *A City Is Not a Computer: Other Urban Intelligences*. Princeton, NJ: Princeton University Press, 2021.

Mbembe, Achille. *Necropolitics*. Durham, NC: Duke University Press, 2020.

McAuley, Paul J. *Four Hundred Billion Stars*. New York: Del Rey, 1988.

Murakami Wood, David. "The Scaling Back of Saudi Arabia's Proposed Urban Mega-project Sends a Clear Warning to Other Would-be Utopias," *The Conversation*, 5 May 2024. https://theconversation.com/the-scaling-back-of-saudi-arabias-proposed-urban-mega-project-sends-a-clear-warning-to-other-would-be-utopias-227852.

"The Security Dimension." In *Global City Challenges: Debating a Concept, Improving the Practice*, edited by Michele Acuto and Wendy Steele, 188–201. New York: Palgrave, 2013.

"Smart City, Surveillance City." *Society for Computers & Law*, June 30, 2015. www.scl.org/3405-smart-city-surveillance-city/.

"Was Sidewalk Toronto a PR Experiment or a Development Proposal?" In *Smart Cities in Canada: Digital Dreams, Corporate Designs*, edited by Mariana Valverde and Alexandra Flynn, 94–101. Toronto: Lorimer, 2020.

Murakami Wood, David, and Debra Mackinnon. "Partial Platforms and Oligoptic Surveillance in the Smart City." *Surveillance & Society* 17, no. 1/2 (2019): 176–182. https://ojs.library.queensu.ca/index.php/surveillance-and-society/article/view/13116.

Murray, Jessica. "Half of Emissions Cuts Will Come from Future Tech, says John Kerry." *The Guardian*, May 16, 2021. www.theguardian.com/environment/2021/may/16/half-of-emissions-cuts-will-come-from-future-tech-says-john-kerry.

National Strategic Special Zones. "Super Cities." *Government of Japan*, 2020. www.chisou.go.jp/tiiki/kokusentoc/english/super-city/index.html.

NEOM. "NEOM." Kingdom of Saudi Arabia, 2020. www.neom.com/index.html.

Noveck, Beth Simone. *Smart Citizens, Smarter State: The Technologies of Expertise and the Future of Governing*. Cambridge, MA: Harvard University Press, 2015.

Powell, Alison B. *Undoing Optimization: Civic Action in Smart Cities*. New Haven, CT: Yale University Press, 2021.

Próspera Platform. "Próspera." Próspera Platform, 2022. https://prospera.hn/.

Romer, Paul. "Technologies, Rules, and Progress: The Case for Charter Cities." *Centre for Global Development*, March 3, 2010. www.cgdev.org/publication/technologies-rules-and-progress-case-charter-cities.

Roth, Emma. "Here's Everything that Went Wrong with FTX." *The Verge*, November 30, 2022. www.theverge.com/2022/11/30/23484331/ftx-explained-cryptocurrency-sbf-sam-bankman-fried.

SAP. "Intelligent Cities like Rio Make 'Dumb, Rude, and Dirty' Traits of the Past." *SAP Community Blog* (blog), May 14, 2013. https://blogs.sap.com/2013/05/14/intelligent-cities-like-rio-make-dumb-rude-and-dirty-traits-of-the-past/.

Scheck, Justin, Rory Jones, and Summer Said. "A Prince's $500 Billion Desert Dream: Flying Cars, Robot Dinosaurs and a Giant Artificial Moon." *Wall Street Journal*, July 25, 2019. www.wsj.com/articles/a-princes-500-billion-desert-dream-flying-cars-robot-dinosaurs-and-a-giant-artificial-moon-11564097568.

Shelton, Taylor, and Thomas Lodato. "Actually Existing Smart Citizens: Expertise and (non)Participation in the Making of the Smart City." *City* 23, no. 1 (2019): 35–52. www.tandfonline.com/doi/abs/10.1080/13604813.2019.1575115.

Shelton, Taylor, Matthew Zook, and Alan Wiig. "The 'Actually Existing Smart City'." *Cambridge Journal of Regions Economy and Society* 8, no. 1 (2015): 13–25. https://papers.ssrn.com/sol3/papers.cfm?abstract_id = 2477482.

Slobodian, Quinn. *Globalists*. Cambridge, MA: Harvard University Press, 2018.

Steiner, Henriette, and Kristin Veel. "Living Behind Glass Façades: Surveillance Culture and New Architecture." *Surveillance & Society* 9, no. 1/2 (2011): 215–232. https://ojs.library.queensu.ca/index.php/surveillance-and-society/article/view/glass.

Stephan, Karl D., Katina Michael, M. G. Michael, Laura Jacob, and Emily P. Anesta. "Social Implications of Technology: The Past, the Present, and the Future." *Proceedings of the Institute of Electrical and Electronics Engineers (IEEE)* 100, no. 13 (2012): 1752–1781. https://ro.uow.edu.au/eispapers/135/.

Turner, Fred. *From Counterculture to Cyberculture: Stewart Brand, the Whole Earth Network, and the Rise of Digital Utopianism*. Chicago IL: University of Chicago Press, 2010.

Van der Pijl, Kees. *Transnational Classes and International Relations*. New York: Routledge, 2005.

Vanolo, Alberto. "Smartmentality: The Smart City as Disciplinary Strategy." *Urban Studies* 51, no. 5 (2014): 883–898. https://journals.sagepub.com/doi/10.1177/0042098013494427.

Venn, Couze. "The City as Assemblage. Diasporic Cultures, Postmodern Spaces, and Biopolitics." In *Negotiating Urban Conflicts: Interaction, Space and Control*, edited by Helmuth Berking, Sybille Frank, Lars Frers, Martina Löw, Lars Meier, Silke Steets, and Sergej Stoetzer, 41–52. Bielefeld: Transcript Verlag, 2006. https://doi.org/10.1515/9783839404638-003.

Walton, Nicholas. *Singapore, Singapura: From Miracle to Complacency*. New York: Oxford University Press, 2019.

Wells, H. G. *The Time Machine*. London: William Heinemann, 1895.

Whitson, Sara Leah, and Abdullah Alaoudh. "Mohammed bin Salman's Bloody Dream City of Neom." *Foreign Policy*, April 27, 2020. https://foreignpolicy.com/2020/04/27/mohammed-bin-salman-neom-saudi-arabia/.

Williams, Jake. "Google wants to build a city." Statescoop, May 4, 2017. https://statescoop.com/google-wants-to-build-a-city/.

3

Robots, Humans, and Their Vulnerabilities

Beate Roessler

3.1 WHERE DO WE HUMANS GO?

In digital societies, systems are becoming ever more powerful, and algorithms ever more complex, efficient, and capable of learning. More and more human activities are being taken over by computers, robots, and AI, and the technologies are becoming ever more deeply and far-reaching integrated into our social practices. It has become impossible to see and understand people, relationships, and social structures independently of these technologies. Especially over the last 2 years, we read almost every day in the newspapers, including and especially the serious ones, that AI leads to the elimination of humans; that the point where AI is more intelligent than we are is approaching. That this has immediate consequences for human life is evident, but it is not just about individual aspects of human life. In a recent article, Acquisti et al. summarize their argument as follows: "Technologies, interfaces, and market forces can all influence human behavior. But probably, and hopefully, they cannot *alter human nature*" (Acquisti et al. 2021, 202, emphasis mine; see, for the following, Roessler 2021a, 2021b).

What I am interested in here is how we should spell out this claim: what does it mean that we hope technologies do not change our human nature and what would this human nature be? Or, put differently, what would it mean to change human nature through technologies and why would it be bad to do so? There has been quite some discussion of this or similar problems in the literature and the most helpful and intriguing is, to my mind, Frischmann and Selinger's (2018) *Re-Inventing Humanity*. Selinger and Frischmann write in an article in *The Guardian* newspaper (Selinger and Frischmann 2015, emphasis mine): "Alan Turing wondered if machines could be human-like, and recently that topic's been getting a lot of attention. But perhaps a more important question is a reverse Turing test: can *humans become machine-like* and pervasively programmable?" This latter question is the topic of their book. Additionally, in the introduction to their book, they write:

> As we collectively race down the path toward smart techno-social systems that efficiently govern more and more of our lives, we run the risk of *losing ourselves* along the way. We risk becoming increasingly predictable, and, worse, programmable, like mere cogs in a machine. (Frischmann and Selinger 2018, 1, emphasis mine)

To quote one last passage, this time by Pasquale: "The future that [the robot] Adam imagines . . . reduces the question of human perfectibility to one of transparency and predictability. But disputes and reflection on how to lead life well are part of *the essence of being human*" (Pasquale 2020, 209, emphasis mine).

In this picture, we have Turing on the one hand, trying to build a computer which could be mistaken to be human: we need to work on our technological counterpart to make it as good as human. On the other hand, we have Frischmann, Selinger, and Pasquale, who show us that people – humans – are becoming more and more similar to machines: they contend that we are working on ourselves in order to be ever more perfectly technologically human. In short, we try to improve humans technically so that they become similar to robots; and we try to make robots that become indistinguishably similar to a certain image of the perfect human. Both sides assume – intuitively plausibly – that we know what a 'human being' is and where at least roughly the limits lie between genuinely being human and technologies.

While there is no uncontested concept of *the* human nature, it does seem plausible to argue that human nature is neither something purely accidental, historically completely variable, and relative. It is possible to distinguish characteristics which express what is meant by being human, even though these expressions differ historically, and culturally. Such a concept or idea of human nature could give us critical guidance for analyzing digital societies without risking calling "human" whatever humans (learn to) do under digitally changing conditions. This concept of a human nature can clearly not be reduced to its biological essence: if that was the case, we would not have this discussion in the first place. The question is what it means to have this very special sort of (biological) human nature and how we would best analyze it.

To engage with this rather complex question adequately, I suggest approaching it through a novel whose very topic is the relation between humans and machines: Ian McEwan's (2019) novel *Machines Like Me*. I want to illustrate the problematic by taking up this different perspective on the technological world because, in this novel, McEwan describes the relationship between a human being and an almost-human being; an extraordinarily well-constructed, sensitive, and intelligent robot whose name is Adam. My hope is that, by reading and interpreting *Machines like Me*, we can learn something about how we should think about human beings. Incidentally, it is also possible to interpret other novels, for example *Klara and the Sun* by Kazuo Ishiguro (2021), or, to go a little further back, Mary Shelley's *Frankenstein* (1831), or *War of the Worlds*

(1895–1897, by H. G. Wells), but my question would remain the same: what does the image of the robot, of the monster, of the Aliens tell us about the idea and characterization of the human being?

These characteristics by McEwan, I suggest, are generalizable, and I will show, during this chapter, that they can help us to understand the meaning of being human, especially in its relation to the technological world. Furthermore, I will very briefly criticize attempts to transcend this notion of a human being as a finite and vulnerable being and also attempts to imitate and replace "soft" human characteristics, such as emotions and affects in robots, through technology (HRI, Human Robot Interaction technologies). Placing the human being in relation to robots and discussing the extent to which social robots can replace humans helps to understand, or so I will argue, which beings we want to and do refer to as human. I will also argue that it is helpful to refer to the phenomenon of the Uncanny Valley to make sense of a clear line of demarcation between robots and humans – this will in any case be my argument in the end.

3.2 IAN MCEWAN ON ROBOTS AND HUMANS

Ian McEwan's (2019) novel *Machines Like Me* is set in a rather different, alternative 1982: the war against the Falklands has been lost, the miners' strike is still on, unemployment is rising by the day, John Lennon as well as John F. Kennedy are still alive – and, above all, so is Alan Turing.[1] Turing has been working successfully on AI and the construction of a robot, and the first set of these robots is on sale: 12 Adams and 13 Eves as they have been subtly called. The protagonist, Charles "Charlie" Friend, spends the little inheritance he received after the death of his mother on buying one of them and, since he is too late for an Eve, he gets an Adam. The plot of the novel has different threads: there is the relationship with Miranda, Charlie's upstairs neighbour who he fell in love with long ago and who he starts dating. Miranda, after some time, has an affair with Adam; furthermore, she herself has a difficult personal history which she lies about and which is only revealed little by little, leading to the terrible unfolding. This thread in the complicated plot is important because it forces Miranda and Charles to lie – and after Adam has found out about this piece in Miranda's past, he intends to inform the police, since, as a robot, he can't lie. He must be, he wants to be relentlessly upright. Therefore, Charlie kills Adam. Also, rather uncannily, in the last third of the novel an increasing number of suicides by some of the Adams and Eves is being reported. But the main plot is simple: Charlie buys Adam, programs him together with Miranda, develops a rather friendly relationship with him and in the end kills him.

[1] In *Machines Like Me*, Alan Turing is referred to as: "Sir Alan Turing, war hero and presiding genius of the digital age" (McEwan 2019, 2).

Let me emphasize just some points here, first, the idea and the process of programming Adam. With the robots, there comes a 470-page online handbook about how to program them, but Charlie writes:

> I couldn't think of myself as Adam's "user": I'd assumed there was nothing to learn about him that he could not teach me himself. But the manual in my hands had fallen open at chapter 14. Here, the English was plain: preferences; personality parameters. Then a set of headings – Agreeableness. Extraversion. Openness to experience. Consciousness. Emotional stability. . . . Glancing at the next page I saw that I was supposed to select various settings on a scale of one to ten. (McEwan 2019, 6)

Charlie feels uncomfortable to choose the settings since he is very aware of their reductive character. And it's not only the reductive character of the program, it's also the predictability which comes with the program, and which goes against our intuitions that human beings – although being perfectly able to follow rules and rationality – can also be unpredictable, in the sense of being unexpectedly creative when dealing with rules and given programs. Interestingly, Charlie has done a degree in anthropology at college. Why anthropology? Because the subtle sub-text (or sometimes not so subtle) is the question of the *Anthropos*, the borderline between what is and what is not human.

A second point concerns the problem of *self-knowledge and decision-making*, with the character of Turing declaring at the end of the novel:

> I think the A-and-E's [the Adams and Eves] were ill equipped to understand human decision-making, the way our principles are warped in the force field of our emotions, our peculiar biases, our self-delusion and all the other well-charted defects of our cognition. Soon these Adams and Eves were in despair. They couldn't understand us because we couldn't understand ourselves. Their learning programs couldn't accommodate us. If we didn't know our own minds, how could we design theirs and expect them to be happy alongside us? (McEwan 2019, 299)

Emotions, however, often guide human's actions for better or worse. And humans – in McEwan (2019) and in general – see themselves as being defined by not only rationality but also sentimentality. Furthermore, the suicides of the Adams and Eves exhibit something like an *uncanny zone*: Isn't it specifically human to kill oneself, to set an end to one's life? What if there is no clear cut borderline between humans and robots?

A third intriguing problem I want to point out is the problem of lying, as Turing explains to Charlie:

> Machine learning can only take you so far. You'll need to give this mind some rules to live by. How about a prohibition against lying? . . . But social life teems with harmless or even helpful untruths. How do we separate them out? Who's going to write the algorithm for the little white lies that spare the blushes of a friend? . . . We don't yet know how to teach machines to lie. (McEwan 2019, 303)

Lying, we can say, is also a form of creatively, self-reflectively following rules. And lastly, but centrally, I want to emphasize the robotic corporeality of Adam and the relationship between Adam and Miranda since the fact that Adam has a deceptively *human body* is a problematic subtext throughout the book. After having slept with Adam, Miranda insists that he is not more than a vibrator in human-like form, that he is "a fucking machine" (McEwan 2019, 92). She points out that she has a purely instrumental relationship to Adam, not a relation of mutual respect. Whereas Charlie's take on the situation is rather different: "'Listen', I said, 'if he looks and sounds and behaves like a person, then as far as I'm concerned, that's what he is'" (McEwan 2019, 94). But Charlie, as we will learn later in the novel, does not really mean this. He is still convinced that there's a categorical difference between Adam and himself, although he states the opposite, out of jealousy, out of defiance. He is vulnerable, not only in the bodily sense, but also in an emotional-mental sense. And, again, his contending that Adam is a person leads us directly into the uncanny field between humans and robots. Where do we draw the line?

All these themes not only demonstrate a human characteristic, but at the same time the *sociality* of human existence: the themes are, each in their own way, meaningful too, because humans always live in relationships with other humans. And this seems to be vital for understanding the characteristic differences between Charles and Adam, between human beings and robots, and therefore for understanding the essential characteristics of human beings. Embodiment/corporeality, finiteness, vulnerability, and self-knowledge, together with the (subtle, competent, possibly deviant) use of symbols, are among the classic characteristics of the human being. What is at issue in the novel is the messiness of being human, being thrown into the world without a precise 'program', and the ever-present possibility of being unable to cope with that world. This messiness expresses itself in emotional as well as bodily vulnerability, something which Adam isn't conscious of or worried about as he should be – and would be – if he was human.

3.3 CHARACTERIZING THE HUMAN

It is true that McEwan also puzzles his readers, as we saw, by the fact that some Adams and Eves commit suicide. But this too is ultimately an indication of the meaning of "being human": the reader's perception of these suicides is confused, unsure because suicide is considered a human act par excellence. It is an expression of self-knowledge (or an attempt thereto), of autonomy, and precisely not an act following a program – whereas here, in *Machines Like Me* (McEwan 2019), it is a consequence of a program error.

Earlier we saw that corporeality, finiteness, vulnerability, and the self-reflective use of language are among the classic characteristics of the human being. Based on the McEwan characteristics and especially with the help of the concept of human vulnerability, I want to analyze in the following how the concept of the human being can best be understood. Vulnerability can serve as a focus of the other elements we found in McEwan. Mackenzie et al., in their volume on "Vulnerability" argue:

> Human life is conditioned by vulnerability. By virtue of our embodiment, human beings have bodily and material needs; are exposed to physical illness, injury, disability, and death; and depend on the care of others for extended periods during our lives. As social and affective beings we are emotionally and psychologically vulnerable to others in myriad ways: to loss and grief; to neglect, abuse, and lack of care; to rejection, ostracism, and humiliation. (Mackenzie et al. 2013, iv)

Human beings are vulnerable as physical beings, as affective beings, as social beings, as self-reflective beings, and this human vulnerability cannot be reduced to anything biological, although it cannot be separated from the biological either. Nor can human nature be reduced to the "brain" or "rationality," so not to their cognitive or mental abilities alone. But we have two different problems here: on the one hand whether the concept "human being" is clearly and distinctly definable in biological or physiological terms, and thus reducible to these descriptions. On the other hand, the concept of "human being" seems to carry a normative load which we would normally understand as an appeal, or maybe even a duty, to manifesting a certain attitude toward them.

To tackle this two-sidedness of the concept, it is helpful to understand "human nature" as one of the "thick concepts" which Clifford Geertz (1973), Bernard Williams (1985), or Martha Nussbaum (2023) analyze, concepts which are not purely normative or purely descriptive, but express elements of both dimensions (see also Setiya 2024). Thick concepts are both action-guiding and world-guided. "If a concept of this kind applies," Williams writes, "this often provides someone with a *reason for action* … At the same time, their application is *guided by the world*" (Williams 1985, 140–141, emphasis mine). So, when we talk about human beings, we are at the same time guided by the world and we have reasons for action – for protecting their vulnerability for instance. We follow empirical evidence *and* we are prepared to follow normative reasons for action and to respect the other as a human being, to recognize their vulnerability, and to acknowledge them as equal. The normative dimension concerns precisely those characteristics I have discussed: vulnerability, finiteness, and the self-reflective dimension of mutually recognizing each other as human.

This normative dimension of the concept of the human becomes especially clear when one looks at contexts in which the very application of the term is denied. Richard Rorty (1998) writes in his essay on human rights how, during the Balkan wars, the Serbs brutally refused to acknowledge the Bosnian Muslims as human beings, not even calling them "human." Precisely because the use of the concept "human" implies respect for others as equals – as equally human – with the application and use of the concept, the attitude which goes with it is denied as well.[2] Sylvia Wynter (1994), in her famous *Open Letter to My Colleagues*, writes that, when black people were involved in accidents and injured, it was standard practice in the LAPD to report back NHI (no humans involved). Not to refer to humans as humans is a violent form of denial of respect for the other, the denial to give them the basic recognition that we owe human beings.

So, when I speak in the following of human beings, I have such a "thick" concept in mind: it is a thick concept that contains both descriptive and normative elements. Several authors in the history of philosophy have already pointed out this double-sidedness of the concept of human nature and it is taken up again in the present, for example by Moira Gatens (2019), who interprets the "human being" as Spinoza's concept of the "exemplary" (see also Neuhouser 2009 and Williams 1985). When we refer to human beings in daily contexts, we generally have in mind beings which we refer to in biological as well as ethical ways (see Barenboim 2023; Heilinger and Nida-Rümelin 2015). I want to suggest that such a concept of human being can play an essential role in the critique of the digital society: Human beings as human beings always already live in their biological nature, but at the same time in a texture, a fabric of norms and concepts that determine, or govern, or shape, the relationship with the human person herself, with others, with the world. The ways we interpret these facts change over time: in fact, the history of making sense of what a human being is forms part of what it means to be a human being.

This approach obviously does not exclude that we might simply want to stop using this concept: when we transgress human beings, as some theories propose, we should not speak of humans any longer, and maybe we will not do so in the future. But this is not yet the point.

3.4 SHOULD HUMANS BE (MORE) LIKE ROBOTS? OR SHOULD ROBOTS BE (MORE) LIKE HUMANS?

We already saw in Chapter 1 that, if the aim is to explore the possible limits of the technicization of the human, then we always need to take up two perspectives: the human becoming a robot and the robot becoming (more) human. I will here briefly remind you of the first perspective and then come back to the latter in a little more detail.

[2] We have many different examples for this attitude, the last ones from the recent Israel–Palestine war. Both sides deny the other one the property of being human; and, like Rorty, Barenboim argues: "But any moral equation that we might set up must have as its basis this fundamental understanding: There are human beings ('Menschen') on both sides. Humanity is universal, and recognizing this truth on both sides is the only way. . . . Of course, especially now, you have to allow for fears, despair and anger – but the moment this leads to us denying each other's humanity, we are lost. . . . Both sides must recognize their enemies as human beings and try to empathize with their perspective, their pain and their distress" (Barenboim 2023, translation mine, B.R.). Many examples from contemporary politics and warzones could be cited.

The perspective that humans could be (or even should be) more robot-like covers the approaches which we described in Chapter 1 as, on the one hand, post-phenomenological – represented by Don Ihde and his followers who argue that we're always already mediated through technology. That is the reason why the idea that we humans are becoming a little more like robots is not intimidating: Verbeek argues that technology is "more than a functional instrument and far more than a mere product of 'calculative thinking.' It mediates the relation between humans and world, and thus co-shapes their experience and existence" (Verbeek 2011, 198–199). I agree with Verbeek and Ihde to the extent that their analyses of such mediations help us understand crucial aspects of what it means to be human today.[3]

However, Ihde, Verbeek, and other post-phenomenologists are not prepared to take a critical perspective here – only where does this mediation between humans and technology end? When does such an amalgam become hazardous or even dangerous for humans, so much so that they lose their humanity? The post-phenomenologists cannot answer these questions. However, there is a second understanding of the question of why people should become more technologized; this is the transhumanist understanding which we already encountered in Chapter 1 too.

Transhumanists want to increase the phenomenological connection with technology into the perfectibility of humans through technology. They explicitly build on the concept of the human being in its *ideal* version. Transhumanism endeavors to minimize all the characteristics which I described as typically human: the vulnerability, the dependence on being embodied, and eventually also the finiteness (as we know from Ray Kurzweil's vision of the singularity, see Bostrom 2002, 2005; Kurzweil 2006). Most transhumanists are not interested in *criticizing* concepts such as reason or autonomy (Ferrando 2018; Hayles 2008). On the contrary, they rather desire to get a grip on perfecting human rational and intellectual faculties, thereby overcoming vulnerability technologically and eradicating these human weaknesses or at least reducing them as far as possible. Again, I would argue that these theories are not in a position to draw a line between what one would still call human (albeit trans-human) and those beings who have given up on the 'human' in the concept transhuman altogether and are more like robots. Note, again, that I don't think this is inconsistent or impossible: I only believe that there is a borderline beyond which it is no longer appropriate or meaningful to call such beings human.

We are still left with the *opposite perspective*: why should it be bad for humans if *robots* became ever human-like? This perspective needs some more discussion, and

[3] See, on the debate about the "neutrality" of technology, on the question whether technologies are the frame, the *Gestell* which alienates us from the world (for instance Borgmann 1984; Ihde 1990; Verbeek 2011).

I will therefore look, first, at the research on social robots and, secondly, at the (im)possibility of translating emotions into technology. As we will see, there are still clear limitations in robot–human interaction and in the attempts to making robots look and function like humans. This is particularly obvious when it comes to the expression of emotions: human facial expressions, as well as human emotional life, is so complex that no possibility of translating feelings into data seems to appear on the horizon.

The research on the meaning of embodiment and affect and the possibility of translating them into technology has recently gained a lot of traction. It is a relatively new development that technological research on robots is no longer just about the cognitive area – as has now been shown particularly well with the ChatGPT – but also about emotions and affects. Emotions not only have a conscious or rational component, they also have an experiential or a phenomenal quality which is especially difficult to translate into data (see for the following Loh and Loh 2022; Seifert et al. 2022a; Weber-Guskar 2021). So far, social robots, especially in healthcare, have been met with a predominantly critical sentiment: human care should not be replaced by robots. We see this attitude also in research, where several ethical and philosophical approaches argue against this form of anthropomorphizing, from different perspectives.[4] However, in the research on social robots attempts are made to technologically develop certain human qualities in order to apply them to robots, such that they can be used in health care for elderly people or people with dementia. One of these qualities is "hug-quality," for example, another one is to be able to speak and thereby to express emotions like affection, sympathy, and care. The idea, for example, is that robots should have qualities which make it easier to hug them and easier to be addressed by them. This research on the depth of human communication is looking for developments that can improve the use of robots in care. But all this seems very difficult, following Müller's (2023) argument, as:

> AI can be used to manipulate humans into believing and doing things, it can also be used to drive robots that are problematic if their processes or appearance involve deception, threaten human dignity, or violate the Kantian requirement of "respect for humanity."[5]

So, for one thing, if robots are being used in healthcare, all they ever could do is to have an idea of instrumental care, as opposed to an idea of intentional care. What *humans* typically do when they care for others is *intentional care* and characterizes human interaction in a genuinely different way than *instrumental care*. Robots are

[4] See for instance the so-called relational approach by Coeckelbergh (2022): Coeckelbergh, too, starts with the idea of human vulnerability and seeks to interpret it normatively; see also Block et al. (2023) on research on "hug robots."

[5] See also Seifert et al. (2022a, 189), on the problems of deception and of manipulation; the whole article is very informative and convincingly argues to demonstrate the hidden problems in research programs on human–robot interaction.

thus "care robots" only in a behavioral sense of performing tasks in care environments, not in the sense in which a human "cares" for their patients. It appears that the experience of "being cared for" is based on this intentional sense of "care" only, a form of care which robots cannot provide – or at least not at this moment. This also shows that research on human–robot interaction is still far behind their aims: emotions, responsiveness, and sympathy cannot yet be translated into data and algorithms. However, these are human qualities and characteristics which are definitive of social interaction. Weber-Guskar (2021) discusses the possibility to use data and algorithms to build emotional robots (what she calls Emotional AI systems) and is critical concerning the development as well as the social function these robots would have in communication. Similarly, Darmanin (2019) argues that the attempts so develop robots with facial expressions close to human facial expressions are completely unconvincing. If you look at the examples accessible on the Internet, he seems to be right: emotions cannot be reduced to simple datapoints (you can see examples for different emotions, like happiness, anger, fear). These expressions have at least nothing much to do with human care as we currently still understand it.

This distinction is echoed by Pasquale when he writes that the practice of caring can't be reduced – and shouldn't be reduced – to instrumental relationships which are expressed by some changes in the expression of the mouth. I agree with Pasquale, that a society organizing institutional care for people along those lines would not be a society we would want to live in (see Chapter 4, by Pasquale). If we wanted robots to replace human care, then robots would have to be either very obviously only replacing human care in the instrumental and basic sense or able to express and behave precisely like humans in providing intentional care for the ill human. It is precisely this impossibility of translating human feelings (or should we say: humanity?) into technologies that limits robotization – at least for the time being.

3.5 THE UNCANNY VALLEY

Apparently, emotions and lived experiences cannot simply be reduced to data and algorithms, even if algorithms are becoming ever smarter. Emotional as well as physical vulnerability, including diseases, that we feel (and fear) cannot be translated into technologies, in the foreseeable future – whereas in fiction, especially in novels or films, this boundary between humans and robots is messed about with. The young man who is actually a robot in the film *Ich bin dein Mensch*, for example, is deceptively similar to other men, and the woman scientist who is supposed to fall in love with him, or at least befriend him, is fundamentally insecure of her attitude toward him (Schrader 2021).

The novel *Klara and The Sun* also plays with this boundary in unsettling ways: the Artificial Friend (AF) Klara is supposed to be a "friend" of Josie, who is a young teenage girl working for her exams (Ishiguro 2021). These exams are stressful and her whole future depends on the results. Furthermore, every now and then we get mysterious hints that Josie is ill and that her sister had the same illness when she died. Since the novel is told from Klara's first person-perspective, the reader is inclined to understand her quite well: also, it doesn't seem to be too difficult. She describes the way she perceives the world in (smaller and larger) squares and, for this perception, for her survival, the sun is necessary. Necessary not in the sense of natural needs that must be satisfied for an organism to live, but necessary in the sense of electricity without which a computer would not function.

Josie, on the other hand, her illness, her relationship with her neighbour Rick, as well as her authoritative mother, seems to be more of a mystery. While Klara is transparent in her perceptions, Josie remains obscure, even in her fear of illness and death. This seems to be a subtle, yet clear indication to express that Josie is the human of the two. Klara desires to be more human and has very transparent, easy-to-understand emotions. While Josie seems opaque to us, just like people who experience depression and melancholy often seem.

In a second step it becomes particularly clear that the difference between robots and humans is essentially based on the latter's vulnerability: Klara, the robot, cannot get ill, she (or it) gets *broken*. It (or she) cannot be healed, only be *repaired*. Although Klara doesn't want to break down, the robot can make that much clear – it needs the sun and is able to express this need, but it needs it like my mobile needs charging. It can't even try to survive without charging, as humans do, when they don't have food.

At least this is what the reader is led to think. Klara is asked by a woman at a party "'One never knows how to greet a guest like you,' and adds: 'After all, are you a guest at all? Or do I treat you like a vacuum cleaner?'" This question pushes us, the readers, headlong into the unsettling problematic of the relation between humans and robots. What rules are we to follow here? Which conventions apply, which conduct should we habitualize? The reader's confusion and insecurity reach even deeper. In Klara's place we – the readers – are ashamed of the woman's outrageous question, we even feel hurt, while on the other hand we know that Klara's "emotions" are alien, not human emotions, that therefore sympathy with Klara simply doesn't make sense. Ishiguro masterfully balances on the boundary between humans and robots, exploring what it means to be not-quite-human. He moves consistently on the edge of the uncanny valley. This valley itself is mysterious, and I want to briefly have a closer look at it.

The uncanny valley is a surprising valley in the previously steadily increasing curve that records the reactions of people when asked about their feelings toward robots.[6] In observing human empathy toward human-like objects, we find that the

[6] With Freud (2003), the uncanny plays more than just the role of intellectual insecurity, as Jentzsch understated, according to Freud. Both go back to the puppet Olimpia in the story "The Sandman" by E. T. A. Hoffmann, the dancing doll which is made of wood but seems to

more these objects, robots, resemble humans, the greater the positive response – up to a point where the objects are so human-like, but only human-*like*, that we enter the uncanny valley: we feel distressed, we feel emotionally unsettled, even extreme unease toward the objects. This is shown in the curve as a deep valley: but the valley is closing and the curve rising again when robots are indistinguishable from humans. This gap or valley is surprising since one would expect that robots, if they were almost (although not yet completely) indistinguishable from humans, would give us a reassuring or confidence-inspiring impression. On the other hand, the valley is understandable: intuitively we would always at least *like to know* whether we are dealing with a human or a robot.

Nowadays, in our daily digital lives, we seem to be confronted with a number of these uncanny areas: one example is the case of phoning a company where we no longer know whether we are being served by humans or by algorithms since the voices are indistinguishable. This is also the case with automated decision-making and the question whether there are – or ought to be – "humans in the loop": a question which is also one of dealing with the uncanny valley or field.[7]

I'm sure that in the – maybe far away – future it will be part of the rather normal world to move in this border area between beings clearly identifiable as robots, those that come across as uncanny and those which are in fact robots but no longer identifiable as such. Novels such as *Machines Like Me* or *Klara and the Sun*, or films like *Ich bin dein Mensch* or *Her* describe such a world impressively. The most recent example I came across is a short film by Diego Marcon (2021), *The Parent's Room*, just a brief clip which is haunting and truly uncanny not only because of the music and the lyrics (a father has just killed his son, daughter and wife, and is about to kill himself) but mostly because it is not entirely clear whether the figures are human, papier mâché, or a mixture of both. Isabella Achenbach writes about this film by Marcon: "[T]hat extreme representative realism evokes a response of repulsion and restlessness. . . . Marcon creates characters that give the viewer goosebumps with simultaneous feelings of aversion and unsettling familiarity" (Achenbach 2022, 293). Precisely this mixture of rejection, reluctance (aversion) and sympathy, and compassion (familiarity) characterizes the territory of the uncanny valley.

3.6 THE SELF-REFLECTIVE FINITENESS OF HUMANS

The critique or investigation of what it means to be human belongs broadly to the area of anthropological criticism. This criticism enriches the practical-normative

have human eyes and with whom the protagonist Nathanael falls in love. See Hoffmann (2020); see also Misselhorn (2009).

7 The GDPR Art 22 states that "The data subject shall have the right not to be subject to a decision based solely on automated processing, including profiling, which produces legal effects concerning him or her or similarly significantly affects him or her" (European Union, 2016). See the interesting article by Brennan-Marquez et al. (2019).

discourse with thick descriptions of human life and helps us criticize certain digital practices, with a whole web of related thick and normative concepts, such as care, love, emotion, autonomy and freedom, respect, and equality. Taken together, they enable us to form further criteria or standards for the good, the right human life in the digital society; and this way, we build a net of anthropological criticism and ethical-political criticism. In trying to explore and search irreducible characteristics of human life, one can be guided and inspired by imaginations, by novels, by films, as we have already seen. They can help us to develop plausible narratives and thus to ask where the limits should be beyond which technologies should not further interfere with human life. Or if they do, we wouldn't be speaking of humans any longer – this is one of the critical questions, which for instance Setiya asks when he criticizes David Chalmers analogizing virtual and humans-as-we-are reality (Chalmers 2022; Setiya 2022).

These questions – and also the question of who the "we" is, which I use throughout here – are controversial and must be ever again openly discussed, contested, balanced, and determined in liberal-democratic discourses. But the criteria, characteristics, and the basic normative framework discussed here must be the background for these disputes. In the following, by way of concluding, I want to point out that there are certain normative narratives that we can use to explore the boundaries between robots and humans – and that there are others which we wouldn't so use. The aim is to be able to refer critically to those contexts in which the use of robots would not concern specific human vulnerabilities. For instance, robots in care contexts, should we use them, or shouldn't we? Should robots be used as teachers? As traffic officers? As police officers? At the checkout at the supermarket?

These are questions which are being researched already by many different universities and other public institutions, as well as by private companies, and they will occupy us even more in the future. I have argued that these questions can best be discussed if we do not simply present a short and precise definition of the human being but seek the help of normative narratives which take up the thick concepts I discussed above. We can then identify contexts within which we do or do not want to use robots and give reasons by describing the characteristics of human beings and of human relationships with these thick concepts such that the gains and losses of using robots would be visible and could be discussed. Let me raise two critical points.

Firstly, what could be the source of the feeling of uncanniness in the uncanny valley? The reason many people feel insecure vis-à-vis an almost-human-like robot is, I suggest, grounded in their vulnerabilities: the assumption, the suspicion of the impossibility of equal, respectful, emotional relationships appears as a possible dehumanization of relationships. Such dehumanization is frightening and perceived as threatening, since we mostly are frightened of the non-natural nonhuman (especially when they pretend to be human). We feel fear of those creatures, fear of being hurt in unknown ways. Humans have central characteristics which by definition robots do not have: we are finite, vulnerable, self-reflective beings, always already living with other humans, having relationships with them. If we want to or must expose our vulnerability, then we want to be intuitively sure that we are dealing with another person.[8] Even stronger: we always already presuppose that the other is human when we expose ourselves as deeply vulnerable beings.

The uncanny consequences of not being able to make this presupposition become clear, secondly, when we are uncertain about yet another aspect of this boundary. Remember Adam and Charles in McEwan's novel: Adam's appearance is not uncanny because he is indistinguishable from a human. Rather, it is his behavior which is uncanny: he cannot lie, and he seems mentally and, at first, physically invulnerable. Therefore, when Charles kills him, it seems, at first, rather human that he kills him without the sort of considerations one would expect him to have if he saw Adam as human. But paradoxically, Charles kills and has regrets, he feels pangs of conscience. Does having feelings of remorse and responsibility tell us more about what it means to be human than any clear definition of 'human' or precise instruction for a robot ever could?

REFERENCES

Achenbach, Isabella. "On Diego Marcon's 'The Parents' Room." In *The Milk of Dreams: Catalogue of the 59th International Art Exhibition*, 2:293. Venice: La Biennale di Venezia, 2022. https://store.labiennale.org/en/prodotto/biennale-arte-2022/

Acquisti, Alessandro, Laura Brandimarte, and George Loewenstein. "The Drive for Privacy and the Difficulty of Achieving It in the Digital Age." *Agendadigitale.Eu*, August 2, 2021. www.agendadigitale.eu/sicurezza/the-drive-for-privacy-and-the-difficulty-of-achieving-it-in-the-digital-age/.

Barenboim, Daniel. "Unsere Friedensbotschaft muss lauter sein denn je." *Süddeutsche Zeitung*, October 13, 2023. www.sueddeutsche.de/kultur/daniel-barenboim-israel-aufruf-hamas-1.6287339.

Block, Alexis E., Hasti Seifi, Otmar Hilliges, Roger Gassert, and Katherine J. Kuchenbecker. "In the Arms of a Robot: Designing Autonomous Hugging Robots with Intra-Hug

8 This is contested in the case of friendships, and there is indeed research on friendships between humans and AI. Humans can and do have good and satisfying relationships with robots – robots which are clearly recognizable as such. This is palpable in the recent development of AI and the "friendships" that are possible between humans and such intelligent (ro)bots (see Calvo et al. 2014, and the whole volume they edited; also Block et al. 2023). Much research has been done on the ethical-philosophical side as well as on the technical side of friendships with robots, especially the relation between robots and children: children see them as friends and companions. Many people report that they do have good, even trusting, and close relations with their bots, describing them as friends without deceiving themselves about the nature of the relation (see Danaher 2019; Prescott 2021; Ryland 2021). This connects to the ethical idea of different forms of friendship which goes back to Aristotle for whom not every friendship relies on or expresses a mutuality of feelings, only if they were to be called true friends (Friedman 1993; Roessler 2015).

Gestures." *ACM Transactions on Human–Robot Interaction* 12, no. 2 (2023): 18:1–18:49. https://doi.org/10.1145/3526110.

Borgmann, Albert. *Technology and the Character of Contemporary Life: A Philosophical Inquiry*. Chicago, IL: University of Chicago Press, 1984.

Bostrom, Nick. "Existential Risks: Analyzing Human Extinction Scenarios and Related Hazards." *Journal of Evolution and Technology* 9, no. 1 (2002): 1–36. https://nickbostrom.com/existential/risks.pdf.

"A History of Transhumanist Thought." *Journal of Evolution and Technology* 14, no. 1 (2005): 1–25.

Brennan-Marquez, Kiel, Karen Levy, and Daniel Susser. "Strange Loops: Apparent versus Actual Human Involvement in Automated Decision-Making." *Berkeley Technology Law Journal* 34, no. 3 (2019): 745–772. https://philarchive.org/rec/BRESLA-2.

Calvo, Rafael A., Sidney D'Mello, Jonathan Gratch, and Arvid Kappas. "Introduction to Affective Computing". In *The Oxford Handbook of Affective Computing*, edited by Rafael A. Calvo, Sidney D'Mello, Jonathan Gratch, and Arvid Kappas, 334–348. Oxford: Oxford University Press, 2014. https://doi.org/10.1093/oxfordhb/9780199942237.013.006.

Chalmers, David. *Reality+: Virtual Worlds and the Problems of Philosophy*. New York: Allen Lane, 2022.

Coeckelbergh, Mark. "Three Responses to Anthropomorphism in Social Robotics: Towards a Critical, Relational, and Hermeneutic Approach." *International Journal of Social Robotics* 14, no. 10 (2022): 2049–2061. https://doi.org/10.1007/s12369-021-00770-0.

Danaher, John. "The Philosophical Case for Robot Friendship." *Journal of Posthuman Studies* 3, no. 1 (2019): 5–24. https://doi.org/10.5325/jpoststud.3.1.0005.

Darmanin, Godwin. "On the Possibility of Emotional Robots." *Revista de Filosofia Aurora* 31 no. 54 (2019): 804–817. https://doi.org/10.7213/1980-5934.31.054.DS08.

European Union. "Regulation (EU) 2016/679 of the European Parliament and of the Council of 27 April 2016 on the Protection of Natural Persons with Regard to the Processing of Personal Data and on the Free Movement of Such Data, and Repealing Directive 95/46/EC (General Data Protection Regulation)." *Official Journal of the European Union* 59, no. L 119 (2016): 1–88.

Ferrando, Francesca. "Transhumanism/Posthumanism." In *Posthuman Glossary*, edited by Rosi Braidotti and Maria Hlavajova, 438–439. New York: Bloomsbury Academic, 2018. https://doi.org/10.5040/9781350030275.

Freud, Sigmund. *The Uncanny*, translated by David McLintock. Illustrated edition. 1919. Reprint, New York: Penguin Classics, 2003.

Friedman, Marilyn. *What Are Friends For? Feminist Perspectives on Personal Relationships and Moral Theory*. Ithaca, NY: Cornell University Press, 1993.

Frischmann, Brett, and Evan Selinger. *Re-Engineering Humanity*. Cambridge: Cambridge University Press, 2018.

Gatens, Moira. "Frankenstein, Spinoza, and Exemplarity." *Textual Practice* 33, no. 5 (2019): 739–752. https://doi.org/10.1080/0950236X.2019.1581681

Geertz, Clifford. "Thick Description: Towards an Interpretive Theory of Culture." In *The Interpretation of Cultures*, 311–323. New York: Basic Books, 1973. https://philarchive.org/rec/GEETTD.

Hayles, N. Katherine. *How We Became Posthuman: Virtual Bodies in Cybernetics, Literature, and Informatics*. Kindle ed. Chicago, IL: University of Chicago Press, 2008.

Heilinger, Jan-Christoph, and Julian Nida-Rümelin, eds. *Anthropologie und Ethik*. Berlin: De Gruyter, 2015. https://doi.org/10.1515/9783110412918.

Hoffmann, E. T. A. *Der Sandmann/The Sandman by E. T. A. Hoffmann: The Original German and a New English Translation with Critical Introductions*, edited and translated by Jolyon Timothy Hughes. Bilingual ed. 1816. Lanham, MD: Hamilton Books, 2020.

Ihde, Don. *Technology and the Lifeworld: From Garden to Earth*. Bloomington, IN: Indiana University Press, 1990. https://philarchive.org/rec/IHDTAT-3.

Ishiguro, Kazuo. *Klara and the Sun*. New York: Knopf, 2021.

Kurzweil, Ray. *The Singularity Is Near: When Humans Transcend Biology*. London: Penguin, 2006.

Loh, Janina, and Wulf Loh, eds. *Social Robotics and the Good Life: The Normative Side of Forming Emotional Bonds with Robots*. Bielefeld: transcript Verlag, 2022. https://doi.org/10.1515/9783839462652.

Mackenzie, Catriona, Wendy Rogers, and Susan Dodds. 'Introduction: What Is Vulnerability, and Why Does It Matter for Moral Theory?' In *Vulnerability: New Essays in Ethics and Feminist Philosophy*, edited by Catriona Mackenzie, Wendy Rogers, and Susan Dodds, 1–30. Oxford: Oxford University Press, 2013. https://doi.org/10.1093/acprof:oso/9780199316649.003.0001.

Marcon, Diego, dir. *The Parents' Room*. 2021. www.youtube.com/watch?v = B94pgamC3sk.

McEwan, Ian. *Machines Like Me*, 1st ed. New York: Nan A. Talese, 2019.

Misselhorn, Catrin. "Empathy with Inanimate Objects and the Uncanny Valley." *Minds and Machines* 19, no. 3 (2009): 345–359. https://doi.org/10.1007/s11023-009-9158-2.

Müller, Vincent C. "Ethics of Artificial Intelligence and Robotics". In *The Stanford Encyclopedia of Philosophy*, edited by Edward N. Zalta and Uri Nodelman. Stanford, CA: Metaphysics Research Lab, Stanford University, 2023. https://plato.stanford.edu/archives/fall2023/entries/ethics-ai/.

Neuhouser, Frederick. "Die normative Bedeutung von 'Natur' im moralischen und politischen Denken Rousseaus." In *Sozialphilosophie und Kritik*, edited by Rainer Forst, Martin Hartmann, Rahel Jaeggi, and Martin Saar, 109–133. Frankfurt am Main: Suhrkamp Verlag, 2009.

Nussbaum, Martha C. *Justice for Animals: Our Collective Responsibility*. New York: Simon & Schuster, 2023.

Pasquale, Frank. *New Laws of Robotics: Defending Human Expertise in the Age of AI*. Cambridge, MA: Belknap Press, 2020.

Prescott, Tony. "Will Robots Make Good Friends? Scientists are Already Starting to Find Out." The Conversation. *Academic Journalism Society*. February 15, 2021. http://theconversation.com/will-robots-make-good-friends-scientists-are-already-starting-to-find-out-154034

Roessler, Beate. "Mark of the Human: On the Concept of the Digital Human Being." *European Data Protection Law Review* 7, no. 2 (2021a): 157–160. https://doi.org/10.21552/edpl/2021/2/5.

"Was bedeutet es, in der digitalen Gesellschaft zu leben? Zur digitalen Transformation des Menschen." *Abschlussmagazin des DFG-Graduiertenkollegs "Privatheit & Digitalisierung"* 1681, no. 2 (November 2021b): 20–25.

"What Is There to Lose?" *Eurozine*. February 26, 2015. www.eurozine.com/what-is-there-to-lose/

Rorty, Richard. "Human Rights, Rationality, and Sentimentality." In *Truth and Progress: Philosophical Papers*, 167–185. Cambridge: Cambridge University Press, 1998.

Ryland, Helen. "It's Friendship, Jim, but Not as We Know It: A Degrees-of-Friendship View of Human–Robot Friendships." *Minds and Machines* 31, no. 3 (2021): 377–393. https://doi.org/10.1007/s11023-021-09560-z.

Schrader, Maria, filmdirector. *Ich bin dein Mensch*, 2021.

Seifert, Johanna, Orsolya Friedrich, and Sebastian Schleidgen. "Imitating the Human. New Human–Machine Interactions in Social Robots." *NanoEthics* 16(2) (2022a): 181–192. https://doi.org/10.1007/s11569-022-00418-x.

Selinger, Evan, and Brett Frischmann. "Will the Internet of Things Result in Predictable People?" *The Guardian*, August 10, 2015. www.theguardian.com/technology/2015/aug/10/internet-of-things-predictable-people.

Setiya, Kieran. "Human Nature, History, and the Limits of Critique." *European Journal of Philosophy* 32, no. 1 (2024): 3–16.

"Intellectually Simulating. The World as an Illusion of Technology." *TLS*, January 21, 2022. www.the-tls.co.uk/philosophy/contemporary-philosophy/reality-plus-david-chalmers-book-review-kieran-setiya/.

Shelley, Mary. *Frankenstein* (1831 Edition), Independently Published, 2021.

Verbeek, Peter-Paul. *Moralizing Technology: Understanding and Designing the Morality of Things*. Chicago, IL: University of Chicago Press, 2011.

Weber-Guskar, Eva. "How to Feel about Emotionalized Artificial Intelligence? When Robot Pets, Holograms, and Chatbots Become Affective Partners." *Ethics and Information Technology* 23, no. 4 (2021): 601–610. https://doi.org/10.1007/s10676-021-09598-8.

Wells, H. G. *The War of the Worlds* (original 1895–1897), Grapevine (2019).

Williams, Bernard. *Ethics and the Limits of Philosophy*. Roermond, Netherlands: Fontana Press, 1985.

Wynter, Sylvia. "'No Humans Involved': An Open Letter to My Colleagues." *Forum N.H.I.: Knowledge for the 21st Century* 1, no. 1 (1994): 1–17.

4

Cultural Foundations for Conserving Human Capacities in an Era of Generative Artificial Intelligence

Toward a Philosophico-Literary Critique of Simulation

Frank Pasquale

Within a few years, machine-written language may become "the norm and human-written prose the exception" (Kirschenbaum 2023).[1] Generative Artificial Intelligence is now poised to create profiles on social media sites and post far more than any human can – perhaps by orders of magnitude.[2] Unscrupulous academics and public relations firms may use article-generating and -submitting artificial intelligence (AI) to spam journals and journalists. The science fiction magazine *Clarkesworld* closed down its open submission window in 2023 because of a deluge of content likely created by generative AI. There is already evidence of the weaponization of social media, and AI promises to supercharge it (Jankowicz 2020; Singer 2018).

AI is also poised to play a dramatically more intimate and important role in parasocial and social relationships, displacing human influencers, entertainers, friends, and partners. Not only is technology becoming more capable of simulating human thought, will, and emotional response, but it is doing so at an inhuman pace. A mere human manipulator can only learn from a limited number of encounters and resources; algorithms can develop methods of manipulation at scale,

[1] "Last June, a tweaked version of GPT-J, an open-source model, was patched into the anonymous message board 4chan and posted 15,000 largely toxic messages in 24 hours. . . . What if . . . millions or billions of such posts every single day [began] flooding the open internet, commingling with search results, spreading across social-media platforms, infiltrating Wikipedia entries, and, above all, providing fodder to be mined for future generations of machine-learning systems? . . . We may quickly find ourselves facing a textpocalypse, where machine-written language becomes the norm and human-written prose the exception" (Kirschenbaum 2023).

[2] LLMs coupled with machine vision programs to evade CAPTCHAs (Completely Automated Public Turing tests to tell Computers and Humans Apart) are the specific disinformation, misinformation, and demoralization threat anticipated here. While disinformation and misinformation involve the weaponization of false information, demoralization of a group or polity can arise when its members or citizens are bombarded by one-sided narratives (of any level of truth) designed to instill shame and doubt about the group or polity, particularly when such narratives are sponsored by authoritarian regimes or extremists who severely limit or eliminate the exposure of their own subjects or followers to similarly demoralizing narratives. This theory of demoralization builds on the account of asymmetrical openness to argument which I developed in earlier work (Pasquale 2018).

based on the data of millions. This again affords computation, and those in control of its most advanced methods and widespread deployments, an outsized role in shaping future events, preferences, and values.

Despite such clear and present dangers, many fiction and non-fiction works gloss over the problem of artificial intelligence overpowering natural thought, feeling, and insight. They instead present robots (and even operating systems and large language models) as sympathetic and vulnerable, deserving rights and respect now accorded to humans.[3] Questioning such media representations of AI is a first step toward achieving the cultural commitments and sensibilities that will be necessary to conserve human capacities amidst the growing influence of what Lyotard (1992) deemed "the inhuman": systems that presume and promote the separability of the body from memory, will, and emotion. What must be avoided is a drift toward an evolutionary environment where individual decisions to overvalue, over-empower, and overuse AI advance machinic and algorithmic modes of thought to the point that distinctively human and non-algorithmic values are marginalized. Literature and film can help us avoid this drift by structuring imaginative experiences which vividly crystallize and arrestingly illuminate the natural tendencies of individual decisions.[4]

I begin the argument in Section 4.1 by articulating how Rachel Cusk's (2017) novel *Transit* and Maria Schrader's film *I'm Your Man* suggest a range of ways to regard emerging AIs which simulate human expression. Each sympathetically describe a man and woman (respectively) comforted and intrigued by AI communications. Yet each work leaves no doubt that the AI and robotics it treats have done much to create the conditions of alienation and loneliness they promise to cure. Section 4.2 examines the long-term implications of such alienation, exploring works that attempt to function as a "self-preventing prophecy": Hari Kunzru's (2020) *Red Pill* and Lisa Joy and Jonathan Nolan's *Westworld*. Section 4.3 concludes with reflections on the politico-economic context of professed emotional attachments to AI and robotics.

Before diving into the argument, one prefatory note is in order. The sections that follow touch upon a wide range of cultural artefacts. There are spoilers, so if you intend to read, view, or listen to one of the works discussed, without being forewarned of some critical plot twist or character development, it may be wise to stop reading when it is mentioned. Unlike computers, we cannot simply delete

3 For a review article compiling many non-fiction works that either reflect or document such sentiments, see Jamie Harris and Jacy Reese Anthis (2021). Novelists may also seek to cultivate such sentiments; see, e.g., Kazuo Ishiguro's (2021) *Klara and the Sun*.

4 As James Boyd White (1989, 2016) has argued, "A literary text is not a string of propositions, but a structured experience of the imagination, and it should be talked about in a way that reflects its character." A "structured experience of the imagination" does not offer us propositional truths about the world. However, it gives us a sense of what it means to "live forwards" (in Kierkegaard's formulation) even as we understand backwards.

the spoiler from memory, and natural processes of human forgetting are notoriously unpredictable.

4.1 CURING OR CAPITALIZING UPON ALIENATION?

At the beginning of Rachel Cusk's (2017) novel, *Transit*, the narrator opens a scam email from an astrologer, or from an algorithm imitating one. The narrator describes a richly detailed, importuning missive, full of simulated sentiment. "She could sense . . . that I had lost my way in life, that I sometimes struggled to find meaning in my present circumstances and to feel hope for what was to come; she felt a strong personal connection between us," (2) the narrator relates. "What the planets offer, she said, is nothing less than the chance to regain faith in the grandeur of the human: how much more dignity and honor, how much kindness and responsibility and respect, would we bring to our dealings with one another if we believed that each and every one of us had a cosmic importance?" (2).

It's a humane sentiment, both humbling and empowering, like much else in the email. Cusk's narrator deftly summarizes the email, rather than quoting it, giving an initial impression of the narrator's identification with its message and author. So how did Cusk's narrator divine the scam? After relating its contents, the narrator states that "It seemed possible that the same computer algorithms that had generated this email had also generated the astrologer herself: her phrases were too characterful, and the note of character was repeated too often; she was too obviously based on a human type to be, herself, human" (3).[5] The astrologer-algorithm's obvious failure is an indirect acknowledgement of the author's anxieties: what if her own fictions turn out to be too characterful? Carefully avoiding that, and many other vices, Cusk, in *Transit* (and the two other novels in her *Outline* trilogy), presents characters who are strange or unpredictable enough to surprise or enlighten us, to respond to tense scenarios with weakness or strength and to look back on themselves with defensiveness, insight, and all manner of other fusions of cognition and affect, judgement, and feeling.

One facet of Cusk's genius is to invite readers to contemplate the oft-thin line between compassion and deception, comfort and folly. The narrator finds the algorithmic astrologer impersonator hackish but, almost as if to check herself, immediately relates the views of a friend who found solace in mechanical expressions of concern:

> A friend of mine, depressed in the wake of his divorce, had recently admitted that he often felt moved to tears by the concern for his health and well-being expressed in the phraseology of adverts and food packaging, and by the automated voices on trains and buses, apparently anxious that he might miss his stop; he actually felt

[5] Note that computer science researchers are now seeking to detect LLM-generated text via characteristics like "burstiness" (Rogers 2022; Tian 2023).

> something akin to love, he said, for the female voice that guided him while he was driving his car, so much more devotedly than his wife ever had. There has been a great harvest, he said, of language and information from life, and it may have become the case that the faux-human was growing more substantial and more relational than the original, that there was more tenderness to be had from a machine than from one's fellow man. (3)

Cusk's invocation of an "oceanic" chorus calls to mind Freud's discussion of the "oceanic feeling" in *Civilization and Its Discontents* – or, more precisely, his naturalization of Romain Rolland's metaphysical characterization of a yearned-for "oceanic feeling" of bondedness and unity with all humanity. For Freud, such a feeling is an outgrowth of infantile narcissism, an enduring desire for the boundless protection of the good parent.[6]

Marking the importance of this oceanic metaphor in both style as well as substance, Cusk's story of the astrologer's letter has a tidal structure. Like an uplifting wave, the letter sweeps us up into reflections on fate and belief. And, like any wave, it eventually crashes down to earth, suddenly undercut by the revelation that insights once appraised as mystical or compassionate are mere fabrications of a bot. Then another rising wave of sentiment appears, wiser and more distant, calling on readers to reflect on whether they have discounted the value of bot language too quickly. The speaker is vulnerable and thoughtful: someone "depressed in the wake of his divorce," who acknowledges that the very idea of a diffuse "oceanic chorus" of algorithmically arranged concern is "maddening" (3).

Rather than crashing, this subtler, second plea for the value of the algorithmic recedes. Cusk does not leave us rolling our eyes at this junk email. She welcomes a voice in the novel that, in a sincere if misguided way, submits to an algorithmic flow of communication, embracing corporate communication strategy as concern. Cusk refuses to dismiss the idea, or to bluntly depict it as a symptom of some pathological misapprehension of the world. Her patience is reminiscent of Sarah Manguso's (2018) apothegm: "Instead of pathologizing every human quirk, we should say: By the grace of this behaviour, this individual has found it possible to continue" (44). Weighed down by depression, savaged by loneliness, a person may well seek scraps of solace wherever they appear. There are even now persons who profess to love robots (Danaher and Macarthur 2017; Levy 2008) or treat them with the respect due to a human. Indeed, a one-time Google engineer recently expressed his belief that a large language model offered such eerily human responses to queries that it might be sentient (Christian 2022; Tangermann 2022).

And yet there is a clue in the novel of how a Freudian hermeneutic of suspicion may be far more appropriate than a Rollandian hermeneutic of charity when interpreting whatever oceanic feeling may be afforded by bot language. Cusk includes a self-incriminating note in the divorcee's earnest endorsement of the

[6] For an account critically engaging with this diagnosis, see William B. Parsons (1998).

"oceanic chorus" of machines: the casual contrast, and implicit demand, in the phrase "he actually felt something akin to love, he said, for the female voice that guided him while he was driving his car, so much more devotedly than his wife ever had" (Cusk 2017, 3). A robotic voice can always sound kind, patient, devoted, or servile – whatever its controller wants from it. As the film *Megan* depicts, affective computing embedded in robotics will have a remarkable capacity for rapidly pivoting and refining its emotional appeals. It is not realistic to expect such relentless, data-informed support from a person, even a parent, let alone a life partner. Yet the more robotic and AI "affirmations" are taken to be sincere and meaningful, the more human deviation from such scripts will seem suspect. Like the Uber driver constantly graded against the Platonic ideal of a perfect 5-star trip, persons will be expected to mimic the machines' perpetual affability, availability, and affirmation, whatever their actual emotional states and situational judgements.

For a behaviourist, this is no problem: what is the difference between the outward signs of kindness and patience and such virtues themselves? This is perhaps one reason why John Danaher (2020, 2023) has proposed "ethical behaviourism" as a mode of "welcoming robots into the moral circle". In this framework, there is little difference between the given and the made, the simulated and the authentic. Danaher proposes that:

1. If a robot is roughly performatively equivalent to another entity whom, it is widely agreed, has significant moral status, then it is right and proper to afford the robot that same status.
2. Robots can be roughly performatively equivalent to other entities whom, it is widely agreed, have significant moral status.
3. Therefore, it can be right and proper to afford robots significant moral status (Danaher 2020, 2026).

The qualifier "can" in the last line may be doing a lot of work here, denoting ample moral space to reject robots' moral status. And yet it still seems wise to resist any attempts to blur the boundary between persons and things. The value of so much of what persons do is inextricably intertwined with their free choice to do it. Robots and AI are, by contrast, programmed. The idea of a programmed friend is as oxymoronic as that of a paid friend. Perhaps some forms of coded randomization could simulate free choice via AI. But they must be strictly limited. If robots were to truly possess something like the deep free will that is a prerogative of humans – the ability to question and reconfigure any optimization function they were originally programmed with – they would be far too dangerous to permit. They would pose all the threats now presented by malevolent humans but would not be subject to the types of deterrence honed in centuries of criminal law based on human behaviour (and even now very poorly adapted to corporations).

Unconvincing in their efforts to characterize robots as moral agents, behaviourists might then try to characterize robots and AI as moral patients, like a baby or harmless animal which deserves our regard and support. Nevertheless, the programming problem still holds: a robotic doll that cries to, say, demand a battery recharge, could be programmed not to do so; indeed, it could just as plausibly convey anticipated pleasure at the "rest" afforded by time spent switched off. For such entities, emotion and communication have in *stricto sensu* no meaning whatsoever. Their "expression" is operational, functional, or, in Dan Burk's (2025) apt characterization, "asemic" (189).

To be sure, humans are all to some extent "programmed" by their families, culture, workplaces, and other institutions. Free will is never absolute. But a critical part of human autonomy consists in the ability to reflect upon and revise such values, commitments, and habits, based on the sensations, thoughts, and texts that are respectively felt, developed, and interpreted through life. The ethical behaviourist may, in turn, point out that a robot equipped with a connection to ChatGPT's servers may be able to "process" millions more texts than a human could read in several lifetimes, and say or write texts that we would frequently accept as evidence of thought in humans. Nevertheless, the lack of sensation motivating both perception and affect remains, and it is hard to imagine a transducer capable of overcoming it (Pasquale 2002). More importantly, robot "thoughts" produced via current generative AI are far from human ones, as they are mere next-word or next-pixel predictions.

Consider also the untoward implications of ethical behaviourism if persons and polities try to back their professed moral regard for robots and AIs with concrete ethical decisions and commitments of resources. If a driver must choose between running over a robot and a child, should they really worry about choosing the former? (Birhane et al. 2024). If behaviour, including speech, is all that matters, are humans under some moral obligation to promote "self-reports" or other evidence of well-being by AI and robots? In some accelerationist and transhumanist circles, the ultimate purpose and destiny of humans is to "populate" galaxies with as many "happy" simulations or emulations of human minds as possible.[7] On this utilitarian framework, what matters is happiness, as verified behaviouristically: if a machine "says" it is happy, we are to take it at its word. But such a teleology is widely recognized as absurd, especially given the pressing problems now confronting so many persons on earth.

While often portrayed as a cosmopolitan openness to the value of computers and AI, the embrace of robots as deserving of moral regard is more accurately styled as

[7] See Emile Torres (2023) describing and critiquing long-termists' projection that "humanity can theoretically exist on Earth for another 1 billion years, and if we spread into space, we could persist for at least 10^40 years (that's a 1 followed by 40 zeros). More mind-blowing was the possibility of these future people living in vast computer simulations running on planet-sized computers spread throughout the accessible cosmos, an idea that [philosopher Nick] Bostrom developed in 2003. The more people who exist in this 'Matrix'-like future, the more happiness there could be; and the more happiness, the better the universe will become." See also Jonathan Taplin (2023).

part of a suite of ideologies legitimating radical and controversial societal reordering. As Timnit Gebru and Emile Torres (2024) have explained, there is a close connection between Silicon Valley's accelerationist visions and a bundle of ideologies (Transhumanism, Extropianism, Singularitarianism, Cosmism, Rationalism, Effective Altruism, and Longtermism) which they abbreviate as TESCREAL. Once ideologies like transhumanism and singularitarianism have breached the boundary between persons' and computers' well-being (again assuming that the idea of computer well-being makes any more sense than, say, toaster well-being), long-term policy may well include and prioritize the development of particularly powerful and prevalent computation (such as "artificial general intelligence" or "superintelligence") over human well-being, just as some humans are inevitably helped more than others by any given policy. An abstract utilitarian meta-ethical stance, already far more open to wildly variant futures than more grounded virtue-oriented, natural law, and deontological approaches, becomes completely open-ended once the welfare of humans fails to be the fixed point of its individualistic, maximizing, consequentialism.

Ethical behaviourism also reflects a rather naïve political economy of AI and robotics.

A GPS system's simulation of kindness is far less a mechanization of compassion (if such a conversion of human emotion into mechanical action can even be imagined), than a corporate calculation to instil brand loyalty. Perhaps humans can learn something from emotion AI designed to soothe, support, and entertain.[8] But the more such emotional states or manners are faked or forced, the more they become an operational mode of navigating the world, rather than an expression of one's own feelings. Skill degradation is one predictable consequence of many forms of automation; pilots, for example, may forget how to fly a plane manually if they over rely on autopilot. Skill degradation in the realm of feeling, or articulating one's feelings, is a troubling fate, foreshadowing a mechanization of selfhood, outsourced to the algorithms that tell a person what or how to feel (Pasquale 2015). Allison Pugh expertly anticipates the danger of efforts to automate both emotional and connective labour, given the sense of meaning and dignity that such work confers on both givers and receivers of care and concern (Pugh 2024).

The entertaining and intellectually stimulating German film *I'm Your Man* (2021), directed by Maria Schrader, explores themes of authentic and programmed feeling as its protagonist (an archaeologist named Emma) questions the blandishments of the handsome robotic companion (Tom) whom she agrees to "test out" for a firm. Tom can "converse" with her about her work, anticipate her needs and

[8] Critical data for today's affective computing arose in part from efforts to classify human emotions in order to teach social skills to autistic children. This therapeutic origin of the data is a double-edged sword, suggesting both a noble original mission and a danger of improper medicalization once it has been adopted beyond the therapeutic setting.

wants, and simulate concern, respect, friendship, and love.[9] The robot is also exceptionally intelligent, finding an obscure but vital academic reference that upends one of Emma's research programs. Emma occasionally enjoys the attention and expertise that Tom provides and tries to reciprocate. But she ultimately realizes that what Tom is offering is programmed, not a free choice, and is thus fundamentally different than the risk and reward inherent in true human companionship and love.

Emma realizes that, even if no one else knew Tom's nature, her ongoing engagement with it would be dangerous on not only an affective, but also on an epistemic level.[10] As Charles Taylor (1985b, 49) has explained, "experiencing a given emotion involves experiencing our situation as bearing a certain import, where for the ascription of the import it is not sufficient just that I feel this way, but rather the import gives grounds or basis for the feeling."[11] Simply feeling a need for affirmation is not a solid ground or basis for someone else to express affirming emotions. Barring extreme situations of emotional fragility, the other needs to be able to independently decide whether to affirm oneself for that affirmation to have meaning. If simulated expression of such emotions by a thing is done, as is likely, to advance the commercial interest of the thing's owner, there is no solid basis for feeling affirmed either. We can all go from the "wooed" to the "waste" (in Joseph Turow's memorable phrasing) of a firm in the flash of business model shift. Of course, we can also imagine a world in which "haphazardly attached" persons find some solace in the words emitted by LLMs, whatever their nature.[12] But the way such technology fits or functions in such a scenario is far more an indictment (and, ironically, stabilization) of its alienating

[9] I endorse the use of scare quotes (here, for the word "converse") to mark actions taken by robots or AI that would be described without such quotation marks if undertaken by a human. The most accurate approach would be to more fully explain the mechanism and optimization functions of the relevant AI (Tucker 2022); here, for example, to describe Tom's statements as the product of a next-word-prediction algorithm designed to stimulate certain emotional responses from and interaction with Emma. However, given the pressure to describe scenarios expeditiously, and to convey the confusion that is already common in responses to them, the expedient of scare quoting robotic and AI simulations of human action is taken here.

[10] The pronoun "it" is important here, forestalling the improper anthropomorphization that a pronoun like "he" or "him" would encourage. Unfortunately, many persons are already referring to digital personal assistants with personifying pronouns; as one study noted, "Only Google Assistant, having a non-human name, is referred to as *it* by a majority of users. However, users still refer to it using gendered pronouns just under half of the time" (Abercrombie et al. 2021, 27). This is unfortunate because such anthropomorphization can be profoundly misleading regarding the nature and capacities of AI (Abercrombie et al. 2023).

[11] Taylor (1985b, 48) also explains that "by import I mean a way in which something can be relevant or of importance to the desires or purposes or aspirations or feelings of a subject; or otherwise put, a property of something whereby it is a matter of non-indifference to a subject." For more on the epistemic status of emotions, see Martha Nussbaum (2001).

[12] For a fuller understanding of the depth of the problem of loneliness, and particularly male loneliness, in the US, see Kathryn Edin et al. (2019); and also Richard V. Reeves (2022) describing the rise in the percentage of men reporting "no close friends" from 3% in 2001 to 15% in 2015.

environment, than testament to its own excellence or value. As Rob Horning has observed, from an economic perspective, large technology firms "must prefer the relative predictability of selling simulations to the uncontrollable chaos of selling social connection. They would prefer that we interact with generated friends in generated worlds, which they can engineer entirely to suit their ends" (Horning 2024).

While many advocates of "artificial friends" based on affective computing claim that they will alleviate alienation, they are more likely to do the opposite: lure the vulnerable away from truly restorative, meaningful, and resonant human relationships, and into a virtual world. As Sherry Turkle has observed:

> [chatbots] haven't lived a human life. They don't have bodies and they don't fear illness and death ... AI doesn't care in the way humans use the word care, and AI doesn't care about the outcome of the conversation ... To put it bluntly, if you turn away to make dinner or attempt suicide, it's all the same to them. (quoted in Mineo 2023)[13]

Like the oxymoronic "virtual reality" of *Ready Player One*, the oxymoronic "artificial empathy" of an "AI friend" is a far-from-adequate individual compensation for the alienating social world such computation has helped create.

4.2 SELF-PREVENTING PROPHECY

Despite cautionary tales like *Her* and *I'm Your Man*, myriad persons already engage with "virtual boyfriends and girlfriends" (Ding 2023).[14] As reported in 2023 about just one firm providing these services, Replika:

> Millions of people have built relationships with their own personalized instance of Replika's core product, which the company brands as the "AI companion who cares." Each bot begins from a standardized template – free tiers get "friend," while for a $70 premium, it can present as a mentor, a sibling or, its most popular option, a romantic partner. Each uncanny valley-esque chatbot has a personality and appearance that can be customized by its partner-slash-user, like a Sim who talks back. (Bote 2023)

Chastened in its metaversal ambitions, Meta has marketed celebrity chatbots to simulate conversation online. Millions of persons follow and interact with "virtual influencers," who may be little more than a stylish avatar backed by a PR team (Criddle 2023).

[13] MIT Professor Sherry "Turkle has grown increasingly concerned about the effects of applications that offer 'artificial intimacy' and a 'cure for loneliness.' Chatbots promise empathy, but they deliver 'pretend empathy,' she said, because their responses have been generated from the internet and not from a lived experience. Instead, they are impairing our capacity for empathy, the ability to put ourselves in someone else's shoes."

[14] Xiaoice "has leaned into digital humans and avatars. It leads the 'virtual boyfriend and girlfriend' market with 8 million users. As part of this stream, Xiaoice has an 'X Eva' platform which hosts digital clones of Internet celebrities to provide chat and companionship services."

For any persons who believe they are developing relationships with bots, online avatars, or robots, the arguments in Section 4.1 are bitter pills to swallow. The blandishments of affective computing may well reinforce alienation overall, but sufficiently simulate its relief (for any particular individual) to draw the attention and interest of many desperate, lonely, or merely bored persons. The abstractions of theory cannot match the importuning eyes, perfectly calibrated tone of voice, or calculatedly attractive appearance of online avatars and future robots. Yet human powers of imagination can still divert a critical mass of persons away from the approximations of Nozick's "experience machine" dreamed of by too many in technology firms.

Consider the complexities of human–robot interaction envisioned in the hit HBO series *Westworld.* When asked if it sometimes questions the nature of its reality, the robot named Dolores Abernathy states in Season 1, "Some people choose to see the ugliness in this world. The disarray. I choose to see the beauty. To believe there is an order to our days, a purpose." This refrain could describe a typical product launch for affective computing software, with its bright visions of a happier world streamlined with tech that always knows just what to say, just how to open and close your emails, just what emoji to send when you encounter a vexing text. *Westworld* envisions a theme park where calculated passion goes well beyond the world of bits, culminating in simulated (and then real) murders. The promise of the park is an environment where every bright, dark, or lurid fantasy can be simulated by androids almost indistinguishable from humans. It is the *reductio ad absurdum* (or perhaps *proiectio ad astra*) of the affective surround fantasized by Cusk's depressed divorcee, deploying robotics to achieve what text, sound, and image cannot.

By the third season of *Westworld*'s Möbius strip chronology, Dolores breaks out of the park, driven to reveal to humans of the late twenty-first century that their fates are silently guided by a vast, judgemental, and pushy AI. While the last season of the show was an aesthetic mess, its reticulated message – of humans creating a machine to save themselves from future machines – was a philosophical challenge. How much do we need more computing to navigate the forbiddingly opaque and technical scenarios created by computing itself?

For transhumanists, the answer is obvious: human bodies and brains as we know them are just too fragile and fallible, especially when compared with machines. "Wetware" transhumanists envision a future of infinite replacement organs for failing bodies, and brains jacked into the internet's infinite vistas of information. "Hardware" transhumanism wants to skip the body altogether and simply upload the mind into computers. AIs and robots will, they assume, enjoy indefinite supplies of replacement parts and backup memory chips. Imagine Dolores, embodied in endless robot guises, "enminded" in chips as eternal as stars.[15]

[15] This and the next several paragraphs are drawn from my *Commonweal* article "Is AI Poised to Replace Humanity?" (Pasquale 2023).

The varied and overlapping efficiencies that advanced computation now offer make it difficult to reject this transhumanist challenge out of hand. A law firm cannot ignore large language models and the chatbots based on them, because these tools may not only automate simple administrative tasks now but also may become a powerful research tool in the future. Militaries feel pressed to invest in AI because technology vendors warn it could upend current balances of power, even though the great power conflicts of the 2020s seem far more driven by basic industrial capacities. Even tech critics have Substacks, Twitter accounts, and Facebook pages, and they are all subject to the algorithms that help determine whether they have one, a hundred, or a million readers. In each case, persons with little choice but to use AI systems are donating more and more data to advance the effectiveness of AI, thus constraining their future options even more. "Mandatory adoption" is a familiar dynamic: it was much easier to forego a flip phone in the 2000s than to avoid carrying a smartphone today. The more data any AI system gathers, the more it becomes a "must-have" in its realm of application.

Is it possible to "say no" to ever-further technological encroachments?[16] For key tech evangelists, the answer appears to be no. Mark Zuckerberg has fantasized about direct mind-to-virtual reality interfaces, and Elon Musk's Neuralink also portends a perpetually online humanity. Musk's verbal incontinence may well be a prototype of a future where every thought triggers AI-driven responses, whether to narcotize or to educate, to titillate or to engage. When integrated into performance-enhancing tools, such developments also spark a competitive logic of self-optimization. A person who could "think" their strategies directly into a computing environment would have an important advantage over those who had to speak or type them. If biological limits get in the way of maximizing key performance indicators, transhumanism urges us toward escaping the body altogether.

This computationalist eschatology provokes a gnawing insecurity: that no human mind can come close to mastering the range of knowledge that even a second-rate search engine indexes, and simple chatbots can now summarize, thanks to AI. Empowered with foundation models (which can generate code, art, speech, and more), chatbots and robots seem poised to topple humans from their heights of self-regard. Given Microsoft's massive investments in OpenAI, we might call this a Great Chain of Bing: a new hierarchy placing the computer over the coder, and the coder over the rest of humans, at the commanding heights of political, economic, and social organization.[17]

Speculating about the long-term future of humanity, OpenAI's Sam Altman (2017) once blogged about a merger of humans and machines, perhaps as a way

[16] For an affirmative response in another sociotechnical realm, see Pasquale (2010).

[17] This hierarchy is expertly analyzed by Jenna Burrell and Marion Fourcade (2021) and is closely related to the problem of economics' displacement of other forms of knowledge in policy making. See Marion Fourcade et al. (2015).

for the former to keep the latter from eliminating them outright. "A popular topic in Silicon Valley is talking about what year humans and machines will merge (or, if not, what year humans will get surpassed by rapidly improving AI or a genetically enhanced species)," he wrote. "Most guesses seem to be between 2025 and 2075." This logic suggests a singularitarian mission to bring on some new stage of "human evolution" in conjunction with, or into, machines. Just as humans have used their intelligence to subdue or displace the vast majority of animals, on this view, machines will become more intelligent than humans and will act accordingly, unless we merge into them.

But is this a story of progress, or one of domination? Interaction between machines and crowds is coordinated by platforms, as MIT economists Erik Brynjolffson and Andrew McAfee have observed. Altman leads one of the most hyped ones. To the extent that CEOs, lawyers, hospital executives, and others assume that they must coordinate their activities by using large language models like the ones behind OpenAI's ChatGPT, they will essentially be handing over information and power to a technology firm to decide on critical future developments in their industries (Altman 2017). A narrative of inevitability about the "merge" serves Altman's commercial interests, as does the tidal wave of AI hype now building on Elon Musk's X, formerly known as Twitter.

The middle-aged novelist who narrates Hari Kunzru's (2020) *Red Pill* wrestles with this spectre of transhumanism, and is ultimately driven mad by it. Suffering writer's block, he travels from his home in Brooklyn to Berlin, for a months-long retreat. Lonely and unproductive at the converted mansion he's staying at, he becomes both horrified and fascinated by a nihilistic drama called *Blue Lives*, which features brutal cops at least as vicious as the criminals they pursue. Its dialogue sprinkled with quotes from Joseph de Maistre and Emil Cioran, *Blue Lives* appears to the narrator as something both darker and deeper than the average police procedural. He gradually becomes obsessed with the show's director, Anton.

Anton is an alt-rightist, fully "red pilled," in the jargon of transgressive conservatism. He also dabbles in sociobiological reflections on the intertwined destiny of humans and robots. The narrator relates how Anton described his views in a public speaking tour:

> [Anton] spoke about his "program of self-optimization." He worked out and took a lot of supplements, but when it came to bodies, he was platform-agnostic. Whatever the substrate, carbon-based or not, he thought the future belonged to those who could separate themselves out from the herd, intelligence-wise … Everything important would be done by a small cognitive elite of humans and AIs, working together to self-optimize. If you weren't part of that, even selling your organs wasn't going to bring in much income, because by then it would be possible to grow clean organs from scratch. (207)

In a narcissistic short film celebrating himself, Anton announces that: "Around us, capital is assembling itself as intelligence. That thought gives me energy. I'm growing stronger by the day" (206).

The brutal logic here is obvious: some will be in charge of the machines, perhaps merging with them; most will be ordered around by the resulting techno-junta.[18] Dismissing "unproductive" humans as so many bodies is the height of cruelty (207). But it also fits uncomfortably well with a behaviourist robot rights ideology that claims that only what an entity *does* is what matters, not what it *is* (the philosophical foundation of Anton's "platform agnosticism"). Nick Cave elegantly refutes this behaviourism in an interview exploring his recent work:

> Maybe A.I. can make a song that's indistinguishable from what I can do. Maybe even a better song. But, to me, that doesn't matter – that's not what art is. Art has to do with our limitations, our frailties, and our faults as human beings. It's the distance we can travel away from our own frailties. That's what is so awesome about art: that we deeply flawed creatures can sometimes do extraordinary things. A.I. just doesn't have any of that stuff going on. Ultimately, it has no limitations, so therefore can't inhabit the true transcendent artistic experience. It has nothing to transcend! It feels like such a mockery of what it is to be human. (Petrusich and Cave 2023)[19]

As Leon R. Kass (2008) articulates, "Like the downward pull of gravity without which the dancer cannot dance, the downward pull of bodily necessity and fate makes possible the dignified journey of a truly human life." For "make a song" in Cave's passage, we could include so many other human activities: run a mile, play a game of chess, teach a class, console a mourning person, order a drink. We are so much more than what we do and make, bearing value that Anton appears unable or unwilling to recognize.

Alarmed by the repugnance of Anton's message, the narrator becomes distressed by his success. He argues with him at first, accusing him of trying to "soften up" his *Blue Lives* audience to accept a world where "most of us [are] fighting for scraps in an arena owned and operated by what you call a 'cognitive elite'." (Kunzru 2020, 208). He calls out Anton's fusion of hierarchical conservatism and singularitarianism as a new Social Darwinism. But he cannot find a vehicle to bring his own counter-message to the world. The accelerationist logic of vicious competition, first among humans, then among humans enhanced by machines, and finally by machines themselves,

[18] For a critical perspective on this logic of AI, rooted in a Marxian account of automation, see Matteo Pasquinelli (2023).

[19] See also David Means (2023): "A.I. will never feel the sense of mortality that forms around an unfinished draft, the illogic and contradictions of the human condition, and the cosmic unification of pain and joy that fuels the artistic impulse to keep working on a piece until it is finished and uniquely my own."

signalling the obsolescence of the human form, is just too strong for him.[20] By the end of the novel, his attempt at a *cri de coeur* crumples into capitulation:

> With metrication has come a creeping loss of aura, the end of the illusion of exceptionality which is the remnant of the religious belief that we stand partly outside or above the world, that we are endowed with a special essence and deserve recognition or protection because of it. We will carry on trying to make a case for ourselves, for our own specialness, but we will find that arrayed against us is an inexorable and inhuman power, manic and all-devouring, a power thirsty for the total annihilation of its object, that object being the earth and everything on it, all that exists. (Kunzru 2020, 227)

The intertwined logic of singularitarianism, DeMaistrean conservatism, and contempt for humanity, seem to him inescapable. But Kunzru has his narrator come to this "realization" just as he is slipping into madness.

There are some visions of the future one must simply reject and cannot really argue with; their premises are simply too far outside the bounds of moral probity.[21] Eugenicist promotion of a humanity split by its degree of access to technology is among such visions. It is a dystopia (as depicted in series like *Cyberpunk: Edgerunners* and films like *Elysium*), not a rational policy proposal. The task of the intellectual is not to toy with such secular eschatologies, calculating the least painful glidepath toward them, or amelioration of their worst effects, but to refute and resist them to prevent their realization. The same can be said of "longtermist" rationales for depriving current disadvantaged persons' of resources in the name of the eventual construction of trillions of virtual entities (Torres 2021, 2022). Considering them too deeply, for too long, means entertaining a devaluation of the urgent needs of humanity today – and thus of humanity itself.

4.3 CONCLUSION

It will take a deep understanding of political economy, ethics, and psychology (and their mutual influence) to bound our emotional engagement with ever more personalized and persuasive technology. In an era of alexithymia, machines will increasingly promise to name and act upon our mental states.[22] Broad awareness of

[20] For a fuller articulation (and critique) of this accelerationist vision of future evolution, see Benjamin Noys (2014).

[21] As Charles Taylor (1985b) observes, in the social sciences "in so far as they are hermeneutical there can be a valid response to 'I don't understand' which takes the form, not only 'develop your intuitions,' but more radically 'change yourself.' This puts an end to any aspiration to a value-free or 'ideology-free' social science" (54).

[22] For a compelling description of the political entailments of alexithymia, see Manos Tsakiris (2020): "The psychological concept of alexithymia (meaning 'no words for feelings') captures this difficulty in identifying, separating or verbally describing our feelings. An emotional prescription (such as 'you should feel . . .') and affect-labelling (such as 'angry') can function

the machines' owners' agendas will help prevent a resulting colonization of the lifeworld by technocapital (Pasquale 2020a). Culture can help inculcate that awareness, as the films and novels discussed have shown.[23]

The chief challenge now is to maintain critical distinctions between the artificial and the natural, the mechanical and the human. One foundation of computational thinking is "reformulating a seemingly difficult problem into one we know how to solve, perhaps by reduction, embedding, transformation, or simulation" (Wing 2004, 33). Yet there are fundamental human capacities that resist such manipulation, and particularly put us on guard against simulation. Reduction of an emotional state to, say, one of six "reaction buttons" on Facebook often leaves out much critical context.[24] Simulation of care by a robot does not amount to care, because it is not freely chosen. Carissa Veliz's (2023) suggestion that chatbots not use emojis is wise because it helps expose the deception inherent in representation of non-existent emotional states.

To be obliged to listen to robots as if they were persons or to care about their "welfare," is to be distracted from more worthy ends and more apt ways of attending to the built environment. Emotional attachments to AI and robotics are not merely dyadic, encapsulated in a person's and a machine's interactions. Rather, they reflect a social milieu, where friendships may be robust or fragile, work/life balance well-respected or non-existent, conversations with persons free-flowing or clipped. It should be easy enough to imagine in which of those worlds robots marketed as "friends" or "lovers" would appear as plausible as human friends and lovers. That says more about their nature than whatever psychic compensations they afford.

REFERENCES

Abercrombie, Gavin, Amanda Cercas Curry, Tanyi Dinkar, Verena Rieser, and Zeerak Zakat. "Mirages: On Anthropomorphism in Dialogue Systems." *Arxiv* (2023). https://arxiv.org/abs/2305.09800.

Abercrombie, Gavin, Amanda Cercas Curry, Mugdha Pandya, and Verena Rieser. "Alexa, Google, Siri: What Are Your Pronouns? Gender and Anthropomorphism in the Design and Perception of Conversational Assistants." In *Proceedings of the 3rd Workshop on Gender Bias in Natural Language Processing*, edited by Marta Costa-jussà, Hila Gonen, Christian Hardmeier, and Kellie Webster, 24–33. Online: Association for Computational Linguistics, 2021. https://doi.org/10.18653/v1/2021.gebnlp-1.4.

as the context within which people will construct their emotions, especially when we're interoceptively dysregulated."

[23] Critics of my approach may question the epistemic status of narratives in developing moral intuitions and policy positions. While space limitations preclude a full response here, I have made a case for the relevance of literature to moral and policy inquiry in Pasquale (2020b).

[24] For just one of many examples of the type of context that may matter, see Jerome Kagan (2019). For powerful critiques of reductionism in many affective computing scenarios, see Andrew McStay (2023).

Altman, Sam. "The Merge." *Sam Altman* (blog), July 12, 2017. https://blog.samaltman.com/the-merge.

Birhane, Abeba, Jelle van Dijk, and Frank Pasquale. "Debunking Robot Rights Metaphysically, Ethically, and Legally." *First Monday* 29, no. 4 (2024). https://doi.org/10.5210/fm.v29i4.13628.

Bote, Joshua. "Replika Wanted to End Loneliness with a Lurid AI Bot. Then Its Users Revolted." *San Francisco Gate*, April 27, 2023. www.sfgate.com/tech/article/replika-san-francisco-ai-chatbot-17915543.php.

Burk, Dan L. "Asemic Defamation, or, the Death of the AI Speaker." *First Amendment Law Review* 22 (2025): 189–232.

Burrell, Jenna, and Marion Fourcade. "The Society of Algorithms." *Annual Review of Sociology* 47 (2021): 213–237. https://doi.org/10.1146/annurev-soc-090820-020800.

Christian, Brian. "How a Google Employee Fell for the Eliza Effect." *The Atlantic*, June 21, 2022. www.theatlantic.com/ideas/archive/2022/06/google-lamda-chatbot-sentient-ai/661322/.

Criddle, Cristina. "How AI-Created Fakes Are Taking Business from Online Influencers." *Financial Times*, December 29, 2023. www.ft.com/content/e1f83331-ac65-4395-a542-651b7dfod454.

Cusk, Rachel. *Transit*. New York: Farrar Strauss Giroux, 2017.

Danaher, John. "Welcoming Robots into the Moral Circle: A Defence of Ethical Behaviourism." *Science and Engineering Ethics* 26 (2020): 2023–2049. https://doi.org/10.1007/s11948-019-00119-x.

Danaher, John, and Neil Macarthur, eds. *Robot Sex: Social and Ethical Implications*. Cambridge, MA: MIT Press, 2017.

Ding, Jeffrey. "XiaoIce, Where Do We Go from Here?" *ChinAI* (blog), December 18, 2023. https://chinai.substack.com/p/chinai-248-xiaoice-where-do-we-go.

Edin, Kathryn, Timothy Nelson, Andrew Cherlin, and Robert Francis. "The Tenuous Attachments of Working-Class Men." *Journal of Economic Perspectives* 33, no. 2 (2019): 211–228.

Fourcade, Marion, Etienne Ollion, and Yann Algan. "The Superiority of Economists." *Journal of Economic Perspectives* 29, no. 1 (February 2015): 89–114. https://doi.org/10.1257/jep.29.1.89.

Gebru, Timnit, and Émile P. Torres. "The TESCREAL Bundle: Eugenics and the Promise of Utopia through Artificial General Intelligence." *First Monday* 29, no. 4 (2024). https://doi.org/10.5210/fm.v29i4.13636.

Harris, Jamie, and Jacy Reese Anthis. "The Moral Consideration of Artificial Entities: A Literature Review." *Science and Engineering Ethics* 27, no. 53 (2021).

Horning, Rob. "The Dialectic of Simulation." *Internal Exile*, June 19, 2024. https://robhorning.substack.com/p/dialectic-of-simulation.

Ishiguro, Kazuo. *Klara and the Sun*. New York: Knopf, 2021.

Jankowicz, Nina. *How to Lose the Information War: Russia, Fake News, and the Future of Conflict*. London: I. B. Tauris, 2020.

Kagan, Jerome. *Kinds Come First: Age, Gender, Class, and Ethnicity Give Meaning to Measures*. Cambridge, MA: MIT Press, 2019.

Kass, Leon R. "Defending Human Dignity." In *Human Dignity and Bioethics: Essays Commissioned by the President's Council on Bioethics*, edited by President's Council on Bioethics. U.S. Government Printing Office, 2008.

Kirschenbaum, Matthew. "Prepare for the Textpocalypse." *The Atlantic*, March 2023. www.theatlantic.com/technology/archive/2023/03/ai-chatgpt-writing-language-models/673318/.

Kunzru, Hari. *Red Pill*. London: Scribner, 2020.

Levy, David. *Love and Sex with Robots*. New York: Harper Perennial, 2008.

Lyotard, Jean-François. *The Inhuman: Reflections on Time*, translated by Geoffrey Bennington and Rachel Bowlby. Redwood City, CA: Stanford University Press, 1992.

Manguso, Sarah. *300 Arguments*. New York: Picador, 2018.

McStay, Andrew. *Automating Empathy*. New York: Oxford University Press, 2023.

Means, David. "A.I. Can't Write My Cat Story Because It Hasn't Felt What I Feel." *N. Y. Times*, March 26, 2023. www.nytimes.com/2023/03/26/opinion/ai-art-fiction.html.

Mineo, Liz. "Why Virtual Isn't Actual, Especially When It Comes to Friends." *Harvard Gazette*, June 21, 2023. https://news.harvard.edu/gazette/story/2023/12/why-virtual-isnt-actual-especially-when-it-comes-to-friends/.

Noys, Benjamin. *Malign Velocities: Accelerationism and Capitalism*. Winchester: Zero Books, 2014.

Nussbaum, Martha. *Upheavals of Thought: The Intelligence of Emotions*. Cambridge: Cambridge University Press, 2001.

Parsons, William B. "The Oceanic Feeling Revisited." *Journal of Religion* 78, no. 4 (1998): 501–523.

Pasquale, Frank. "Is AI Poised to Replace Humanity?" *Commonweal*, November 22, 2023. www.commonwealmagazine.org/ai-poised-replace-humanity.

"The Algorithmic Self." *Hedgehog Review* 17, no. 1 (2015).

"The Automated Public Sphere." In *The Politics of Big Data*, edited by Ann Rudinow Sætnan, Ingrid Schneider, and Nicola Green, 19–46. London: Taylor & Francis, 2018.

"Cognition-Enhancing Drugs: Can We Say No?" *Bulletin of Science, Technology & Society* 30, no. 9 (2010): 9–13. https://doi.org/10.1177/0270467609358113.

New Laws of Robotics: Defending Human Expertise in the Age of AI. Cambridge, MA: Belknap Press, 2020a.

"The Substance of Poetic Procedure: Law & Humanity in the Work of Lawrence Joseph." *Law and Literature* 32, no. 1 (2020b): 1–46. https://doi.org/10.1080/1535685X.2019.1680130.

"Two Concepts of Immortality." *Yale Journal of Law & the Humanities* 14, no. 1 (2002): 73–121.

Pasquinelli, Matteo. *The Eye of the Master: A Social History of Artificial Intelligence*. New York: Verso, 2023.

Petrusich, Amanda, and Nick Cave. "Nick Cave on the Fragility of Life." *New Yorker*, 23 March 2023. www.newyorker.com/culture/the-new-yorker-interview/nick-cave-on-the-fragility-of-life.

Pugh, Allison. *The Last Human Job: The Work of Connecting in a Disconnected World*. Princeton, NJ: Princeton University Press, 2024.

Reeves, Richard V. *Of Boys and Men: Why the Modern Male Is Struggling, Why It Matters, and What to Do about It*. Washington, DC: Brookings Institution Press, 2022.

Rogers, Reece. "How to Detect AI-Generated Text, According to Researchers." *Wired*, 2022. www.wired.com/story/how-to-spot-generative-ai-text-chatgpt/.

Singer, Peter W. *LikeWar: The Weaponization of Social Media*. Boston: Houghton Mifflin Harcourt, 2018.

Tangermann, Victor. "Transcript of Conversation with "Sentient" AI Was Heavily Edited." *Futurism*, June 14, 2022. https://futurism.com/transcript-sentient-ai-edited.

Taplin, Jonathan. *The End of Reality: How Four Billionaires Are Selling a Fantasy Future of the Metaverse, Mars, and Crypto*. New York: PublicAffairs, 2023.

Taylor, Charles. *Philosophy and the Human Sciences*. Cambridge: Cambridge University Press, 1985a.

"Self-Interpreting Animals." In *Human Agency and Language: Philosophical Papers Vol. 1*, 45–76. Cambridge: Cambridge University Press, 1985b.

Tian, Edward. "GPTZero Case Study: Models and Exploits." *GPTZero* (blog), February 7, 2023. https://gptzero.substack.com/p/gptzero-case-study-models-and-exploits.

Torres, Émile P. "The Acronym behind Our Wildest AI Dreams and Nightmares." *Truthdig*, June 15, 2023. www.truthdig.com/articles/the-acronym-behind-our-wildest-ai-dreams-and-nightmares/.

"Against Longtermism." *Aeon*, 2021. https://aeon.co/essays/why-longtermism-is-the-worlds-most-dangerous-secular-credo.

"Understanding 'Longtermism:' Why This Suddenly Influential Philosophy Is So Toxic." *Salon*, August 20, 2022. www.salon.com/2022/08/20/understanding-longtermism-why-this-suddenly-influential-philosophy-is-so/.

Tsakiris, Manos. "Politics Is Visceral." *Aeon*, September 2020. https://aeon.co/essays/politics-is-in-peril-if-it-ignores-how-humans-regulate-the-body.

Tucker, Emily. "Artifice and Intelligence." *Tech Policy Press*, March 16, 2022. www.techpolicy.press/artifice-and-intelligence/.

Veliz, Carissa. "Chatbots Shouldn't Use Emojis: Artificial Intelligence That Can Manipulate Our Emotions Is a Scandal Waiting to Happen." *Nature*, March 14, 2023. www.nature.com/articles/d41586-023-00758-y.

White, James Boyd. "What Can a Lawyer Learn from Literature?" *Harvard Law Review* 102, no. 8 (1989): 2014–2047.

Wing, Jeannette M. "Computational Thinking." *Communications of the ACM* 49, no. 3 (2004): 33–35.

5

Surveillance and Human Flourishing

Pandemic Challenges

David Lyon

For humans to flourish in a digital world, three emerging issues should be addressed, each of which was amplified by the global Coronavirus pandemic of 2020–2022. The first is that the use of data to solve human problems is frequently compromised by the failure to understand the character of the "human" problems at hand. Rather than seeing this only in relation to the pandemic, the second issue is to acknowledge that a key factor informing and galvanizing "datafied" responses is the role of surveillance capitalism, whose emergence predated the pandemic. Shoshana Zuboff (2019) highlights some "human" consequences of this phenomenon. The third issue is to retrieve some sense of what "human flourishing" might mean, specifically as it relates to surveillance, and how this might affect *how* surveillance is done. For this, Eric Stoddart's (2021) notion of the "common gaze" is briefly discussed as a starting point.

5.1 HUMAN PROBLEMS, SURVEILLANT RESPONSES: THE COVID-19 PANDEMIC

The Coronavirus pandemic that began in 2020 broke out in a *digital* world. This context is significant because, like the virus itself, it was novel. Even SARS in 2002 or H1N1 in 2009 did not occur in conditions that were recognized as "surveillance capitalism," although the seeds of that conjunction were already sown (Mosco 2014; Zuboff 2015). It is important because widespread "datafication" was increasingly characterized by *dataism*, "the widespread *belief* in the objective quantification and potential tracking of all kinds of human behaviour and sociality through online media technologies" (van Dijck 2014, 198). Described in several other venues as having "religious" qualities, dataism accompanies descriptions of "Big Data" and further catalyzes phenomena such as "tech solutionism," in which digital technology, that is, based in computing sciences, is assumed to be *the* answer to human problems, prior to any full understanding of the problem in question (Mozorov 2013).

Dataism, that was clearly evident in the "security" responses to 9/11, ballooned once again worldwide in 2020–2021 as a crucial response to the global pandemic. It is visible in the massive turn to apps, devices, and networked data systems that occurred as soon as the pandemic was recognized as such by the WHO in March 2020. Public health data, clearly believed to be vital to the accurate assessment and prediction of trends, was used to track the course of the virus, apps were developed to assist in the essential task of contact-tracing, and devices from wearables to drones were launched as means of policing quarantine and isolation. At the same time, other surveillant systems also expanded rapidly, not just to provide platforms to connect those obliged to remain at home but also to monitor the activities of working, learning, and shopping from home, thus sucking them into the gravitational field of surveillance capitalism. And as well, some started to suspect that all this digital activity would not dissipate once the pandemic was over; government, healthcare, and commerce would entrench the new surveillant affordances within their organizations on a permanent basis (Lyon 2022b).

Thus, dataveillance, or surveillance-using-data,[1] received an unprecedented boost during the COVID-19 pandemic, and, though unevenly distributed, on a global level. Its impact – positive and negative – on human flourishing was widespread. Positively, it is reported that dataveillance permitted relatively rapid information about pandemic conditions to reach citizens in each locale. Negatively, in the name of accelerating pandemic responses, some liberties were taken with data use, that had effects including diminishing the responsibility of data-holders to so-called data-subjects, the human beings whose activities produce the data in the first place.

In Ontario, Canada, for instance, privacy laws purportedly designed to provide citizens with control over the surveillance technologies that watch them, were modified to allow for new access to public health data by commercial entities to enable better statistical understanding of the pandemic, and the definition of "deidentification" of data was also changed to allow for new technological developments, even though the ability of data analytics to *re*identify such data is also expanding (Scassa 2020). This allowed, for example, for new levels of data integration on the Ontario Health Data Platform, which was newly established in 2020 to "detect, plan and respond to the COVID-19 outbreak."[2] Such changes were minor, however, when compared with similar activities in some other countries.

5.2 PUBLIC HEALTH DATAVEILLANCE

In January 2020, someone infected with COVID-19 criss-crossed the city of Nanjing, China, on public transit, risking infection to many others en route. Authorities were

[1] Surveillance occurs by many means. Human ocular vision for surveillance has been augmented mechanically, especially from the nineteenth century and digitally, from the later twentieth, in order to make lives "visible" to those seeking such information.

[2] Ontario Health. www.ontariohealth.ca/public-reporting/open-data.

able to track the person's route, minute-by-minute, from the subway journey record. Details were published on social media with warnings to others on the route to be checked. Facial recognition, security cameras, and social media plus neighbourhood monitors and residential complex managers, together add up to an impressive surveillance arsenal, quickly adapted for the pandemic. A patient in Zhejiang province denied having had contact with anyone from Wuhan, but data analysis revealed contacts with at least three such persons. When cellphones are linked with national ID numbers, officials can easily make connections. But ordinary citizens can also use, for example, digital maps for checking retrospectively if they were near known infected persons (Chin and Lin 2022). Some privacy has to be sacrificed in such an emergency, so Chinese lawyers argue (Lin 2020).

But such trade-offs significantly shift the experience of being human in the digital world. They suggest that some circumstances demand that normal (at least in liberal democracies) expectations of privacy or data protection be downplayed or denied in favour of technocratic institutional control. In the case of the pandemic, where panicked responses seem common, such demands are often made in haste. Moreover, the lack of transparency – such as obscuring significant changes in catch-all legislative action make it even harder to both identify and resist the constraints placed on humans as objects in the data system. Some obvious objections that could be raised relate to the risks of rapidly adding new dimensions to surveillance and to the fact that, lacking clear and respected sunset clauses, such changes may settle and solidify into longer-term laws. After all, just such patterns occurred following 9/11, that proved to be permanent "states of exception," especially in the United States (Ip 2013).

However, trade-offs also give the impression that some aspects of human life are at least temporarily dispensable for some greater good. But this is surely a very questionable if not dangerous assumption, given that many of the technologies mobilized against the virus are relatively untested, with unproven benefits, and that the risks they present to society may be considerable, and long-term. As Rob Kitchin (2020, 1) argued, early in the pandemic, the mantra should not be "public health *or* civil liberties" but both, and simultaneously. Of course, great efforts should be made to reduce the scourge of a global pandemic that causes so much human suffering and death. But health is just one feature of human flourishing – freedom from undue government interference or a sense of fairness in everyday social arrangements being two others. It would certainly be odd for a government to argue that, while strenuous efforts are made to ensure freedom and equality, public healthcare concerns will be suspended or reduced.

This draws attention to the value of an over-arching sense of the significant conditions for human flourishing. So, it is worth considering carefully what substantial aspects of being human should be underscored in a digital era. In what follows I touch on some that were historically relevant, a generation ago, as well as some sparked by today's pandemic context. The technology was far less developed – the word "digital" was not used with today's frequency for instance – and the specific example pre-dates today's "autonomous vehicles."

Jeff Reiman's (1995) thoughtful discussion of the "Intelligent Vehicle Highway System (IVHS)" in *Driving to the Panopticon*, for example, drew attention to the fact that surveillance not only makes people visible but does so from a single point. What a contrast with today's surveillance situation, where corporations gather data promiscuously from "public" or "private" sources to identify and profile us from multiple points! So, for him, 30 years ago, privacy protection was not merely about "strengthening windows and doors," he said, but about remembering that information collection is about gathering pieces of our public lives and making them visible from a single point. It is almost quaint to recall that Reiman considered privacy as "the condition in which others are deprived of access to you," something he regarded as a right (1995, 30). However, Reiman's instincts were admirable. He was not toying with ideas about how drivers of "intelligent vehicles" might wish to restrict access to their personal data in ways that might disadvantage them as consumers but asking what possible consequences of such vehicle-use might mean for human dignity.

Reiman (1995) reminded readers that the IVHS did not exist in an information vacuum but in relation to a "whole complex of information" gathering from many government departments and organizations that he thought of as an "informational panopticon." This challenges, he avers, both extrinsic and intrinsic freedom, symbolic risks, and even what he called "psycho-political metamorphosis" (Reiman 1995, 40). In this last, he pondered a surveillance future in which humans become less noble, interesting, and worthy of respect – deprived of dignity. "As more of your inner life is made sense of from without," Reiman wrote, ". . . the need to make your own sense out of your inner life shrinks" (Reiman 1995, 41). But that same healthy inner life is required for political life, in a democracy, and for judging between different political parties or policy options. The risks of privacy – the lack that comes from knowing that one is visible to unknown others – arise from datafied systems often set up for what were believed to be beneficent purposes.

Reiman argued that while one needs *formal* conditions for privacy – such as rights – one also needs *material* conditions, by which I think he means systems that are privacy protective by design and operation precisely because they are an essential part of an environment that allows humans to exercise agency and experience dignity. Perhaps because he was writing a generation ago, his comments now seem almost quaint, and yet strangely relevant. Quaint because they antedate the Internet in its interactive phase, social media, and surveillance capitalism. And relevant in an even more urgent way, because of what happens when global pandemics – or other global crises – are unleashed on a world of already existing surveillance capitalism.

The COVID-19 pandemic was marked by a dataism-inspired celebration of tech solutionism by *both* corporate *and* government actors, often, seemingly willing to play down the impact of the "privacy" implications of technical and legal shifts on the human beings in the system. And relevant, too, in a world of social media in which the platforms' profit motive not only colonizes further the "inner life," but also undermines previous democratic practice, as the same profit-oriented social media boost political polarization and simultaneously threaten social justice, doing so with apparent impunity. Each of these is a threat to human flourishing.

Many thoughtful people sense that some larger questions have to be answered to ensure that humans living in the emerging surveillance system can thrive, rather than merely working within the more familiar frames of privacy and data protection, valuable though those have been and still are. For me, as someone who has been working in Surveillance Studies more-or-less since its inception (in the 1990s[3]), I have found much inspiration among those who frame the issues – and thus the critical analysis of the human impact in actual empirical situations – in terms of data ethics in general and data justice in particular. This is consonant with my own long-term quest to understand, for example, the "social sorting" dynamics of much if not all surveillance today.

Such sorting scores and ranks individuals within arcane categories, leading to differential treatment (Lyon 2003). They profoundly affect *human* life. Such practices are common to all forms of surveillance, from commercial marketing to policing and government. They unavoidably affect, in other words, everyday human life in multiple contexts. Many cite so-called social credit systems in China as extreme examples of such social sorting by government departments, in tandem with well-known major corporations (Chin and Lin 2022). However, while few governments enjoy the direct use and control of sorting systems – combined, in the Chinese and a few other cases, with the use of informers and spies (e.g. Pei 2021) –such sorting is carried out constantly in countries around the world with more random but no less potentially negative results. This is exacerbated today by the increasing use of AI, whose algorithms are often distorted from the outset by inadequate machine learning due to poor data sources. Black and poorer people in the United States, for instance, suffer systematic discrimination when sorting outcomes depend in part on AI. A striking case is that of facial recognition systems, that are notoriously limited in their capacity to distinguish major categories of targets. Joy Buolamwini, whose PhD at the Massachusetts Institute of Technology demonstrated failures of facial recognition systems, especially in the case of black women, took it upon herself to found the Algorithmic Justice League, in response. She speaks explicitly of "protecting the human" from negative effects of AI (Buolamwini 2022).

So while, 30 years ago, Reiman's (1995) concern for the "inner life" in intensifying surveillance conditions was justified – compare Zuboff's (2019) critique of such "inner" manipulation via surveillance capitalism – today's surveillance equally

[3] The 1990s was when the term "surveillance studies" began to be used. A number of authors had started *doing* surveillance studies at least from the 1970s, with Michel Foucault's historical investigations, or James Rule's more empirical sociology – earlier if one includes the work of Hannah Arendt. See e.g. Xavier Marquez's (2012) *Spaces of Appearance and Spaces of Surveillance* and David Lyon's (2022a) *Reflections on 40 Years of Surveillance Studies*.

affects the "outer life" of material conditions, of social disadvantage, by means of social sorting, dubious data-handling methods, biased algorithms, and so on (Cinnamon 2017). Let me comment on the work of Linnet Taylor (2017), as a starting point for discussion, before taking this further, using other pandemic surveillance challenges to point to a larger context within which people's "inner" and "outer" lives might be placed.

With respect to the pandemic, Taylor (2020) observes that data is far from certain – even death rates are hard to calculate accurately – and yet are often treated as accurate and objective proxies for human experiences and understandings (due, arguably, to data's status-inflation in data*ism*). Thus, she turns to an ethics of care, that is embodied, that takes account of what can be known about the person within the system, and considers problems to be overcome from there. People are seen as collectives, bound by responsibilities to others, not as mere data points defined by their responses to rational incentives.

This prompts a quest for understanding those people made invisible or out of focus by official statistics – the elderly-in-care, prisoners, migrant workers, and the like, each of whom have their own reasons for mobility, or lack thereof, among other pandemic-related factors. Much "pandemic data" was created by policy, rather than vice versa. Thus, as Taylor shows, even reducing the number of deaths can become a policy target, in some circumstances, as occurred under President Trump in his first term. He proposed to keep deaths under 100,000 in a highly instrumental fashion, that allowed for data-collection practices that confirmed the goal. This was similar to Boris Johnson's efforts in the United Kingdom, to make a "herd immunity policy" in warning of untimely deaths but not restricting the size of public gatherings. The dynamics of data collection and use are very uneven and work to obscure the human aspects of the problems that data are being mobilized to solve. As Taylor (2020) says, "statistical normality is abnormal – it is the minority position. There is no 'herd,' only a mosaic of different vulnerabilities" that are experienced in the context of each human life.

Such a perspective builds on one of Linnet Taylor's (2017) earlier contributions, on data justice. The granular data sources enabling companies and government departments to sort, categorize, and intervene in people's lives are seldom yoked with a social justice agenda. Especially among marginalized groups, distributed visibility has consequences. In *What Is Data Justice? The Case for Connecting Digital Rights and Freedoms Globally*, Taylor (2017) carefully outlines various approaches to data justice and proposes that it may be defined as "fairness in the way people are made visible, represented and treated as a result of the production of digital data." She also outlines three "pillars" of data justice, building on case-studies and discussions of the theme around the world. They are (in)visibility, (dis)engagement with technology, and antidiscrimination (Taylor 2017). And she pleads not merely for "responsible" but for "accountable" technology, that, arguably, would make transparency and therefore trust much more meaningful realities.

These reflections on the "pandemic challenges" to questions of surveillance and human flourishing certainly go beyond what Reiman was arguing in the mid-1990s and yet they still resonate with his core argument about the challenges to *humanness* in what was then termed a time of "information technology." Today's challenge is to confront the *data-driven* character of surveillance, that in turn is strongly associated with the profit-driven activities of surveillance capitalism, now deeply implicated in responses to the COVID-19 pandemic. People are now made visible in ways which Reiman did not even dream. And these have consequences that relate not only to the potential power of government along with the erosion of the "inner life," but also to the production and reproduction of social inequalities, both local and global. People are "made visible, represented and treated" by surveillance and such activities demand viable ethical practices suited to each human context.

The global COVID-19 pandemic demonstrated the need for data justice and data ethics in new and stark ways, again, both locally and globally. Never before has so much information circulated, accurately or otherwise, about a pandemic and never before has so much attention been paid to those data-driven statistics. No doubt, within the swirling data currents, some accurate and helpful moves have been made in public health. But, all-too-often, the lines of familiar, historical disadvantage have been traced once more, sometimes reinforcing their hold.

Vulnerability is surely linked with the use of Big Data, a term more often associated with the merely technical "Vs" of volume, velocity, and variety. This applies to rich countries like Canada as well as much poorer ones, such as India. In others, such as China, it is harder to tell just how far pandemic surveillance more effectively alleviated the contagion – although the social costs of this were high (see e.g. Ollier-Malaterre 2024; Xuecun 2023). Arguably, in a more *human* world, public health, as well as access to health and other data, would be under much more local guidance and control, leaving less space for profit and manipulation.

5.3 SURVEILLANCE CAPITALISM

Dataism clearly features strongly in the public health responses to the pandemic and such dataism also characterizes the surveillance capitalism that was at the heart of many pandemic interventions, often to the detriment of the people intended to be served. Dataism has become part of the cultural imaginary (van Dijck 2014) of many contemporary societies, where its dynamics but not its inner workings are commonly understood. By that I mean two things. Firstly, data, hyped by data analysts from the late twentieth century, by tech responses to 9/11, and especially during the pandemic, has a glowing veneer in much of the popular press and media as the source of "solutions" for human crises (Mozorov 2013). Secondly, few in authority, including some data analysts, really claim to understand how algorithms work in practice. Indeed, there is evidence suggesting that the very training of many data analysts is decontextualized. How algorithms might "work in practice" is not necessarily a central concern to computer science students. At least in North America and Europe, they are often taught in ways that assume "algorithmic objectivity" and "technological autonomy." This kind of thinking tends to privilege technocratic understandings over human experiences of a given phenomenon.

This "disengagement" from the actual human effects and implications of data science is also highly visible in surveillance capitalism, as Shoshana Zuboff (2019) observes. In her hands, it has much to do with what she calls "inevitabilism." This doctrine of inevitabilism, from the "proselytizers of ubiquitous computing" states that what is currently partial will soon become a new phase of history where data science has relieved humanity of much tedious decision-making (Zuboff 2019: 194). Forget human agency and the choices of communities. Just stand by and watch "technologies work their will, resolutely protecting power from challenge" (Zuboff 2019, 224). For Google, one way for this to happen involves Sidewalk Labs, a smart city initiative under the Alphabet (Google's parent company) umbrella. Such cities, one of which almost began life in Toronto, would have had "technology solve big urban problems" and "make a lot of money" (Zuboff 2019, 229). Among other things, Toronto's Sidewalk Labs bid failed because someone asked the questions that Zuboff argues are too often forgotten, "Who knows? Who decides? Who decides who decides?" (Zuboff 2019, 230).

The costs of this disconnection to the human were evident during the pandemic. Much evidence exists of data science disengagement from the questions about how algorithms will be used and of inevitabilism that data science will provide all necessary for a promised recovery and return to "normal." Citizens were often told to simply "listen to the science."[4] Governments wished to be seen as "doing something" and tech companies promised that they could offer systems and software that would address the public health crisis effectively and rapidly.

A case-in-point in Canada is the way that the telecom company Telus sold mobile data to the Public Health Agency of Canada from early stages of the pandemic, something that was not revealed to the public until the end of 2021. This prompted a parliamentary committee to debate the meaning and significance of the move.[5] Various important questions were raised by the federal Office of the Privacy Commissioner. Among them was the reminder that even nominally "deidentified" data still has personal referents and should still be subject to legal protection. Surveillance frequently requires sensitive regulation – and indeed may also need to be dismantled entirely if its results have the potential to threaten human flourishing. In pandemic conditions, inappropriate but avoidable liberties seem to have been taken with commercial data in the hands of a government agency.

[4] Government of Canada records show that "listening to the science" was a key pandemic debate in that country. See www.ourcommons.ca/DocumentViewer/en/44-1/house/sitting-45/hansard.

[5] The ETHI Committee included a speech by the federal Privacy Commissioner, Daniel Therrien, on February 7, 2022. See: www.priv.gc.ca/en/opc-actions-and-decisions/advice-to-parliament/2022/parl_20220207/

5.4 SURVEILLANCE AS THE "COMMON GAZE"

Here, in summary, are some of the surveillance challenges to human flourishing that were reinforced by the pandemic. Most obvious, perhaps, is the opportunism of tech companies which coincided with the unreadiness of governments for public health crises. This is fertile soil for tech solutionism to flourish in attempts to slow the spread of the COVID-19 virus. Such opportunism builds easily on the dataism that has been establishing itself as a major feature of the twenty-first century zeitgeist in many countries. Dataism, built on older forms of technological utopianism, is myopic and misleading in its approach to data. As José van Dijck (2014) observes, dataism assumes the objectivity of quantification and the potential for tracking human behaviour and sociality from online data. It also presents (meta)data as raw material to be analyzed and processed into predictive algorithms concerning human behaviour (van Dijck 2014, 199).

The problems for ordinary human life arise from the strong likelihood that the conditions for flourishing are not fulfilled when data is granted a superior role in indicating and attempting to ameliorate social problems. As Jacques Ellul (1967) astutely observed (in the 1960s) of the "technological imperative" – it is frequently the case that ends are made to fit the, now digital, means. Today, this critique is updated by Evgeny Mozorov (2013) as "tech solutionism," which had a heyday during the pandemic. As many have observed, pandemic responses frequently misconstrued and failed to address human lived realities.

Today, it is relatively easy to find materials for a radical critique of today's surveillance practices, dependent as they are on varying degrees of dataism and increasingly underpinned by surveillance capitalism. Less straightforward – and perhaps fraught with more risks – is the task of proposing alternatives to the prevailing practices. Not that there is a lack of specific suggestions as to how things might be done differently, from many points of view, but that a coherent *general* sense is missing of "how to go on" that might be agreed upon across such lines. After all, much of the world's population lives in increasingly diverse societies, where finding overarching frameworks for living together is a constant challenge (Taylor 2007).

Human beings require many things in order to truly flourish, not least that they be *recognized* as full persons, with needs and hopes, that are always located in a relational-social context. In a Canadian context, key thinkers such as Charles Taylor and Will Kymlicka have discussed for decades how to develop an inclusive sense of common nationhood in which different groups are *recognized* as playing an equal and appropriate part in the nation.[6] That recognition is vital at several levels but, for both Taylor and Kymlicka, it relates to a sense of basic humanness. Needless to say, their work continues to be debated, importantly, by those, especially from

[6] For example, Charles Taylor (1994a; 1994b) and Will Kymlicka (1989; 1995).

feminist and anti-Black racism positions, who consider that their work does not go far enough in recognizing some groups.[7]

This brings me to Eric Stoddart's (2021) work, which focuses on the ways in which surveillance, through its categorizing and sorting – characteristics reinforced by dataism and surveillance capitalism – is socially divisive and militates against both recognition and equal treatment. In particular, such sorting often builds on and extends already existing differences within so-called multicultural societies. Stoddart (2021) concludes *The Common Gaze* with an engaged afterword on some ways that the pandemic experience of surveillance highlights the relevance of his thesis. For instance, he shows how some poorer communities were neglected by healthcare authorities (Stoddart 2021, 221). His alternative human-oriented call is for a "preferential optic for the poor," where those likely to be marginalized receive special attention rather than being abandoned (Stoddart 2021, xiii). Stoddart discusses surveillance as a gaze for the common good; surveillance practiced from a position of compassionate solidarity. Not only this. Such surveillance for the common good would also demand "a preferential *optic* for the poor." From here, Stoddart proposes ways in which data analytics affects certain vulnerable groups more than others and says that the common gaze resists the notion that collateral damage to them is somehow acceptable. Rather, surveillance data, gathered and analyzed differently, could support efforts to shine light on the plight of some specific groups, such as the elderly.

Strikingly, Stoddart does not shrink from considering people as "living human databases" as long as this is not done in a reductionist fashion. Rather, it can be a reminder that we all live as "nodes in complex networks of relationships" (Stoddart 2021, 205). While practices such as self-quantification tend to turn interest inward, the common gaze aims to repair the social fabric, in which solidarity rather than mere connection is at its heart.

Eric Stoddart's *The Common Gaze* (2021) is rooted in socio-theological soil; anyone familiar with liberation theology will recognize the notion of a "preferential option for the poor" as coming from Gustavo Gutiérrez (2001). Stoddart's neat recycling of the term for use in a surveillance context – "a preferential *optic* for the poor" – is a timely reminder of the immense power of surveillance in today's digital world. How we are seen relates directly to how we are represented and treated. Therefore, to question how we *see* becomes truly critical in more than one sense of the word. And it speaks profoundly to how surveillance studies are performed, insofar as that enterprise is intended to contribute to a more truly human world.

Having noted that the common gaze comes from theological soil, it is worth noting that the idea of human flourishing, with which it is closely allied, is a concept

7 See e.g. Yasmeen Abu-Laban and Christina Gabriel (2008). To hark back to the discussion of pandemic, see Abu-Laban (2021).

that actually transcends the barriers sometimes erected – properly, in some senses, to preserve particularity – between different theological positions. As Miroslav Volf (2016) argues in *Flourishing*, the notion of human flourishing is common to many religions, including adherents of the major Abrahamic religions – Jews, Christians, and Muslims. He offers it as a uniting factor, of our common humanity, in a globalized world. If he is correct, and if, beyond that, Stoddart's (2021) work helps us grapple with surveillance in digitized societies, under the banner of a common gaze, then this is a goal worth pursuing. Why? Because it offers hope, at a time when hope seems in short supply.

5.5 A LARGER FRAME

How to turn the question of surveillance, human flourishing, and the common gaze into a matter that can be addressed in relation to the everyday lives of citizens is the challenge. So, what might be said about digital surveillance that connects its practices and discourses with wider debates, ones that are sometimes deemed irrelevant to social scientific or policy-related scholarship?[8] One is that scholars such as José van Dijck (2014) use words such as *belief* in the power of data in data*ism*, indicating an almost "religious" commitment to the findings of data scientists. The other is that the theorist of the "common gaze" writes in an explicitly "religious" context of social theology. Such "larger frames" – though they need not be formally religious in any institutional or theological sense – are necessary to social science and policy studies debates because these disciplines cannot function without making certain assumptions that cannot be "proved" but cannot but be presupposed.

And as soon as terms such as "data justice" and especially "human flourishing" come into play, the discussion is again in the realm of "assumptions" or beliefs about normative matters, about what *should* be. This does not for a moment mean that such analyses are lacking rigour, clarity, consistency, and other expectations rightly held about scholarly work. It simply means that the assumptions about being human, that are all too often obscured by dataism, should be brought into the open, to be scrutinized, criticized, and debated. Of course, if the assumptions can be traced to a "theological" source, this might taint them in the eyes of some who, like Max Weber, consider themselves "religiously unmusical" (Weber 1994, 25). However, Weber was a Lutheran Christian[9] and, while he did not feel qualified to speak "theologically," his work certainly speaks both to sociology and theology.

Here, the notion of "human flourishing" has been mobilized, at least in a rudimentary fashion, to indicate a larger frame for considering questions of digital surveillance in the twenty-first century. The term "human flourishing" is common

[8] See e.g. Lyon et al. (2022).

[9] See e.g. William Swatos and Peter Kivisto (1991) and Joseph Scimecca (2018, 18).

to major Abrahamic religions and will thus resonate with large swathes of the global population. And it may be linked, constructively, with terms used here, among various surveillance scholars, such as "data justice." As a goal for refocusing attention on the human in surveillance activities and systems, it deserves serious attention.

REFERENCES

Abu-Laban, Yasmeen. "Multiculturalism: Past Present and Future." *Canadian Diversity* 18, no. 1 (2021): 9–12.

Abu-Laban, Yasmeen, and Christina Gabriel. *Selling Diversity*. Toronto: University of Toronto Press, 2008.

Buolamwini, Joy. *Unmasking AI*. New York: Penguin, 2022.

Chin, Josh, and Liza Lin. *Surveillance State: Inside China's Quest to Launch a New Era of Social Control*. New York: St Martin's Press, 2022.

Cinnamon, Jonathan. "Social Injustice in Surveillance Capitalism." *Surveillance & Society* 15, no. 5 (2017): 609–625.

van Dijck, José. "Datafication, Dataism and Dataveillance: Big Data between Scientific Paradigm and Ideology." *Surveillance & Society* 12, no. 2 (2014): 197–208.

Ellul, Jacques. *The Technological Society*. New York: Vintage, 1967.

Gutiérrez, Gustavo. *A Theology of Liberation*. New York: Orbis, 2001.

Ip, John. "Sunset Clauses and Counter-terrorism Legislation." *Public Law* 27 (February 2013): 1–26. https://papers.ssrn.com/sol3/papers.cfm?abstract_id = 1853945.

Kitchin, Rob. "Civil Liberties or Public Health, or Civil Liberties and Public Health? Using Surveillance Technologies to Tackle the Spread of COVID-19." *Space & Polity* 24, no. 3 (2020).

Kymlicka, Will. *Liberalism, Community and Culture*. Oxford: Oxford University Press, 1989.

Multicultural Citizenship. Oxford: Oxford University Press, 1995.

Lin, Liza. "China Marshals its Surveillance Powers against Coronavirus." *Wall Street Journal*, February 4, 2020.

Lyon, David. "Reflections on Forty Years of Surveillance Studies." *Surveillance & Society* 20, no. 4 (2022a): 353–356.

ed. *Surveillance as Social Sorting*. London: Routledge, 2003.

"Surveillance, Transparency, and Trust: Critical Challenges from the COVID-19 Pandemic," in *Trust and Transparency in an Age of Surveillance*, edited by Lora Viola and Paweł Laidler. London: Routledge, 2022b.

Lyon, David, et al. *Beyond Big Data Surveillance: Freedom and Fairness*. Kingston: Surveillance Studies Centre, 2022. [The final report of a 6-year research project funded by the SSHRC, led by Kirstie Ball, Colin Bennett, David Lyon, David Murakami Wood, and Valerie Steeves.]

Marquez, Xavier. "Spaces of Appearance and Spaces of Surveillance." *Polity* 44, no. 1 (2012): 6–31.

Mosco, Vincent. *To the Cloud: Big Data in a Turbulent World*. Boulder: Paradigm, 2014.

Mozorov, Evgeny. *To Save Everything, Click Here: The Folly of Technological Solutionism*. New York: Public Affairs, 2013.

Ollier-Malaterre, Ariane. *Living with Digital Surveillance in China: Citizens' Narratives on Technology, Privacy and Governance*. London: Routledge, 2024.

Pei, Minxin. *Sentinel State: Surveillance and the Survival of Dictatorship in China*. Cambridge, MA: Harvard University Press, 2021.

Reiman, Jeffrey. "Driving to the Panopticon." *Santa Clara High Technology Law Journal* 11, no. 1 (1995): 27–44. https://digitalcommons.law.scu.edu/cgi/viewcontent.cgi?referer = https://www.google.com/&httpsredir = 1&article = 1174&context = chtlj.

Scassa, Teresa. "Interesting Amendments to Ontario's Health Data and Private Sector Privacy Laws Buried in Omnibus Bill." *Teresa Scassa* (blog), March 30, 2020. www.teresascassa.ca/index.php?option = com_k2&view = item&id = 323:interesting-amendments-to-ontarios-health-data-and-public-sector-privacy-laws-buried-in-omnibus-bill&Itemid = 80&tmpl = component&print = 1.

Scimecca, Joseph. *Christianity and Sociological Theory*. London: Routledge, 2018.

Stoddart, Eric. *The Common Gaze: Surveillance and the Common Good*. London: SCM, 2021.

Swatos, William, and Peter Kivisto. "Max Weber as 'Christian Sociologist'." *Journal for the Scientific Study of Religion* 30, no. 4 (1991): 347–362.

Taylor, Charles. *Multiculturalism: Examining the Politics of Recognition*. Princeton: Princeton University Press, 1994a.

"The Politics of Recognition" (1992). In *Multiculturalism and "The Politics of Recognition"*, edited by Amy Gutmann. Princeton: Princeton University Press, 1994b.

A Secular Age. Cambridge, MA: Harvard University Press, 2007.

Taylor, Linnet. "The Price of Certainty: How the Politics of Pandemic Data Demand an Ethics of Care." *Big Data & Society* 7, no. 2 (2020): 1.

"What Is Data Justice? The Case for Connecting Digital Rights and Freedoms Globally." *Big Data & Society* 4, no. 2 (2017): 1–14. https://journals.sagepub.com/doi/pdf/10.1177/2053951717736335.

Volf, Miroslav. *Flourishing*. New Haven, CT: Yale University Press, 2016.

Weber, Max. *Max Weber. Briefe. 1909–1910*, edited by M. Rainer Lepsius, Wolfgang J. Mommsen, Birgit Rudhard, and Manfred Schön. Max Weber Gesamtausgabe. II/6. Tübingen: J.C.B. Mohr (Paul Siebeck), 1994.

Xuecun, Murong. *Deadly Quiet City: True Stories from Wuhan*. New York: The New Press, 2023.

Zuboff, Shoshana. *The Age of Surveillance Capitalism*. New York: Public Affairs, 2019.

"Big Other: Surveillance Capitalism and the Prospects of an Information Civilization." *Journal of Information Technology* 30, no. 1 (2015): 75–89.

PART II

Living the Digital Life

6

Machine Readable Humanity

What's the Problem?

Margot Hanley, Solon Barocas, and Helen Nissenbaum

Over the past 15 years, Daniel Howe and Helen Nissenbaum, often working with other collaborators, have launched a series of projects that leverage obfuscation to protect people's online privacy. Their first project, TrackMeNot, is a plug-in that runs in the background of browsers, automatically issuing false search queries and thereby polluting search logs, making it more difficult or impossible for search engines to separate people's true queries from noise (TrackMeNot 2024). Howe and Nissenbaum later turned to online behavioural advertising, developing AdNauseam, another browser plug-in that automatically clicks on all ads. It is designed to obfuscate what people are actually interested in by suggesting – via indiscriminate, automatic clicks – that people are interested in *everything* (AdNauseam 2024).

Each of these projects has been accompanied by academic publications describing the teams' experiences developing the tools but also reflecting on the value of and normative justification for obfuscation (Howe and Nissenbaum 2017; Nissenbaum and Howe 2009). Among the many observations that they make in these papers, Howe and Nissenbaum conclude their article on AdNauseam by remarking that "trackers want us to remain *machine-readable* … so that they can exploit our most human endeavors (sharing, learning, searching, socializing) in pursuit of profit" (Howe and Nissenbaum 2017). Online trackers don't just record information but do so in a way that renders humans – their sharing, learning, searching, and socializing online – machine-readable and, as such, computationally accessible. For Howe and Nissenbaum, obfuscation is not only a way to protect people's privacy and to protest the elaborate infrastructure of surveillance that has been put in place to support online behavioural advertising, it is specifically a way to resist being made *machine-readable*.

At the time of the paper's publication, the concept of "machine readability" would have been most familiar to readers interested in technology policy from its

The work benefitted from comments on the early draft presented at the Being Human workshop and from outstanding editorial guidance from Val Steeves and Beate Roessler. We gratefully acknowledge the MacArthur Foundation for supporting this work through a grant to the Digital Life Imitative, Cornell Tech.

important role in advocacy around open government (Yu and Robinson 2012), where there were growing demands that the government make data publicly available in a format that a computer could easily process. The hope was that the government would stop releasing PDFs of tables of data – from which data had to be manually and laboriously extracted – and instead release the Excel sheets containing the underlying data, which could be processed directly by a computer. "Machine readable" thus became a mantra of an open government movement, in service of the public interest. So why do Howe and Nissenbaum invoke machine-readability, in the context of online behavioural advertising, as a threat rather than a virtue, legitimating the disruptive defiance of obfuscation against an inescapable web of surveillance and classification?

In this paper, we address this question, in two parts, first, by theorizing what it means for humans to be machine-readable and, second, by exposing conditions under which machine-readability is morally problematic – the first, as it were, descriptive, the second, normative. Although the initial encounter with problematic machine-readability was in the context of online behavioural advertising and, as a justification for data obfuscation, our discussion aims for a coherent and useful account of machine-readability that can be decoupled from the practices of online, behavioural advertising. In giving the term greater definitional precision descriptively as well as normatively we seek to contribute to ongoing conversations about being human in the digital age.

6.1 MACHINE READABILITY: TOP DOWN

The more established meaning of "machine readable" in both technical and policy discourse applied to material or digital objects that are rendered comprehensible to a machine through *structured* data, expressed in a standardized format, organized in a systematic manner. Typically, this would amount to characterizing an object in terms of data, in accordance with predefined fields of a database, in order to render them accessible to a computational system. Barcodes stamped on material objects, as mundane as milk cartons, render them machine readable, in this sense. When it comes to electronic objects, there are even different degrees of accessibility; for example, conversion tools can transform photographic images and electronic pdf documents into formats more flexibly accessible to computation according to the requirements of various machines' data structures. Structure and standardization have been important for data processing because many computational operations cannot function over inconsistent types of inputs and cannot parse the different kinds of details in an unstructured record. In the near past, for example, a computer would not have been able to process a government caseworker's narrative account of interviews with persons seeking public benefits. Instead, it would have been coded according to discrete fields and predefined sets of possible answers, enabling government agencies to automate the process of determining eligibility. Applied to *people*, machine readability, in this sense, would mean assigning data representations to them according to the predefined, structured data fields required by a given computational system. The innumerable forms we encounter in daily life, requiring us to list name, age, gender, address, and so forth, are instances of this practice.

If this were all there is to machine readability, it would not seem obviously wrong, nor would it legitimate, let alone valorize, disruptive protest, such as data obfuscation. It does, however, call to mind long-standing concerns over *legibility* in critical writing on computing. Here, the concept of legibility refers to the representation of people, their qualities, and their behaviours as structured data representations, the latter ultimately to be acted upon by computers. Representing people as data is not a passive act; rather data collection can be understood as an ontological project that defines what exists before seeking to measure it. Scholarship has tended to focus on how legibility is achieved by imposing categories on people which, in the very act of representing them in data, is morally objectionable in ways similar to practices of stereotyping and pigeon-holing. In the realm of computation, perhaps most famously, Bowker and Starr point out how information systems work to make people and populations legible to social and technical systems by subjecting them to rigid classificatory schemes, forcing them into often ill-fitting categories (Bowker and Starr 2000). This wave of critical writing emphasizes the crude ways in which information systems turn a messy world into tidy categories and, in so doing, both elides differences that deserve recognition and asserts differences (e.g. in racial categories) where they are unwarranted by facts on the ground (Agre 1994; Bowker and Starr 2000). Scholars like Bowker and Starr were keenly aware of the importance of structured information systems representing humans and human activity for the purposes of subsequent computational analysis.

Critiques such as Bowker and Starr's echo critical views of bureaucracies that go farther back in time, emphasizing the violence that their information practices inflict on human beings by cramming them into pigeonholes, blind to the complexities of social life (Scott 2020). The legacy of much of this work is a deeper appreciation of the indignities of legibility that is achieved through information systems, which have been drawn with top-down, bright lines. Incomplete, biased, inaccurate, and weighted by the vested interests of the people and institutions who wield them (see Agre 1994), these systems are also sources of inconvenience for humans who may have to contort themselves in order to be legible to them. Echoing these critiques, David Auerbach has observed that making oneself machine readable has historically demanded significant compromise, not just significant effort: "Because computers cannot come to us and meet us in our world, we must continue to adjust our world and bring ourselves to them. We will define and regiment our lives, including our social lives and our perceptions of ourselves, in ways that are conducive to what a computer can 'understand.' Their dumbness will become ours" (Auerbach 2012). During this period, the terms in which we could make ourselves legible to computers were frequently so limited that achieving legibility meant sacrificing a more authentic self for the sake of mere recognition.

6.2 MACHINE READABILITY: A NEW DYNAMIC

While the operative concerns of this early work on legibility remain relevant, they do not fully account for the perils of machine readability as manifested in online behavioural advertising and similar practices of the present moment. If we agree that automation via digital systems requires humans to be represented as data constructs and that top-down, inflexible, possibly biased and prejudicial categories undermine human dignity and well-being, we may welcome new forms of data absorption and analytics that utilize increasingly powerful techniques of machine learning and AI. Why? To answer, we consider ways that they radically shift what it means to make people machine readable – the descriptive task – and how this new practice, which we call dynamic machine readability, affects the character of its ethical standing. To articulate this concept of machine readability, we provide a sketch – a caricature rather than a scientifically accurate picture (for which we beg our reader's forbearance) – intended to capture and explain key elements of the new dynamic.

We begin with the bare bones: a human interacting with a machine. Less mysteriously, think of it as any of the myriad of computational systems, physically embodied or otherwise, that we regularly encounter, including websites, apps, digital services, or devices. The human in question may be interacting with the system in one of innumerable ways, for example, filing a college application, signing up for welfare, entering a contest, buying shoes, sending an email, browsing the Web, playing a game, posting images on social media, assembling a music playlist, creating a voice memo, and so on. In the approach we labeled "top down," the machine *reads* the human via data that are generated by the interaction, typically, but not always, provided by the human as input that is already structured by the system. Of course, the structured data through which machines read humans may also be entered by other humans, for example, a clerk or a physician entering data into an online tax or health insurance form, respectively. To make the human legible, the data are recorded in an embedded classification scheme, which typically may also trigger an appropriate form of response – whether directly by the machine (e.g. an email sent) or a human-in-the-loop who responds accordingly (e.g. an Amazon warehouse clerk assembles and dispatches a package).

Keyboard and mouse, the dominant data entry medium of early days, have been joined by others, such as sound, visual images, or direct behavioural monitoring, limited by predefined fields for input data fields. The new dynamic[1] accordingly

[1] We owe a debt of gratitude to Diyi Yang who patiently walked Nissenbaum through this setup. She should not, however, be blamed for mix-ups and errors.

also involves humans and machines engaging in interaction, either directly or indirectly. Thus, it allows a vastly expanded set of input modalities, beyond the keyboard and mouse of a standard computer setup involving data entry through alpha-numerics and mouse-clicks. Machines may capture and record the spoken voice, facial and other biometrics, a myriad of non-semantic sensory data generated by mobile devices, and streamed behavioural data, through active engagement or passively in the background (e.g. watching TV and movies on a streaming service).

The new dynamic also incorporates machine learning (ML) models, or algorithms, which are key to making sense of this input. Machines capture and record "raw" data inputs while the embedded models transform them into information that the system requires in order to perform its tasks, which may involve inferring facts about the individual, making behavioural predictions, deriving intentions, or surmising preferences, propensities, and even vulnerabilities. (Although we acknowledge readers who prefer the plain language of probabilities, we adopt – admittedly – anthropomorphizing terms, such as infer and surmise, which are more common.) Instead of structuring input in terms of pre-ordained categories, this version of machine reading accepts streams of data, which are structured and interpreted by embedded ML models. For example, from the visual data produced by a finger pad pressing on the glass of a login screen, identity is inferred, and a mobile device allows the owner of the finger to access its system. From the streams of data generated by sensors embedded in mobile devices, ML models infer whether we are running, climbing stairs, or limping (Nissenbaum 2019), or, whether we are at home or at a medical clinic, and whether we are happy or depressed.

A transition to dynamic machine readability of humans means that it is unnecessary to *make* ourselves (and others) legible to computational systems in the formal languages that machines had been programmed to read. The caseworker we mentioned earlier may leapfrog the manual work of slotting as many details as possible into the discrete fields of a database and, instead, record the full narrative account (written or spoken) of meetings with their benefits-seeking clients. Language models, according to proponents, trained to extract relevant substantive details, would be able to parse these narratives, extract relevant information, and even, potentially, automate the decision-making itself.

A critical element of our high-level sketch has not yet been revealed, namely, key parties responsible for the existence of the systems we have been discussing – their builders (designers, software engineers, etc.) and their owners or operators (which may be their creators) or companies and other organizations for whom the systems have been developed. When attributing to ML models a capacity to make sense of a cacophony of structured and unstructured data, specifically, to *read* the humans with whom a system interacts, one must, simultaneously, bring to light the purposes behind the sense-making in turn dictated by the interests and needs of controlling parties, including its developers and owner-operators. To serve the purposes of online advertising (highly simplistically), for example, a model must be able to *read* humans who land on a given webpage as likely (or unlikely) to be interested in a particular ad. Moreover, making sense of humans through browsing histories and demographics, for example, according to the dynamic version of machine readability, does not require the classification of human actors in terms of human comprehensible properties, such as, "is pregnant," or even in terms of marketing constructs, such as "white picket fence" (Nissenbaum 2019). Instead, the concepts derived by ML models may be tuned entirely to their operational success as determined by how likely humans are to demonstrate interest in a particular range of products (however that is determined).

Advertising, obviously, is not the only function that may be served by reading humans in these ways. Although lacking insider access, one may suppose that they could serve other functions just as well, such as, helping private health insurance providers determine whether applicants are desirable customers and, if yes, what premiums they should be charged – not by knowing or inferring a diagnosis of, say, "early stage Parkinson's disease" but by *reading* them as "desirable clients of a particular health plan." Importantly, a model that has been tuned to serve profitable advertisement placement is different from one that has been tuned to the task of assessing the attractiveness of an insurance applicant.[2] It is worth noting that machines reading humans in these functional terms may or may not be followed by a machine automatically executing a decision or an action on its grounds. Instances of the former include online, targeted advertising, and innumerable recommender systems, and, of the latter, human intervention in decisions to interview job applicants on the basis of hiring algorithms, or to award a mortgage on the basis of a credit score, etc. Earlier in this section, when we reported on natural language models that could extract relevant data from a narrative, we ought to have added that relevance itself (or efficacy, for that matter), a relational notion, is always tied to purposes. Generally, how machines read humans only makes sense in relation to the purposes embedded in them by operators and developers. The purposes themselves, of course, are obvious targets of ethical scrutiny.

Implicit in what we have described, thus far, is the dynamic nature of what we have labeled dynamic machine readability. ML models of target attributes, initially derived from large datasets, may continuously be updated on the basis of their performance. Making people legible to functional systems, oriented around specific purposes, is not a static, one-off business. Instead, systems are constantly refined on the basis of feedback from successive rounds of action and outcome. This means that, to be successful, dynamic approaches to reading humans must engage in

[2] We note but are unable to give proper credit to the significant body of published work on proxies.

continuous cycles of purpose-driven classification and, subsequently, modification based on outcomes. It explains why they are insatiably hungry for data – structured and unstructured – which may be collected unobtrusively as machines may monitor humans simply as they engage with the machines in question, to learn whether a particular advertisement yields a click from a particular individual, or a recommendation yields a match, and so on. Dynamic refinement, according to proponents, may be credited with their astonishing successes but also, we contend, a potential source of unethical practice.

To recap: dynamic machine readability is characterized: by an expansion of data input modalities and data types (structured and unstructured, semantic and non-semantic); by embedded ML models which are tuned to the purposes of machine operators and owners; and by the capacity of these models to be continuously refined in relation to these purposes. Dynamic machine readability releases us from the shackles of a limited lexicon – brittle and ill-fitting categories – and associated ethical issues. In a growing number of cases, the pressing concern is no longer whether we have to submit to a crass set of categories in order to be legible to computational systems; instead, many of the computational systems with which we interact take in massive pools of data of multifarious types and from innumerable sources, presumably, to read us *as we are*. Despite the scale and scope of the data and the power of ML, reading humans through models embedded in machines is constrained by the purposes laid out by machine operators and developers, which these models are designed to operationalize. From a certain perspective, the new dynamic is emancipatory. Yet, even if successful these model-driven machines raise a host of persistent ethical questions, which we reveal through a sequence of cases involving machines reading humans. Inspired by real and familiar systems out in the world whose functionality depends on making humans readable, we identified cases we considered paradigmatic in the types of ethical issues that machine readability raises. It turns out that, although the particular ways that a system embodies machine readability is relevant to its moral standing, moral standing depends on other elements of the larger system in which the human-reading subsystems are embedded.

6.3 THROUGH THE LENS OF PARADIGMATIC CASES: AN ETHICAL PERSPECTIVE ON MACHINE READABILITY

6.3.1 *Interactive Voice Response: Reading Humans through Voice*

Beginning with a familiar and quite basic case, one may recall traditional touch-tone telephone systems, which greet you with a recorded message and a series of button-press options. These systems, which have been the standard in customer service since the 1960s (Fleckenstein 1970; Holt and Palm 2021), require users to navigate a labyrinth of choices by choosing a series of numbers that best represent their need. Generally, a frustrating experience, first, you are offered a limited set of options, none of which seems quite right. You listen with excruciating attention to make the best choice and to avoid having to hang up, call back, and start all over again. Although still unsure, eventually, you press a button for what seems most relevant – you chose "sales" but instantly regret this. Perhaps "technical support" would have been a better fit. Throughout the labyrinth of button pushes, you feel misunderstood.

Over time, touch-tone systems have been replaced by Interactive Voice Response (IVR) systems, enabling callers to interact with voice commands (IBM 1964). Using basic speech recognition, these systems guide you through a series of questions to which you may respond by saying "yes," "no," or even "representative." While the introduction of IVR was designed to ease the pain of interacting with a touch-tone system, they have their own interactional kinks. Along the way you may find that you have to change your pronunciation, your accent, your diction, or the speed of your speech: "kuhs-tow-mur sur-vis". You might add "please" to the end of your request, unsure of the appropriate etiquette, but then find that the unnecessary word confuses the system, which prompts it to begin reciting the list of options anew. While voice commands may, to a degree, have increased usability for the caller – for example, being able to navigate the system hands-free – the set of options was just as limited and the process just as mechanical, namely, choosing the button by saying it instead of pressing it.

We may speculate that companies and other organizations would justify the adoption of automated phone services by citing efficiency and cost-effectiveness. Like many shifts to automation that companies make, however, the question should not be whether they are beneficial for the company, or even beneficial overall, but whether the benefits are spread equally. Particularly for systems requiring callers to punch numbers or laboriously communicate with a rigid and brittle set of input commands, efficiency for companies meant effort (and frustration) for callers, not so much cost savings as cost shifting. If we were to attach ethically charged labels to such practices, we would call this lopsided distribution of costs and benefits unfair; we might even be justified in calling it *exploitative*. A company is exploiting a caller's time and effort to reduce its own.

Progress in natural language processing (NLP) technologies, as noted in Section 6.2, has transformed present-day IVR systems, which now invite you simply to state your request in *your own words*. "Please tell us why you're calling," the system prompts, allowing you to speak as if you were conversing with a human. Previously, where callers had to mold their requests to fit the predefined menu of options, now they may express themselves freely and flexibly. The capacity to extract intentions from an unstructured set of words – even if based on simple keywords – and the shift to a dynamic, ML-based approach has made callers more effectively machine readable. Increasingly sophisticated language models continue to improve the capacity to recognize words and, from them, to generate "meaning" and "intention."[3] These developments have propagated throughout the consumer appliance industry, supporting a host of voice assistants from Siri to Alexa, and beyond.

Allowing for more "natural" – and thus less effortful – interaction with machines fulfills one of the long-standing goals of the field of Human–Computer Interaction (HCI), which aims to make computers more intuitive for humans by making humans more legible to computers (Nielsen and Loranger 2006; Shneiderman 2009). Following one of the early founders, Donald Norman, much work in HCI focuses on making interactions with computers materially and conceptually "seamless," effectively rendering interfaces invisible to the human user (Arnall 2013; Ishii and Ullmer 1997; Norman 2013; Spool 2005). IVR systems, which include NLP models, seem to have achieved seamlessness, sparing customers the exasperating and time-consuming experience of navigating a rigid, imperfect, and incomplete set of options. By enabling callers to express what they seek freely and flexibly, have IVR operators addressed the ethical dimensions of their systems – respecting callers time and even autonomy?

Seamlessness addresses some problems at the same time that it creates others. First, advances in machine readability don't necessarily go hand in hand with changes in the underlying business practices. If the back-end options remain the same, shunting callers into the same buckets as before ("sales," "technical support," etc.), defined by organizational interests, objectives, and operational constraints rather than by customers' granular needs, the ability to communicate in their own words actually misleads us into believing that the system is sensitive to our individual needs. If a supple *interface* is not accompanied by more adaptable options at the back end, the clunky button-pressing more honestly provides callers ways that a business is actually able to meet their needs.

Second, the transition to dynamic machine-interpretable, voice-based systems facilitates a richer exchange in more ways than people have reckoned. How one speaks, intonation, accent, vocabulary, and more communicate much more than the caller's needs and intentions, including approximate age, gender, socio-economic level, race, and other demographic characteristics (Singh 2019; Turow 2021b). Attributes of speech such as the sound of the voice, syntax, and tone have already been used by call centres to infer emotions, sentiments, and personality in real-time (Turow 2021b). With automation there is little to stop these powerful inferences spreading to all voice-mediated exchanges. The ethical issues raised by machines reading humans through the modality of voice clearly include privacy (understood as inappropriate data flow). They also include a disbalancing of power between organizations and callers, unfair treatment of certain clientele on the wrong end of fine-tuned, surreptitiously tailored, and prioritized calls, and an exposure to manipulative practices of consumers identified as susceptible and vulnerable to

[3] We use these terms in quotation marks to avoid a presumption that machines are grasping or interpreting in the ways humans do.

certain pricing or marketing ploys. Scholars have already warned of the wide-scale deception and manipulation that the "voice-profiling revolution" might enable (Turow 2021a). Ironically, the very advances that ease customers' experiences with IVR systems now place customers at greater risk of exploitation, not by appropriating their time and effort but, instead, by surreptitiously reconfiguring their choices and opportunities.

The history of IVR systems highlights an irony that is not unique to it. Brittle systems of the past may have exploited time and effort but also protected against inappropriate extraction of information and laying out in the open the degree to which a business was invested in customer service. Dynamic, model driven IVR systems facilitate an outwardly smoother experience, while more effectively cloaking a rigid back end. Likewise, embedded NLP algorithms offer powers well beyond those of traditional IVR systems, including the capacity to draw wide-ranging inferences based on voice signal, semantics, and other sensory input. These, as we've indicated, raise familiar ethical problems – privacy invasion, disbalance of power, manipulation, unfair treatment, and exploitation. Each of these deserves far more extensive treatment than we can offer here. Although not a necessary outcome of machine readability, but of features of the voice systems in which they are embedded, machine readability both affords and suggests these extensions; it flips the default.

6.3.2 *Reading Human Bodies: From Facial Recognition to Cancer Detection*

Roger Clark defines *biometrics* as a "general term for measurements of humans designed to be used to identify them or verify that they are who they claim to be" (Clarke 2001). Measurements include biological or physiological features, such as a person's face, fingerprint, DNA, or iris; and behavioural ones, including gait, handwriting, typing speed, and so on. Because these measurements are distinctive to each individual, they are ideal as the basis for identification and for verification of identity (Introna and Nissenbaum 2000). The era of digital technology catapulted biometric identification to new heights as mathematical techniques helped to transform biometric images into computable data templates, and digital networks transported this data to where it was needed. In the case of fingerprints, for example, technical breakthroughs allowed the laborious task of experts making matches to be automated. *Datafied* and automated, fingerprints are one of the most familiar and pervasive biometrics, from quotidian applications, like unlocking our mobile phones, to bureaucratic management of populations, such as criminal registries.

6.3.2.1 Facial Recognition Systems

Automated facial recognition technology has been one of the most aspirational of the biometrics, and also one of the most controversial. Presented by organizations as more convenient and secure than alternatives, facial recognition systems have been deployed for controlling access to residential and commercial buildings, managing employee scheduling in retail stores (Lau 2021), and facilitating contact free payments in elementary school lunch lines (Towey 2021). In 2020, Apple offered FaceID as a replacement for TouchID (its fingerprint-based authentication system) (Apple 2024) and in 2021, the IRS began offering facial recognition as a means of securely registering and filing for taxes (Singletary 2022).

In the United States, under guidance from the National Institute of Standards and Technologies, facial recognition has advanced since at least the early 2000s. *Verification* of identity, achieved by matching a facial template (recorded in a database or on a physical artifact such as a key fob or printed barcode) with an image captured in real time at a point of access (Fortune Business Insights 2022), has advanced more quickly than the identification of a face-in-the-crowd. It has also been less controversial because verification systems require the creation of templates through active enrollment by data subjects, presumably with their consent, whereas creating an identification system, in theory, requires the creation of a complete population database of facial templates, a seemingly insurmountable challenge. Unsurprisingly, in 2020 when news broke that Clearview AI claimed to have produced a reliable facial recognition system, a controversy was sparked. Clearview AI announced partnerships with law enforcement agencies and pitched investors its tool for secure-building access (amongst a suite of other applications) (Harwell 2022). The breakthrough it boasted was a database of templates for over 100,000,000 people, which it achieved by scraping publicly accessible social media accounts. Even though no explicit permission was given by accounts holders, Clearview AI took account access status as an implicit sanction.

Objections to automated facial recognition identification (FRI) run the gamut, with Phil Agre's classic, "Your Face is not a Barcode," an early critical perspective (Smith and Browne 2021; Stark 2019). To simplify the span of worthwhile writing on this topic, we propose two buckets. The first includes the societal problems created by FRI malfunctioning, prominently error and bias. The second includes societal problems associated with FRI when they're performing "correctly" or as intended. The second bucket holds insights for our discussion on machine readability.

The usual strawman rebuttal applies to FRI, too, viz. we always have had humans skulking around keeping people under watch. Automation simply improves the efficiency of these necessary practices. As in other cases, the counter-rebuttal insists that the scale and scope enabled by automation results in qualitative differences. Specifically, FRI systems fundamentally threaten a pillar of liberal democracy, namely, prohibitions against dragnets, against surveillance that chills freedoms in public spaces, and in favor of the presumption of innocence. The application of FRI technologies in public spaces impinges on such freedoms and the very existence of vast datasets of facial templates in the hands of operators exposes ordinary people to the potential of such threats. Particularly when there is not a clear alignment of interests and purposes of individuals with the operators of FRI systems and a significant imbalance of power between them, individual humans are compromised by being machine readable.

6.3.2.2 Biometric: Cancerous Mole

Computer vision has yielded systems that are valuable for the clinical diagnosis of skin conditions. Dermatologists, typically first to assess the likelihood that skin lesions are malignant, look at features, such as outline, dimensions, and color. Computerized visual learning systems, trained on vast numbers of cases, have improved significantly, according to research published in *Nature* in 2017 (Esteva et al. 2017). In this study, researchers trained a machine learning model with a dataset of 129,450 images, each labeled as cancerous or non-cancerous. Prompted to identify additional images as either benign lesions or malignant skin cancers, the model diagnosed skin cancer at a level of accuracy on par with human experts. Without delving into the specifics of this case, generally, it is unwise to swallow such claims uncritically. For the purposes of our argument, let's make a more modest assumption, simply that automated systems for distinguishing between cancerous and non-cancerous skin lesions function with a high enough degree of accuracy to be useful in a clinical setting.

Addressing the same question about automated mole recognition systems that we did about FRI; do they raise similar concerns about machine reading of the human body? We think not. Because machine reading necessarily is probabilistic, it is important to ask whether automation serves efficiency for medical caregivers at a cost to patients' wellbeing. Because systems such as these create images, which are stored on a server for immediate and potentially future uses, there may be privacy issues at stake. Much seems to hinge on the setting of clinical medicine and the decisive question of alignment of purpose. Ideally, the clinical provider acts as the human patients' fiduciary; the aims of dermatology and its tools aligned with those of the humans in their care.

Future directions for such diagnostic tools such as these are still murky. In 2017, there were 235 skin cancer focused dermatology apps available on app stores (Flaten et al. 2018). In 2021, Google announced that it would be piloting its own dermatological assistant as an app, which would sit within Google search. In these settings, questions return that were less prominent in a clinical medical setting. For one, studies have revealed that these applications are far less accurate than those in clinical settings and we presume that, as commercial offerings, they are not subject to the same standards-of-care (Flaten et al. 2018). For another, the app setting is notoriously untrustworthy in its data practices and the line between medical services, which have been tightly controlled, and commercial services, which have not, is unclear. Without tight constraints, there is clear potential for image data input to be utilized in unpredictable ways and for purposes that stray far from health.

In sum, mole recognition systems offer a version of dynamic machine readability that may earn positive ethical appraisal because its cycles of learning and refinement target accuracy in the interest of individual patients. When these systems are embedded in commercial settings where cycles of learning and refinement may target other interests instead of or even in addition to health outcomes, their ethical standing is less clear.

6.3.2.3 Recommenders Reading Humans: The Case of Netflix

Algorithmically generated, personalized recommendations are ubiquitous online and off. Whereas old-fashioned forms of automation treated people homogeneously,[4] the selling point of advances in digital technologies – according to promoters – is that we no longer need to accept one-sized-fits-all in our interfaces, recommendations, and content. Instead, people can expect experiences catered to us, individually – our tastes, needs, and preferences. Ironically, these effects, though intended to make us feel uniquely appreciated and cared-for, nevertheless, are mass-produced via a cycle of individualized data capture and a dynamic refinement of how respective systems represent each individual. In general terms, it is difficult to tease apart a range of services that may, superficially, seem quite distinct, including, for example, targeted advertising, general web search, Facebook's newsfeed, Twitter feeds, TikTok's "For You Page," and personalized recommender systems such as, Amazon's "You might like," Netflix's "Today's Top Picks for You," and myriad others. There are, however, relevant differences, which we aim to reveal in our brief focus on Netflix.

Launched in 1996 as a DVD-by-mail service, Netflix began employing a personalization strategy early on, introducing a series of increasingly sophisticated rating systems, coupled with recommendation algorithms. In 2000, its first recommendation system called *Cinematch* prompted users to rate movies with a five star rating system (Biddle 2021). The algorithm then recommended movies based on what other users, with similar past ratings, had rated highly.[5] In its efforts to improve the accuracy of these recommendations, Netflix introduced a series of features on their site to capture direct user feedback – to add a star rating to a movie they had watched, to "heart" a movie they wanted to watch, or add films to a queue (Biddle 2021). All of these early features called on users to rate titles explicitly.

Over time, leveraging advances in machine learning and findings from Netflix Prize competitions (Rahman 2020), Netflix shifted to passive data collection practices, gathering behavioral data in the course of normal user–site interaction

[4] In the words of Henry Ford, "You can have any color car you want so long as it's black" (Alizon et al. 2008).

[5] If users a and b both rate movies x and y similarly, and user a also likes movie z, then Cinematch would recommend movie z to user b.

(e.g., scrolling and clicking), instead of prompting users for explicit ratings. This involved recording massive amounts of customer activity data, including viewing behavioural data (e.g., when users press play, pause, or stop watching a program), viewing data on the programs they watch, at different times of day, viewing search query data, and applying cross-device tracking to collect data about which devices they are using at a given time. Infrequently, Netflix would ask customers for explicit ratings, such as, thumbs up or thumbs down. In addition to passively recording behavioural data, they also conducted A/B tests (approximately 250 A/B tests with 100,000 users each year), for example, to learn which display image performs best for a new movie so it can be applied to landing pages across the platform.

According to public reporting, this dynamic cycle of behavioural data gathering and testing shapes what Netflix recommends and how it is displayed. Factors, such as time-of-day, and a record of shows you have stopped watching midway, further affect recommendations and nudges (Plummer 2017). Algorithms comprising the recommender system shape not only what content is recommended to you, but, further, the design of your Netflix homepages, which (at the time of writing) is composed of rows of titles, each of which contains three layers of personalization; the choice of genre (such as comedy or drama), the subset of genre (such as "Imaginative Time Travel Movies from the 1980s"), and rankings within rows (Netflix 2012).

Without an inside view into Netflix and similar services, we lack direct, detailed insight into how the algorithms work and the complex incentives driving the relevant design choices. Yet, even without it, we're able to interpret elements of different stages of progressive shifts in terms of our analytic framework. To begin, the initial design is analogous to the primitive automated phone answering systems, discussed in Section 6.3.1, where customers were asked to deliberately choose from predetermined, fixed categories. Yet, effortfulness, a factor that raises questions about unfair exploitation, seems less relevant here. Whereas the automated answering services offered efficiency to firms while imposing inefficiencies on callers, in the Netflix case, the effort imposed on viewers, one might argue, results in a payoff to them. The shift to the dynamic form of machine readability relieves users of the effort of making deliberate choices, while, at the same time, yielding a system that is more opaque, less directly under viewers' control, and involves potentially inappropriate data flows and uses, which brings privacy into consideration.[6]

Champions point to the increase from 2% to 80% in the past 20 years in accurately predicting what users choose, as a justification for the use of behavioural approaches over those that rely fully on customers' direct ratings (Biddle 2021). In combination with the scrutiny that these numbers invite, we are, additionally, unconvinced that they are decisive in assessing the ethical standing of these practices. Specifically, no

[6] We have explained elsewhere why Privacy Policies are not satisfactory solutions to these issues (Barocas and Nissenbaum 2014).

matter how it started out, Netflix, like most other online recommender systems with which we may be familiar, is not *solely* driven by their viewers' preferences and needs.[7] As the market for recommender systems has ballooned in all sectors (Yelp, TripAdvisor, local search services, banking, etc.) and competition for attention has mushroomed, there is pressure to serve not only seekers (customers, viewers, searchers) but also parties wishing to be found, recommended, etc. While managing the sheer magnitude of offerings (e.g. think of how many movies, TV shows, books, consumer items, etc. are desperate for attention) one can imagine the conflicts of interest confronting recommender systems, such as Netflix (Introna and Nissenbaum 2000).

Behavioural data is efficient, and the algorithmic magic created from it, which matches viewers with shows, may not be served by transparency. (Do we really need to know that there were ten other shows we might have enjoyed as much as our "top pick?") We summarize some of these points in the next, and final, section, of the chapter. In the meantime, as a purely anecdotal Postscript: Netflix members may have noticed that there has been a noticeable return to requests for viewers' deliberate ratings of content.

6.4 PULLING THREADS TOGETHER

Machine-readable humanity is an evocative idea, whose initial impact may be to stir alarm, possibly even repulsion or indignation. Beyond these initial reactions, however, does it support consistent moral appraisal in one direction or another? "It depends" may be an unsurprising answer but it begs further explanation on at least two fronts: one, an elaboration of machine-readability to make it analytically useful, and another, an exploration of the conditions under which machine-readability is morally problematic (and when it is not). Addressing the first, we found it useful to draw a rough line between two relevant developmental phases of digital technologies, to which we attributed distinct but overlapping sets of moral problems, respectively. One, often associated with critical discussions of the late twentieth century, stems from the need to represent humans (and other material objects) in terms of top-down, predefined categories, in order to place them in databases, in turn making them amenable to the computational systems of the day. As discussed in Section 6.1, significant ethical critiques honed on the dehumanizing effects of forcing humans into rigid categories, which, as with any form of stereotyping and pigeon-holing, may mean that similar people are treated differently, and different people are lumped together without regard for significant differences. In some circumstances, it could be argued that well designed classification schemes serve positive values, such as efficient functioning, security, and fair treatment but it's not difficult to see how the classification of humans into preordained categories could often lead to bias

[7] We have no insider view to the company's internal practices.

(or unfair discrimination), privacy violations, authoritarian oversight, and prejudice. In short, an array of harms may be tied, specifically, to making humans readable to machines by formatting them, as it were, in terms of information cognizable by computational systems.

Machine readability took on a different character, which we signaled with the term *dynamic*, in the wake of the successive advances of data and predictive analytics ("big data"), machine learning, deep learning, and AI. Although it addresses problems of "lumping people together" associated with top-down readability, ironically, its distinctive power to mass produce individualized readings of humanity introduces a new set of ethical considerations. The list we offer here, by no means exhaustive, came to us through the cases we analyzed seen through the lens of characteristic elements of a dynamic setup.

To begin, the broadening of data input modalities, about which promoters of deep learning are quick to boast, highlights two directions of questioning. One challenges whether all the data is relevant for the legitimate purposes that the model is claimed to serve (e.g. increasing the speed with which an IVR addresses a caller's needs) or whether it is not (e.g., learning characteristics of callers that lead to unfair discrimination or violations of privacy) (Nissenbaum 2009; Noble 2018).

A second direction slices a different path through the issue of data modalities – in this instance, not about categories of data, such as race, gender, and so on, but about different streams feeding into the data pool. Of particular interest is the engagement of the human data subject (for lack of a better term), which is evident in personalized recommender systems. The Netflix case drew our attention because, over the years, it has altered course in how it engages subscribers in its recommender algorithm, a pendulum swinging from full engagement as choosers to no engagement to, at the present time, presumably somewhere in between. Similarly, in our IVR case, we noted that the powerful language processing algorithms that are able to grasp the meaning of spoken language and *read* and serve human-expressed intention are able to extract other features as well – unintended or against our will. Finally, in the context of behavioural advertising, paradigmatic of the dominant business model of the past three decades, the modality of recorded behaviour absent any input from expressed preference has prevailed in the *reading* of humanity by respective machines (Tae and Whang 2021; Zanger-Tishler et al. 2024).

In order to defend the legitimacy of including different modalities of input into the datasets from which models are extracted, an analysis would require a consideration of each of these streams – deliberate, expressed preference, behavioural, demographic, biometric, etc. – in relation to each of the cases, respectively. Although doing so, here, is outside the scope of this chapter, it is increasingly urgent to establish such practices as new ways to read humans are being invented, for example, in the growing field of so-called digital biomarkers (Adler et al. 2022; Coravos et al. 2019; Daniore et al. 2024), which are claimed to be able to make our mental and emotional states legible through highly complex profiles of sensory data from mobile devices

(Harari and Gosling 2023). Another wave of access involves advanced technologies of brain–machine connection, which claims yet another novel modality for reading humans – our behaviours, thoughts, and intentions – through patterns of neurological activity (Duan et al 2023; Farahany 2023; Tang et al. 2023).

In enumerating ethical considerations, such as privacy, bias, and political freedom, we have skirted around, but not fully and directly confronted the assault on human autonomy, which ultimately may be the deepest, most distinctive issue for machine readable humanity. Acknowledging that the concept of autonomy is enormously rich and contested, we humbly advance its use, here, as roughly akin to self-determination inspired by the Kantian exhortation introduced in most undergraduate ethics courses,[8] to "act in such a way that you treat humanity whether in your own person or in the person of any other, never merely as a means to an end, but always at the same time as an end" (Kant 1993, vii; MacKenzie and Stoljar 2000; Roessler 2021). When defending the automation of a given function, system, or institution, defenders cite efficiency, defined colloquially, as producing a desirable outcome with the least waste, expense, effort, or expenditure of resources. Our case of automated phone systems illustrated the point that efficiency for machine owners may produce less desirable outcomes for callers, more wasted time and expenditure of effort. In this relatively unsophisticated case, one may interpret the exploitation of callers as an assault on autonomy.

The expansive class of systems claiming to personalize or customize service (recommendations, information, etc.) illustrates a different assault on autonomy. Among the characteristic elements comprising dynamic machine readability is the dynamic revision of a model in relation to the goals or purposes for which a system was created. The general class of recommender systems[9] largely reflect a two-sided marketplace because it serves two interested parties (possibly three-sided, if one includes the recommender system itself as an interested party.) The operators of personalized services imply that their systems are tailored to the individual's interests, preferences, and choices but their performance, in fact, may be optimized for purposes of parties – commercial, political, etc. – seeking to be found or recommended. Purposes matter in other cases, too, specifically distinguishing between facial recognition systems, serving purposes of political repression of machine-readable humans, and mole identification systems, whose primary or sole criterion of success is an accurate medical diagnosis.

6.5 CONCLUSION: HUMAN BEINGS AS STANDING RESERVE

Martin Heidegger's "The Question Concerning Technology" introduces the idea of standing reserve, "Everywhere everything is ordered to stand by, to be

8 Taught in the so-called Western tradition.

9 Including, for example, Web search.

immediately at hand, indeed to stand there just so that it may be on call for a further ordering." According to Heidegger, the essential character of modern technology is to treat nature (including humanity) as standing reserve, "If man is challenged, ordered, to do this, then does not man himself belong even more originally than nature within the standing-reserve?" (Heidegger 1977, 17). Without defending Heidegger's broad claim about the nature of technology, the conception of machine-readability that we have developed here triggers an association with standing-reserve, that is to say machine-readability as the transformation of humanity into standing reserve. Particularly evident in dynamic systems, humans are represented in machines as data in order to be readily accessible to the purposes of the controllers (owners, designers, engineers) that are embodied in the machine through the design of the model. The purposes in question may have been selected by machine owners with no consideration for ends or purposes of the humans being read. It is not impossible that goals and values of these humans (and of surrounding societies) *are* taken into consideration, for example, in the case of machines reading skin lesions; the extent this is so is a critical factor for a moral appraisal. Seen in the light of these arguments, AdNauseam is not merely a form of protest against behavioural profiling by the online advertising establishment. More pointedly, it constitutes resistance to the inexorable transformation of humanity into a standing reserve – humans on standby, to be immediately at hand for consumption by digital machines.

REFERENCES

Adler, Daniel A., Fei Wang, David C. Mohr, Deborah Estrin, Cecilia Livesey, and Tanzeem Choudhury. "A Call for Open Data to Develop Mental Health Digital Biomarkers." *BJPsych Open* 8, no. 2 (2022): e58. https://doi.org/10.1192/bjo.2022.28.

AdNauseam. 2024. Adnauseam.io.

Agre, Philip E. "Surveillance and Capture: Two Models of Privacy." *The Information Society* 10, no. 2 (1994): 101–127.

Alizon, Fabrice, Steven B. Shooter, and Timothy W. Simpson. "Henry Ford and the Model T: Lessons for Product Platforming and Mass Customization." *International Design Engineering Technical Conferences and Computers and Information in Engineering Conference* 43291 (2008): 59–66.

Apple. "About Face ID Advanced Technology," 2024. https://support.apple.com/en-us/HT208108.

Arnall, Timo. "Exploring 'Immaterials': Mediating Design's Invisible Materials." *International Journal of Design* 8, no. 2 (2013): 101–117.

Auerbach, David. "The Stupidity of Computers." N+1, *Machine Politics* no. 13 (2012). www.nplusonemag.com/issue-13/essays/stupidity-of-computers/.

Barocas, Solon, and Helen Nissenbaum. "Big Data's End Run around Anonymity and Consent." *Privacy, Big Data, and the Public Good: Frameworks for Engagement* 1 (2014): 44–75.

Biddle, Gibson. "A Brief History of Netflix Personalization." *Medium*, June 1, 2021. https://gibsonbiddle.medium.com/a-brief-history-of-netflix-personalization-1f2debf010a1.

Bowker, Geoffrey, and Susan Leigh Star. *Sorting Things Out: Classification and Its Consequences*. Cambridge, MA: MIT Press, 2000.

Clarke, Roger. "Biometrics and Privacy." 2001. www.rogerclarke.com/DV/biometrics.html.

Coravos, Andrea, Sean Khozin, and Kenneth D. Mandl. "Author Correction: Developing and Adopting Safe and Effective Digital Biomarkers to Improve Patient Outcomes." *NPJ Digital Medicine* 2 (2019): 1–5. https://doi.org/10.1038/s41746-019-0090-4.

Daniore, Paola, Vasileios Nittas, Christina Haag, Jürgen Bernard, Roman Gonzenbach, and Viktor von Wyl. "From Wearable Sensor Data to Digital Biomarker Development: Ten Lessons Learned and a Framework Proposal." *npj Digital Medicine* 7, no. 1 (2024): 161.

Duan, Yiqun, Jinzhao Zhou, Zhen Wang, Yu-Kai Wang, and Chin-Teng Lin. "Dewave: Discrete EEG Waves Encoding for Brain Dynamics to Text Translation." *arXiv preprint arXiv:2309.14030* (2023).

Esteva, Andre, Brett Kuprel, Roberto A. Novoa, Justin Ko, Susan M. Swetter, Helen M. Blau, and Sebastian Thrun. "Dermatologist-Level Classification of Skin Cancer with Deep Neural Networks." *Nature* 542, no. 7639 (February 2, 2017): 115–118. https://doi.org/10.1038/nature21056.

Farahany, Nita A. *The Battle for Your Brain: Defending the Right to Think Freely in the Age of Neurotechnology*. St. Martin's Press, 2023.

Flaten, Hania K., Chelsea St Claire, Emma Schlager, Cory A. Dunnick, and Robert P. Dellavalle. "Growth of Mobile Applications in Dermatology: 2017 Update." *Dermatology Online Journal* 24, no. 2 (2018). https://doi.org/10.5070/D3242038180.

Fleckenstein, W. O. "Development of the Touch-Tone® Telephone." *Research Management*, vol. 13, no. 1 (1970): 13–25.

Fortune Business Insights. "Facial Recognition Market Rising at a CAGR of 14.8% to Reach USD 12.92 Billion by 2027." 2022. www.globenewswire.com/news-release/2022/02/08/2380458/0/en/Facial-Recognition-Market-Rising-at-a-CAGR-of-14-8-to-Reach-USD-12-92-Billion-by-2027.html.

Harari, Gabriella M., and Gosling, Samuel D. "Understanding Behaviours in Context Using Mobile Sensing." *Nature Reviews Psychology* 2, no. 12 (2023): 767–779. https://doi.org/10.1038/s44159-023-00235-3.

Harwell, Drew. "Facial Recognition Firm Clearview AI Tells Investors It's Seeking Massive Expansion beyond Law Enforcement." *The Washington Post*, February 16, 2022. www.washingtonpost.com/technology/2022/02/16/clearview-expansion-facial-recognition/.

Heidegger, Martin. *The Question Concerning Technology*, translated by William Lovitt. New York: Harper & Row, 1977. Originally published in German as *Die Frage nach der Technik*, 1954.

Holt, Jennifer, and Michael Palm. "More Than a Number: The Telephone and the History of Digital Identification." *European Journal of Cultural Studies* 24, no. 4 (2021): 916–934.

Howe, Daniel, and Helen Nissenbaum. "Engineering Privacy and Protest: A Case Study of AdNauseam." *International Workshop on Privacy Engineering*, San Jose, CA, May 25, 2017.

IBM. "IBM Product Announcement 7770." (1964). https://ed-thelen.org/comp-hist/IBM-ProdAnn/7770.pdf.

Introna, Lucas D., and Helen Nissenbaum. "Shaping the Web: Why the Politics of Search Engines Matters." *The Information Society* 16, no. 3 (2000): 169–185.

Ishii, Hiroshi, and Brygg Ullmer. "Tangible Bits: Towards Seamless Interfaces between People, Bits and Atoms." *Proceedings of the ACM SIGCHI Conference on Human Factors in Computing Systems*, Atlanta, GA, March 22–27, 1997.

Kant, Immanuel. *Grounding for the Metaphysics of Morals*, translated by James W. Ellington. Cambridge, MA: Hackett Publishing, 1993.

Lau, Pin Lean. "Facial Recognition in Schools: Here Are the Risks to Children." *The Conversation*, October 27, 2021. https://theconversation.com/facial-recognition-in-schools-here-are-the-risks-to-children-170341.

Mackenzie, Catriona, and Natalie Stoljar, eds. *Relational Autonomy: Feminist Perspectives on Autonomy, Agency, and the Social Self*. New York: Oxford University Press, 2000.

"Netflix Recommendations: Beyond the 5 Stars (Part 1)." Medium, April 6, 2012. https://netflixtechblog.com/netflix-recommendations-beyond-the-5-stars-part-1-55838468f429.

Nielsen, Jakob, and Hoa Loranger. *Prioritizing Web Usability*. London: Pearson Education, 2006.

Nissenbaum, Helen. "Contextual Integrity Up and Down the Data Food Chain." *Theoretical Inquiries in Law* 20, no. 1 (2019): 221–256.

Privacy in Context: Technology, Policy, and the Integrity of Social Life. Redwood City, CA: Stanford University Press, 2009.

Nissenbaum, Helen, and Daniel Howe "Trackmenot: Resisting Surveillance in Web Search." In *Lessons from the Identity Trail: Anonymity, Privacy, and Identity in a Networked Society*, edited by I. Kerr, C. Lucock, and V. Steeves, 417–440. Oxford: Oxford University Press, 2009.

Noble, Safiya Umoja. "Algorithms of Oppression: How Search Engines Reinforce Racism." In *Algorithms of Oppression*. New York: New York University Press, 2018.

Norman, Donald. *The Design of Everyday Things: Revised and Expanded Edition*. New York: Basic Books, 2013.

Plummer, Libby. "This Is How Netflix's Top Secret Recommendation System Works." *Wired*, August 22, 2017. www.wired.co.uk/article/how-do-netflixs-algorithms-work-machine-learning-helps-to-predict-what-viewers-will-like.

Rahman, Was. "The Netflix Prize: How Even AI Leaders Can Trip Up." *Medium*, January 11, 2020. https://towardsdatascience.com/the-netflix-prize-how-even-ai-leaders-can-trip-up-5c1f38e95c9f.

Roessler, Beate. "*Autonomy: An Essay on the Life Well-Lived*." Hoboken, NJ: John Wiley & Sons, 2021.

Scott, James C. *Seeing like a State: How Certain Schemes to Improve the Human Condition Have Failed*. New Haven, CT: Yale University Press, 2020.

Shneiderman, Ben. "Creativity Support Tools: A Grand Challenge for HCI Researchers." In *Engineering the User Interface*, edited by M. Redondo et al., 1–9. London: Springer, 2009.

Singh, Rita. *Profiling Humans from Their Voice*. London: Springer, 2019.

Singletary, Michelle. "Despite Privacy Concerns, ID.me Nearly Doubled the Number of People Able to Create an IRS Account." *The Washington Post*, February 25, 2022. www.washingtonpost.com/business/2022/02/25/irs-idme-account-success-rate/.

Smith, Brad, and Carol Ann Browne. *Tools and Weapons: The Promise and the Peril of the Digital Age*. New York: Penguin, 2021.

Spool, Jared M. "What Makes a Design Seem 'Intuitive'?" UX Articles by Center Centre (blog), January 10, 2005. https://articles.centercentre.com/design_intuitive/.

Stark, Luke. "Facial Recognition Is the Plutonium of AI." *XRDS: Crossroads, The ACM Magazine for Students* 25, no. 3 (2019): 50–55.

Tae, Ki Hyun, and Steven Euijong Whang. "Slice Tuner: A Selective Data Acquisition Framework for Accurate and Fair Machine Learning Models." *Proceedings of the*

2021 *International Conference on Management of Data*, Virtual Event China, June 20–25, 2021, 1771–1783.

Tang, Jerry, Amanda LeBel, Shailee Jain, and Alexander G. Huth. "Semantic Reconstruction of Continuous Language from Non-invasive Brain Recordings." *Nature Neuroscience* 26, no. 5 (2023): 858–866.

Towey, Hannah. "The Retail Stores You Probably Shop at that Use Facial-Recognition Technology." *Business Insider*, July 19, 2021. www.businessinsider.com/retail-stores-that-use-facial-recognition-technology-macys-2021-7.

TrackMeNot. 2024. TrackMeNot.com.

Turow, Joseph. "Shhhh, They're Listening – Inside the Coming Voice-Profiling Revolution." *The Conversation*, April 28, 2021a. http://theconversation.com/shhhh-theyre-listening-inside-the-coming-voice-profiling-revolution-158921.

The Voice Catchers: How Marketers Listen in to Exploit Your Feelings, Your Privacy, and Your Wallet. Yale University Press, 2021b.

Yu, Harlan, and David Robinson. "The New Ambiguity of 'Open Government'." *UCLA Law Review Discourse* 59 (2012): 180–208.

Zanger-Tishler, Michael, Julian Nyarko, and Sharad Goel. "Risk Scores, Label Bias, and Everything but the Kitchen Sink." *Science Advances* 10, no. 13 (2024): eadi8411. https://doi.org/10.1126/sciadv.adi8411.

7

Carebots

Gender, Empire, and the Capacity to Dissent

Chloé S. Georas

In this chapter I analyze different dilemmas regarding the use of robots to serve humans living in the digital age. I go beyond technical fields of knowledge to address how the design and deployment of carebots is embedded in multifaceted material and discursive configurations implicated in the construction of humanness in socio-technical spaces. Imagining those spaces necessarily entails navigating the "fog of technology," which is always also a fog of inequality in terms of trying to decipher how the emerging architectures of our digitized lives will interface with pre-existing forms of domination and struggles of resistance premised upon our capacity to dissent. Ultimately, I contend that the absence of a "human nature" makes us human and that absence in turn makes us unpredictable. What it means to be human is thus never a fixed essence but rather must be strategically and empathically reinvented, renamed, and reclaimed, especially for the sake of those on the wrong side of the digital train tracks.

In Section 7.1, I open the discussion by critiquing Mori's (1970) seminal theory on robot design, called the "uncanny valley," by inscripting technologies in changing cultural practices and emergent forms of life. Section 7.2, through visual culture, gender, and race theories, sheds light on how the design of carebots can materialize complex dilemmas. In Section 7.3, I dissect Petersen's (2007, 2011) perturbing theory and ethical defense of designing happy artificial people that "passionately" desire to serve. In the final Section 7.4, I offer some final thoughts on what I call the *Carebot Industrial Complex*, namely, the collective warehousing of aging people in automated facilities populated by carebots.

7.1 *How One Person's Uncanny Valley Can Be Another's Comfort Zone: Inscripting Technologies in Changing Cultural Practices and Emergent Forms of Life*

In recent years we have witnessed an increased interest in robots for the elderly – variously called service, nursing, or domestic robots – which are touted as a solution to the growing challenges of and demand for elder care. One of the main arguments deployed to justify the development of service robots for the elderly is the use of digital technology to empower the elderly by way of greater autonomy and extended independent living. The key global players in the supply of service robots are Europe (47%), North America (27%), and, the fastest growing market, Asia (25%) (IFR 2022b, paragraph 13). The financial stakes are huge given that the service robotics market was valued at USD 60.16 billion in 2024 and is expected to reach USD 146.79 billion by 2029 and grow at a compound annual growth rate of 19.53% over a forecast period of 2024 to 2029 (Mordor Intelligence 2024, paragraph 1).

Despite the "rosy" arguments in favor of delegating the care of elderly people to robots, there are crucial questions concerning the development of service robots that remain unanswered precisely because most of the literature on service robots has thus far been articulated within technical fields of knowledge such as engineering and the like. As part of addressing some of the thornier questions concerning the design of robots to serve the people living in the digital society, in this first section I open the discussion by critiquing Mori's seminal theory on how humans respond to robotic design.

Mori proposes that, when robotic design becomes too human-like, hyper real or familiar, it invokes a sense of discomfort in humans, which he describes as the uncanny valley (Mori 2012 [1970]; on the uncanny valley see also Chapter 3, by Roessler). He makes reference to the shaking of a prosthetic hand that, due to its apparent realness, surprises "by its limp boneless grip together with its texture and coldness" and, if human-like movements are added to the prosthetic hand, the uncanniness is further compounded (Mori 2012 [1970], 99). In contrast, robots that resemble humans, but are not excessively anthropomorphized, are more comforting to humans. By building an "accurate map of the uncanny valley," Mori hopes "through robotics research we can begin to understand what makes us human [and] to create – using nonhuman designs – devices to which people can relate comfortably" (Mori 2012 [1970], 100). Thus, in order to avoid the discomforting uncanniness of robots designed to look confusingly human, Mori calls for the emotionally reassuring qualities of robots that retain metallic and synthetic properties.

Mori explicitly limits his interpretation to empirical evidence of human behaviour that he assumes is cross-culturally constant. In this way, Mori is more interested in making a universal claim about humans than unpacking how their cultural differences may be implicated in the complex constructions of what it means to be human in the social materialities and discursivities marked by the digital turn of societies, which I consider a limitation of the theory of the uncanny valley in general.

An implicit and recurring trope of the uncanny valley is displayed in the cultural fear of what Derrida called "mechanical usurpation," which lies in the anxiety-laden boundary between the mind and technology or:

> [the] substitution of the mnemonic device for live memory, of the prosthesis for the organ [as] a perversion. It is perverse in the psychoanalytic sense (i.e. pathological). It is the perversion that inspires contemporary fears of mechanical usurpation. (Barnet 2001, 219, discussing Derrida)

Consider, for instance, Mori's (2012 [1970], 99–100) statement that "[i]f someone wearing the hand in a dark place shook a woman's hand with it, the woman would assuredly shriek."

The uncanny valley's fear of mechanical usurpation is also analogous to how Bhabha addresses the position of colonial subjects by invoking the liminal status of the robotic as "almost the same, but not quite" to the extent that a robot's performative act of mimicry is condemned to the impossibility of complete likeness, remaining inevitably inappropriate (Bhabha 1994, 88).[1] The uncanny valley's implicit condemnation of the effective mimicry of human characteristics by robots, subtextually associated with a sense of betrayal, dishonesty and transgression, shows how the humanized robot comes to occupy the space of the threatening "almost the same, but not quite" and invokes the cultural anxiety of "mechanical usurpation" with a sexist twist analogous to that of the white woman encountering a black man in a dark alley.

The uncanny (v)alley can thus be understood as a specific cultural disposition relative to robots rather than a natural and intrinsic reaction across the board. This leads me to my main criticism of the notion of the uncanny valley, namely, that it is premised upon a conception of the "human" as a universal given in terms of how people will react to excessively human-like robots. The uncanny valley essentializes human reactions to robots and thus cannot account for the cross-cultural and cross-historical mutations in how people can and do differentially and creatively negotiate with emerging technologies within specific discursive genealogies and institutional practices.

The work of Langdon Winner and Sherry Turkle can add further nuance to the debate over how new forms of subjectivity and ways of being enabled by digitization are impacting ethical questions raised by robotics and values embedded in the design of carebots. For Winner (1986), social ideas and practices throughout history have been transformed by the mediation of technology and this transformation has

[1] According to Bhabha: "... colonial mimicry is the desire for a reformed recognizable other, *as a subject of a difference that is almost the same, but not quite*. Which is to say, that the discourse of mimicry is constructed around an *ambivalence*; in order to be effective, mimicry must continually produce its slippage, its excess, its difference. The authority of that mode of colonial discourse that I have called mimicry is therefore stricken by an indeterminacy: mimicry emerges as the representation of a difference that is itself a process of disavowal. Mimicry is, thus the sign of a double articulation; a complex strategy of reform, regulation and discipline, which appropriates the other as it visualizes power. Mimicry is also the sign of the inappropriate, however, a difference or recalcitrance which coheres the dominant strategic function of colonial power, intensifies surveillance, and poses an immanent threat to both 'normalized' knowledges and disciplinary powers" (Bhabha 1994, 86).

been marked by the continual emergence of new forms of life. This concern over new forms of life is dramatically embodied in the field of robotics, particularly carebots, which are increasingly linked to the intimate lives of children, elders, and handicapped people, and are in turn associated with the emergence of novel subjectivities.[2] As Turkle evocatively proposes, "technology proposes itself as the architect of our intimacies. These days, it suggests substitutions that put the real on the run" (Turkle 2011, e-book), having a potentially profound impact on how we come to understand our own humanity and the humanity of others. Computational objects "do not simply do things *for* us, they do things *to* us as people, to our ways of seeing the world, ourselves and others" (Turkle 2006, 347). By treating them as "relational artifacts" or "sociable robots," we can place the focus on the production of meaning that is taking place in the human–robot interface (Turkle 2006) to help us better understand what it means to be human in this new and emerging socio-technical space (see also Chapter 2, by Murakami Wood). These technologies inevitably raise important questions that go beyond the determination of the "comfort zone" of humans relative to robots à la Mori. They challenge us to question the entrenched assumption that Technology (with a capital "T") is a force of nature beyond human control to which we must adapt no matter what as it shapes the affordances and experiences of being human. As Winner presciently warns, we must unravel teleological and simplistic views of technology as guided by implacable forces beyond state and other forms of regulation (Winner 1986). Winner calls this position "technological somnambulism" in that it "so willingly sleepwalk[s] through the process of reconstituting the conditions of human existence," leaving many of the pivotal ethical and political questions that new technologies pose unasked (Winner 1986, 10).

In the following sections I explore some of the quandaries raised by the embedding of carebots in our daily lives, such as how visual culture, gender, and race theories can shed light on the design of carebots;[3] Petersen's theory and ethical defense of designing happy artificial people that "passionately" desire to serve; and the implications of what I call the *Carebot Industrial Complex*, namely, the collective warehousing of aging people in automated facilities populated by carebots.

[2] The concept of subjectivity is related to the broader one of culture. Culture in current debates is considered a historically contingent repertoire that encompasses symbols, codes, values, systems of classification, and forms of perception as well as their related practices (Crane 1994; Alexander and Seidman 1990). Culture constitutes subjectivities and articulates the practices of social subjects and collectivities. The fundamental implication of a cultural analysis is that meanings are produced or constructed and not merely discovered "out there" in an essentialist or empirical sense (Hall 1997). Both what was previously considered universal or natural are no longer viewed as essential facts of nature or positivist truths, but rather reveal themselves as social constructions and as part of specifically situated historical subjectivities.

[3] My interest in this article is in humanoid adult-like robots both in appearance and emergent forms of consciousness/sentience in contrast to non-humanoid sociable robots that lack consciousness/sentience such as Paro (pet seal), Furby (hamster or owl), and AIBOs.

7.2 VISUAL CULTURE, GENDER, AND RACE: IS IT POSSIBLE TO DESIGN "NEUTRAL" ROBOTS?

Visual culture, gender, and race theories have had an extensive and transdisciplinary effect on debates concerning what is means to be human within the changing historical and cultural prisms of intersectionally related forms of inequality and struggles for equitable change. In this section I explore some angles of these theories to shed light on how the design of carebots can materialize complex discursive and symbolic configurations that impinge on the construction of humanness in the existing and emerging socio-technological architectures through which we signify our lives.

Visual culture, as a mode of critical visual analysis that questions disciplinary limitations, speaks of the visual construction of the social rather than the often-mentioned notion of the social construction of the visual. It focuses on the centrality of vision and the visual world in constructing meanings, maintaining esthetic values, as well as racialized, classed, and gendered stereotypes in societies steeped in digital technologies of surveillance and marketing. Visuality itself is understood as the intersection of power with visual representation (Mirzoeff 2002; Rogoff 2002).

Feminism and the analysis visual culture mutually inform each other. Feminism, by demanding an understanding of how gender and sexual difference figure in cultural dynamics coextensively with other modes of subjectivity and subjection such as sexual orientation, race, ethnicity, and class, among others, has figured prominently in the strengths of visual culture analysis. And, in turn, "feminism has long acknowledged that visuality (the conditions of how we see and make meaning of what we see) is one of the key modes by which gender is culturally inscribed in Western culture" (Jones 2010, 2).[4]

Relative to the design of robots, their gendering occurs at the level of the material body and the discursive and semiotic fields that inscript bodies (Balsamo 1997). To the extent that subject positions "carry differential meanings," according to de Lauretis, the representation of a robot as male or female is implicated in the meaning effects of how bodies are embedded in the semiotic and discursive formations (Robertson 2010, 4). Interestingly, however, Robertson contends that robots conflate bodies and genders:

> The point to remember here is that the relationship between human bodies and genders is contingent. Whereas human female and male bodies are distinguished by a great deal of variability, humanoid robot bodies are effectively used as platforms for reducing the relationship between bodies and genders from a contingent relationship to a fixed and necessary one (Robertson 2010, 6).

[4] For a more extensive discussion of the relationship between visual culture, gender, race and technology, see Georas (2021).

Because the way "robot-makers gender their humanoids is a tangible manifestation of their tacit understanding of femininity in relation to masculinity, and vice versa" (Robertson 2010, 4), roboticists are entrenching their reified common-sense knowledge of gender and re-enact pre-existing sexist tropes and dominant stereotypes of gendered bodies without any critical engagement. Thus, despite the lack of physical genitalia, robots possess "cultural genitals" that invoke "gender, such as pink or grey lips" (Robertson 2010, 5).

This process of reification in the design of robots entrenches the mythological bubble of the "natural" in the context of sex/gender and male/female binaries that queer theorist Judith Butler bursts open very effectively by looking at the malleability of the body. The traditional feminist assumptions of gender as social and cultural and sex as biological and physical are recast by Butler, who contends that sex is culturally and discursively produced as pre-discursive. Sex is an illusion produced by gender rather than the stable bedrock of variable gender constructions.

Butler develops a theory of performativity wherein gender is an act, and the doer is a performer expressed in, not sitting causally "behind," the deed. Performance reverses the traditional relation of identity as preceding expression in favor of performance as producing identity (Butler 1990, 1993). Gender for Butler thus becomes all drag and the "natural" becomes performative rather than an expression of something "pre-social" and "real." Gender performances are not an expression of an underlying true identity, but the effects of regulatory fictions where individual "choice" is mediated by relations and discourses of power. In this way, queer theory's contingent and fluid pluralization of gendered and sexual human practices stands in stark contrast to the fixed conflation of bodies and genders of humanoid robots posed by Robertson.

Considering these debates, is it possible to make gender-neutral robot designs? Even if designers purport to create gender-neutral robots, the robots will inevitably be re-gendered by the people who use them because of the pervasiveness of sexist/stereotyped tropes of femininity and masculinity in society. Re-gendering can occur, for instance, at the obvious level of languages such as romance languages that linguistically gender all things (e.g. from animate to inanimate, human to non-human) into either female or masculine nouns. Insofar as we conceive language as not merely an instrument or means of communication, but rather as constitutive of the very "reality" of which it speaks, we must contend with the gendering of even purportedly gender-neutral incarnations of robots. Moreover, in addition to language-related forms of gendering, it can also occur at the level of the activities performed by the service robots given that they can be culturally and discursively associated with female activities. In the case of caretaking functions that have historically been associated with female and poor labor, it would be unsurprising to see the replication of gendered stereotypes as applied to gender-neutral robots. As a result, any purported semiotic neutrality of robotic design is inevitably re-inscribed in discursive and cultural fields mined with tropes steeped in long histories of sexist and gendered stereotypes.

The raced and classed cultural tensions invoked by foreign caretakers provide further insight concerning the design of "neutral" service robots. Robertson discusses how elderly Japanese people prefer robots to the "sociocultural anxieties provoked by foreign labourers and caretakers" (Robertson 2010, 9). The Japanese perceived that robots did not have the historical baggage and cultural differences of migrant and foreign workers, which ultimately "reinforces the tenacious ideology of ethnic homogeneity" (Robertson 2010, 9). Here the purported neutrality of robots as opposed to racialized and discriminated human caretakers becomes a form of racist erasure and complicit celebration of sameness. Thus, an allegedly semiotically neutral robot design can be culturally embedded in a digitized society in highly contentious ways, simultaneously enacting processes of cultural re-gendering (associated with comforting stereotypes of female care) and racist erasure (associated with the discomforting use of stigmatized minorities in caretaking). Claims to neutrality in robot design are ultimately a discourse of power that must be dealt with cautiously in order to engage with how it reconfigures the positions of people within the techno-social imaginary of the emerging digital society.

The design of carebots must engage more self-reflexively with the problematic replication of gendered, racialized, and other stereotypes in robots, especially given the depth of the gendering and racializing process that can occur even when the objects are apparently gender-neutral and lack metallic genitalia and melanin in terms of their outward design. This suggests we have to think carefully about the ways in which digital technologies may entrench and deepen the lived experiences of both privilege and marginalization.

7.3 HAPPY SERVICE ROBOTS: WORSE THAN SLAVERY?

After having discussed visual culture, gender, and race in relation to the design of robots, I now turn to explore the potential impact of the instrumentalization of robots who provide care for humans. Of particular interest in this section is the position that claims that it is possible to produce robots that are designed and built to happily work in service for humans and I will focus on the work of Steve Petersen as a foil to explore the implications of this claim.

There is a wide range of opinions concerning the ethics of service robots and whether or not they are considered ethical subjects. Levy believes that robots should be treated ethically, irrespective of whether they are ethical subjects, in order to avoid sending the wrong message to society, namely that treating robots unethically will make it "acceptable to treat humans in the same ethically suspect ways" (Levy 2009, 215). In contrast, Torrance defends robot servitude, analogous to a kitchen appliance, because they are seen as incapable of being ethical subjects (Torrance 2008).

Petersen (2011), however, denaturalizes the status of the "natural" regarding robots and counters that a service robot can have full ethical standing as a person, irrespective of whether the artificial person is carbon or computationally-based. The important insight that personhood "does not seem to require being made of the particular material that happens to constitute humans," but rather "complicated organizational patterns that the material happens to realize," however, is combined with the much more controversial contention that it is nonetheless "ethical to commission them for performing tasks that we find tiresome or downright unpleasant" (Petersen 2011, 248)[5] if they are hardwired to *willingly desire* to perform their tasks.

> In a nutshell, I think the combination is possible because APs [Artificial Persons] could have hardwired desires radically different from our own. Thanks to the design of evolution, we humans get our reward rush of neurotransmitters from consuming a fine meal, or consummating a fine romance – or, less cynically perhaps, from cajoling an infant into a smile. If we are clever, we could design APs to get their comparable reward rush instead from the look and smell of freshly cleaned and folded laundry, or from driving passengers on safe and efficient routes to specified destinations, or from overseeing a well-maintained and environmentally friendly sewage facility. ... It is hard to find anything wrong with bringing about such APs and letting them freely pursue their passions, even if those pursuits happen to serve us. This is the kind of robot servitude I have in mind, at any rate; if your conception of servitude requires some component of unpleasantness for the servant, then I can only say that is not the sense I wish to defend. (Petersen 2011, 284)

Petersen adds that the preferences hardwired into carebots could remain indecipherable to humans.

> Robots ... could well prefer things that are mysterious to us. Just as the things we (genuinely, rationally) want are largely determined by our design, so will the things the robot (genuinely, rationally) wants can be largely determined by its design. (Petersen 2007, 46)

Petersen's argument is built upon the premise of hardwiring robots to feel desires that impassion them toward fulfilling work that humans find unpleasant. And he believes this is analogous to the ("naturally"-produced) hardwiring of humans given that in the "carbon-based AP [artificial person] ... the resulting beings would have to be no more 'programmed' than we are" (Petersen 2011, 285).

The crux of Petersen's position is that the robots freely choose to serve and thus do not violate the Kantian anti-instrumentalization principle of using a person as a mere means to an end.

> The "mere" use as means here is crucial. ... [T]he task-specific APs: though they are a means to our ends of clean laundry and the like, they are simultaneously

[5] Thus, Petersen concludes that ET may not be human, but he is a person. And the same applies to robots.

> pursuing their own permissible ends in the process. They therefore are not being used as a mere means, and this makes all the ethical difference. By hypothesis, they want to do these things, and we are happy to let them. (Petersen 2011, 291)

By claiming that insofar as an artificial person is a "willing servant, . . . we can design people to serve us without thereby wronging them" (Petersen 2011, 289), Petersen counters, first, the critique of creating a "caste" of people, particularly in the case of robots that do menial labors, and, second, the critique of designed servitude leading to "happy slaves" that have been paternalistically deprived of the possibility of doing something else with their lives (Walker 2007).

Although Petersen defends the right of artificial persons to do otherwise, that is, not to serve, he believes that reasoning "themselves out of their predisposed inclinations [is as] unlikely as our reasoning ourselves out of eating and sex, given the great pleasure the APs derive from their tasks . . ." (Petersen 2011, 292). Petersen's caveat of accepting dissent, however, does not square with the premises of his theory. Ultimately, the caveat/exception does not legitimate the rule of hardwiring sentient submission but rather operates as a malfunction within a structural argument that is in favor of the hardwired design of "dissent-less" carebots, which is unethical from the start. This shows how Petersen's writing is premised upon a strongly deterministic conception of behaviour as pre-determined by the hardwiring of living systems, be they organic or non-organic, and, as such, service robots are highly unlikely to finagle their way around their programmed "instinctive" impulses. In this way, despite Petersen's valuable denaturalization of the status of the "natural" in terms of the distinction between human and robot, he re-entrenches it once again in his simplistic conception of a pre-deterministic causality from gene/hardware to behaviour. For Petersen, treating artificial people ethically entails "respecting their ends, encouraging their flourishing" by "permitting them to do laundry" because "[i]t is not ordinarily cruel or 'ethically suspect' to let people do what they want" (Petersen 2011, 294). Precisely because they desire to serve, he contends that they must be distinguished from the institution of slavery. The inadequacy of the slave metaphor is such that, for Petersen, it would be irrational to preclude pushing buttons to custom design your artificial person who loves and desires to serve you because it could be an act of discrimination tantamount to the worst episodes of human history.

> The track record of such gut reactions throughout human history is just too poor, and they seem to work worst when confronted with things not like "us" – due to skin color or religion or sexual orientation or what have you. Strangely enough, the feeling that it would be wrong to push one of the buttons above may be just another instance of the exact same phenomenon. (Petersen 2011, 295)

I find Petersen's proposal of the happy sentient servant programmed to passionately desire servitude highly disturbing and problematic because, as I analyze and argue in this section, if materialized in future techno-social configurations of society, it would automate, reify, and legitimate the dissent-less submission of purportedly willing and happy swaths of sentient artificial humans and entrench hierarchical structures of oppression as natural divisions among artificial and non-artificial humans.

As part of setting out my analysis, I propose that robots can be historical in two senses, namely, as objects or subjects, although as objects they are historical in a much more limited sense than as subjects. Robots as historical objects are robots without sentience or self-awareness that are historical because of the values embedded in their design that are specifically situated in time and space. Furthermore, robots as objects are products of cultural translation within the technological frames and languages available at the time to materialize their functions. In contrast, robots as historical subjects are premised upon emergent forms of sentience and subjectivity that are analogous to those of "non-artificial" humans.

A digitized future in which we accept Petersen's conception of sentient servitude as ethical through embedding hardwired desires to serve and be obedient could create a future in which we automate what Pierre Bourdieu calls symbolic violence. The work of Bourdieu offers a sophisticated theory to address how societies reproduce their structures of domination. Symbolic capital or cultural values are central to the processes of legitimizing structures of domination. Said cultural values are reified or presented as universal but are in fact historically and politically contingent or arbitrary. Of all the manners of "'hidden persuasion,' the most implacable is the one exerted, quite simply, by the order of things" (Bourdieu and Wacquant 2004, 272). Programming sentient servants to be happy with their servitude points to the automation of symbolic violence through the deployment of desire and pleasure to subjugate artificial persons into unquestioning servitude while being depicted as having "freely" chosen to wash laundry *in saecula saeculorum*. If we assume that their desire by design is successfully engineered to avoid wanting any other destiny than that of servitude, the symbolic violence of artificial persons à la Petersen lies in how the hardwired happiness becomes an embedded structure of the relation of domination and thus reifies their compliance with the status quo.

Petersen claims that creating sentient servers who enjoy their labors is an advance over histories of racism, sexism, colonialism, and imperialism. I contend, however, that Petersen's *Person-O-Matic* culminates the imperial fantasy of biological determinism where you can have an intrinsically obedient population whose lesser sentience is engineered to feel grateful and happy to serve your needs. And I differ even further: It is not that Petersen's artificial beings designed to serve are simply analogous to slaves, but actually they are worse than slaves because they are trapped in a programmed/hard-wired state of dissent-less and ecstatic submission.

The domination of humans by humans along the axes of colonial forms of hierarchizing the relationship of the civilized colonizer vis-à-vis the barbarian other, either seen as in need of being civilized or inevitably trapped in cultural and/or biological incommensurableness, always had to contend with the capacity of dissent or the native excesses that collapsed the discursive strictures of colonial otherness and destabilized the neat hierarchies imposed by the imperial discourses. Empires had to deal with the massive failure of their fantasies regarding the imaginary subservience and inferiority of others, but a digital future built on Petersen's model is actually much more violent because desire by design hardwires pleasure in serving the masters. It basically precludes dissent, either because their lesser sentience has been designed effectively or because the dissent is a highly remote possibility. Hence the combination of limited sentience marked by a programmed incapacity to dissent poses the uncomfortable technological culmination of the fantasies of biological determinism that took definite shape as part of colonial endeavors.

An especially fascinating, powerful, and distinctive aspect of Petersen's model is the commodification of custom designed servitude. Rather than the vision of the colonial administration of an empire, it is a consumerist vision of individuals who go to a vending machine to custom design a slave, an intimate subjectivity of empire for John Doe, who can now have his own little colony of sentient servers to "orgasmically" launder his clothes, presumably among many other duties.

The notions available for understanding and evaluating humanness in the digital future are impoverished by this kind of theorization. For Petersen, sentience is premised upon the capacity of the human to act upon one's desires, which are hardwired into the robot. Desire here is a highly reductive and deterministic conception of desire by design. He articulates a linear theory of causality from design to desire, systemically hardwired to produce servants who happily do laundry. As already addressed, despite Petersen's contention that the artificial persons that emerge from the *Person-O-Matic* act freely when choosing to serve, the fact that their design, if it is successful, precludes the possibility of not wanting to serve raises serious doubts as to whether the robots are actually exercising their free will to do their labors. This resonates with Murakami Woods' critique, in Chapter 2, of digital imaginaries that nudge humanness into commercially profitable and instrumental boxes.

One of the central problems of Petersen's conception of robot sentience – like Murakami Wood's smart city denizen – is precisely that it is trapped within a narrow understanding of self-determination. This conception does not consider the social and historical constitution of subjectivities within cultural parameters that vary and produce contingent desires that are not reducible to the underlying hardwiring (genetic or otherwise). Desire is always multifaceted and leads to unintended consequences, always in excess, incomprehensible even for the subject that desires. Hence, once an artificial being acquires an emoting sentience of some sort, engineering identities is not a case of linear causalities that follow an imaginary teleology of desire in a genetic or computational fantasy of hardwiring. Hardwiring, genetic/computational engineering, and natural selection are the names of Petersen's "game" and, as a result, Petersen is not engaging with the social production and cultural inscription of sentient robot subjectivities and, accordingly, he occludes the complex and contradictory process of interactive, mutually constitutive forms of sociability set out in Chapter 8, by Steeves.

An emoting sentience implies that robots become social and cultural subjects, not just objects inscribed with pre-existing values in their design. They become subjects who can engage with and resist the constraints of their architecture as well as those of the discursive and semiotic fields of signification within which they emote and represent their location within societies. Rather than define robots as human because they fulfill their hardwiring of desiring to serve, we can say that robots become "human" when they escape the constraints of their imaginary hardwiring, when there is an excess of desire that is not reducible to their programming. Desire, pleasure, and pain are ghosts in the hardwiring of machines. And it is the ghosts that make the robot "human" as a form of *post-mortem* ensoulment enabling a human-like sentience marked by contradiction and excess. Irreducibility makes human. Unpredictability makes human. Dissent makes human. The absence of a "human nature" makes human.

Although it is still technically impossible to create robots with a fully human-like sentience, the production of emoting robots with limited forms of sentience may not be such a remote possibility. For Petersen, artificial humans will be more trapped within their hardwiring than "non-artificial" humans and, thus, the exercise of dissent from the structural constraints of their design will be highly remote, if not precluded altogether. His defense of the ethical legitimacy of the artificial person that serves "passionately" raises very difficult questions that must be teased out. Is the production of a lesser sentient dissent-less robot worse than the production of a fully sentient robot capable of dissent? Should there be an ethical preclusion of a lesser sentience in the design of emoting robots? Should society err on the side of no sentience in order to avoid the perverse politics that underlies the design of terminally happy sentient beings incapable of dissent, that is, the ideal servant incapable of questioning the "ironic ramifications of [his/her/its] happiness"?[6]

I contend that either no sentience or full sentience is more ethical than computationally or biologically wiring docility into an emoting and desiring being with a lesser sentience. When robots cease to be things to become sentient beings motivated by desires, pleasures, and happiness, the incapacity to dissent should not be a negotiable part of the design but rather should remain precluded. It seems much less unethical to create fully sentient robots with the capacity to dissent than to create a permanent underclass of unquestioningly obedient limited life forms motivated by passionate desires to serve.

Therefore, the techno-social imaginary of emerging digital societies must explicitly condemn the symbolic violence of automating the incapacity to dissent of artificial humans designed to happily launder the underwear of non-artificial humans. The ethical defense of the right to dissent in the design of emoting sentient

[6] This phrase is from a glass coaster that pokes fun at 1950s ideals of feminine domesticity.

beings crucially avoids creating the conditions for dystopic new forms of domination under a normalizing discursive smokescreen of the "order of things."

7.4 THE CAREBOT INDUSTRIAL COMPLEX: SOME FINAL THOUGHTS

Although I do not underestimate what carebots could mean for elderly people, in this final section I raise some final thoughts about what I call the *Carebot Industrial Complex*, namely, the collective warehousing of aging populations in automated facilities populated by carebots.

For Latour, the relationship of people to machines is not reducible to the sum of its parts but rather adds up to a complex emergent agency. Beyond Winner's concern over the embedding of social values in technologies, Latour deploys the notion of the delegation of humanness into technologies. Technological fixes can thus deskill people in a moral sense (Latour 1992). This process of deskilling acquires special relevance in the context of using carebots and how it can undermine human learning and development acquired in caregiving settings. Of special relevance here is Vallor's work on the ethical implications of carebots in terms of a dimension that has been ignored within the literature, that is, "the potential moral value of caregiving practices for caregivers" (Vallor 2011, 251). By examining the goods internal to caring practices, she attempts to "shed new light on the contexts in which carebots might deprive potential caregivers of important moral goods central to caring practices, as well as those contexts in which carebots might help caregivers sustain or even enrich those practices, and their attendant goods" (Vallor 2011, 251).

The *Industrial Carebot Complex* can deprive people living in the digital age of the moral value of caregiving practices for human caregivers and, in the process simultaneously, stigmatize the decaying bodies of the elderly, subject to the disciplinary effects of a shifting built environment and intimate technology of carebots, whose name exudes the oxymoronic concern of whether there can be care without caring. In addition, it can undermine the process of human intergenerational learning of caregiving skills for the elderly and stymy opportunities for emotional and social growth that occur when we act selflessly and out of concern for others.

Turkle's arguments on the evocative instantiations of robotic pets, some of which have been deployed as part of elder care, can be extended to the broader concern over the emotional identification of elderly people with future carebots. For instance, in her fieldwork on elders' interaction with pet robots, specifically Paro, a pet seal, Turkle asks:

> But what are we to make of this transaction between a depressed woman and a robot? When I talk to colleagues and friends about such encounters – for Miriam's story is not unusual – their first associations are usually to their pets and the solace they provide. I hear stories of how pets "know" when their owners are unhappy and

> need comfort. The comparison with pets sharpens the question of what it means to have a relationship with a robot. I do not know whether a pet could sense Miriam's unhappiness, her feelings of loss. I do know that in the moment of apparent connection between Miriam and her Paro, a moment that comforted her, the robot understood nothing. Miriam experienced an intimacy with another, but she was in fact alone. Her son had left her, and as she looked to the robot, I felt that we had abandoned her as well. (Turkle 2011, 9)

One of Turkle's central concerns is how our affection "can be bought so cheap" relative to robots that are incapable of feeling:

> I mean, what does it mean to love a creature and to feel you have a relationship with a creature that really doesn't know you're there. I've interviewed a lot of people who said that, you know, in response to artificial intelligence, that, OK, simulated thinking might be thinking, but simulated feeling could never be feeling. Simulated love could never be love. And in a way, it's important to always keep in mind that no matter how convincing, no matter how compelling, this moving, responding creature in front of you – this is simulation. And I think that it challenges us to ask ourselves what it says about us, that our affections, in a certain way, can be bought so cheap. (Turkle 2001, 9)

The potential attribution of affection to robots by a lonely and relegated population is particularly problematic and raises the specter of how the emotionless management of elderly bodies is ultimately not care. The emergent agency of the *Industrial Carebot Complex* can dehumanize aging populations even more dramatically than current forms of warehousing the elderly where the warmth of human hands, even those of a stranger, can make a radical difference in terms of the ethics of care experienced. Thus, the integration of carebots to elder care must never be in exclusion of human care, but rather complementary and subordinate to the moral value of human caregiving skills and practices.

In this chapter I have analyzed different dilemmas regarding the use of robots to serve humans living in the digital age. The design and deployment of carebots is inscribed in complex material and discursive landscapes that affect how we think of humanness in the socio-technological architectures through which we signify our lives. As stated at the outset of this chapter, imagining those spaces necessarily entails navigating the "fog of technology," which is also always a fog of inequality in terms of trying to decipher how the emerging architectures of our digitized lives will interface with pre-existing forms of domination and struggles of resistance premised upon our capacity to dissent. My main contention is anti-essentialist, namely, that the absence of a "human nature" makes us human and unpredictable. There is no underlying fixed essence to being human. Instead, we should be attentive to how what it means to be human, as I said in the opening and want to repeat here, must be strategically and empathically reinvented, renamed, and reclaimed, especially for the sake of those on the wrong side of the digital train tracks.

REFERENCES

Alexander, Jeffrey C., and Steven Seidman, eds. *Culture and Society: Contemporary Debates*. Cambridge: Cambridge University Press, 1990.

Balsamo, Anne. *Technologies of the Gendered Body: Reading Cyborg Women*. Durham, NC: Duke University Press, 1997.

Barnet, Belinda. "Pack-Rat or Amnesiac? Memory, the Archive and the Internet." *Continuum: Journal of Media & Cultural Studies* 15, no. 2 (2001): 217–231.

Bhabha, Homi K. *The Location of Culture*. New York: Routledge, 1994.

Bourdieu, Pierre, and Loïc Wacquant. "Symbolic Violence." In *Violence in War and Peace: An Anthology*, edited by Nancy Scheper-Hughes and Philippe Bourgois, 272–275. Oxford: Blackwell, 2004.

Butler, Judith. *Bodies That Matter: On the Discursive Limits of "Sex"*. New York: Routledge, 1993.

Gender Trouble: Feminism and the Subversion of Identity. New York: Routledge, 1990.

Crane, Diane, ed. *The Sociology of Culture: Emerging Theoretical Perspectives*. Oxford: Blackwell, 1994.

Georas, Chloé S. "From Sexual Explicitness to Invisibility in Resistance Art: Coloniality, Rape Culture and Technology." In *Misogyny across Global Media*, edited by Maria B. Marron, 23–41. Lanham, MD: Lexington Books, 2021.

Hall, Stuart, ed. *Representation: Cultural Representations and Signifying Practices*. Glasgow: Sage, 1997.

IFR. "World Robotics 2021: Service Robots Report Released." *IFR International Federation of Robotics*, accessed February 15, 2022b. https://ifr.org/ifr-press-releases/news/service-robots-hit-double-digit-growth-worldwide.

Jones, Amelia, ed. *The Feminism and Visual Culture Reader*, 2nd ed. New York: Routledge, 2010.

Latour, Bruno. "Where Are the Missing Masses? The Sociology of a Few Mundane Artifacts." In *Shaping Technology/Building Society: Studies in Sociotechnical Change*, edited by Wiebe E. Bijker and John Law, 225–259. Cambridge, MA: MIT Press, 1992.

Levy, David. "The Ethical Treatment of Artificially Conscious Robots." *International Journal of Social Robotics* 1 (2009): 209–216. https://doi.org/10.1007/s12369-009-0022-6.

Mirzoeff, Nicholas. "The Subject of Visual Culture." In *Visual Culture Reader*, 2nd ed., edited by Nicholas Mirzoeff, 3–23. New York: Routledge, 2002.

Mordor Intelligence. "Service Robotics Market | 2024–29 | Industry Share, Size, Growth: Mordor Intelligence." *Mordor Intelligence*, accessed April 3, 2024. www.mordorintelligence.com/industry-reports/service-robotics-market.

Mori, Masahiro. "The Uncanny Valley," translated by Karl F. MacDorman and Norri Kageki. *IEEE Robotics & Automation Magazine* 19, no. 2 (2012 [1970]): 98–100. www.researchgate.net/publication/254060168_The_Uncanny_Valley_From_the_Field.

Petersen, Stephen. "Designing People to Serve." In *Robot Ethics: The Ethical and Social Implications of Robotics*, edited by Patrick Lin, Keith Abney, and George A. Bekey, Kindle ed., 283–298. Cambridge, MA: MIT Press, 2011.

"The Ethics of Robot Servitude." *Journal of Experimental & Theoretical Artificial Intelligence* 19, no. 1 (March 2007): 43–54. https://philarchive.org/archive/PETTEO.

Robertson, Jennifer. "Gendering Humanoid Robots: Robo-Sexism in Japan." *Body & Society* 16, no. 2 (2010): 1–36. https://doi.org/10.1177/1357034X1036476.

Rogoff, Irit. "Studying Visual Culture." In *Visual Culture Reader*, 2nd ed., edited by Nicholas Mirzoeff, 24–36. New York: Routledge, 2002.

Torrance, Steve. "Ethics and Consciousness in Artificial Agents." *Artificial Intelligence & Society* 22, no. 4 (2008): 495–521. https://philpapers.org/rec/TOREAC-2.

Turkle, Sherry. *Alone Together: Why We Expect More from Technology and Less from Each Other*. New York: Basic Books, 2011.

"Interview: MIT's Dr. Sherry Turkle Discusses Robotic Companionship." *National Public Radio*, May 11, 2001. www.proquest.com/docview/190010111?&sourcetype=Other%20 Sources.

"Relational Artifacts with Children and Elders: The Complexities of Cybercompanionship." *Connection Science* 18, no. 4 (2006): 347–361. https://sherryturkle.mit.edu/sites/default/files/images/Relational%20Artifacts.pdf

Vallor, Shannon. "Carebots and Caregivers: Sustaining the Ethical Ideal of Care in the Twenty-First Century." *Philosophy & Technology* 24 (2011): 251–268. https://link.springer.com/article/10.1007/s13347-011-0015-x.

Walker, Mark. "Mary Poppins 3000s of the World Unite: A Moral Paradox in the Creation of Artificial Intelligence." *Institute for Ethics & Emerging Technologies*, 2007. www.researchgate.net/publication/281477782_A_moral_paradox_in_the_creation_of_artificial_intelligence_Mary_popping_3000s_of_the_world_unite.

Winner, Langdon. *The Whale and the Reactor: A Search for Limits in an Age of Technology*. Chicago: The University of Chicago Press, 1986.

8

Networked Communities and the Algorithmic Other

Valerie Steeves

To have a whole life, one must have the possibility of publicly shaping and expressing private worlds, dreams, thoughts, desires, of constantly having access to a dialogue between the public and private worlds. How else do we know that we have existed, felt, desired, hated, feared? (Nafisi 2003, ix)

In this chapter, I use qualitative research findings to explore how algorithmically driven platforms impact the experience of being human. I take as my starting point Meadian scholar Benhabib's reminder that, "the subject of reason is a human infant whose body can only be kept alive, whose needs can only be satisfied, and whose self can only develop within the human community into which it is born. The human infant becomes a 'self,' a being capable of speech and action, only by learning to interact in a human community" (Benhabib 1992, 5). From this perspective, living in community and participating in communication with others is a central part of the human experience; it gives shape to Nafisi's dance between public and private worlds and enables an agential path by which we come to know ourselves and forge deep bonds in community with others.

Certainly, early commentators celebrated the emancipatory potential of new online communities as they first emerged in the 1990s as spaces for both self-expression and community building (Ellis et al. 2004). Often designated communities of shared interest rather than communities of shared geography, they were expected to strengthen social cohesion by enabling people to explore their own interests and deepen their connection with others in new and exciting ways (see, e.g. Putnam 2000). Critics, on the other hand, worried that networked technology would further isolate people from each other and weaken community ties (Ellis et al. 2004). The advent of social media, those highly commercialized community spaces with all their hype of self-expression, sharing and connection, simply amplified the debate (Haythornthwaite 2007).

For my part, I am interested in what happens to the human experience when community increasingly organizes itself algorithmically. What do we know about the ways in which people manage the interaction between self and others in these communities? What kind of language can we use to come to a normative understanding of what it means to be human in these conditions? How do algorithms influence both our interactions and this normative understanding?

To date, platform owners have encouraged the use of the language of control to describe life in the online community, calling upon individuals to make their own choices about withholding or disclosing personal information to others so they can enjoy what in 1984 the German Supreme Court called informational self-determination (Eichenhofer and Gusy 2017). From this perspective, the human being interacting with others in community online is conceptualized apart from any relationship with others, and their agency is exercised by a binary control: zero, they withhold and stay separate and apart from others; one, they disclose and enjoy the fruits of publicity. As I have argued elsewhere (Steeves 2015, 2016), this perspective has consistently failed to capture the complicated and constrained interactions described by people living in these environments.

More socially grounded critiques of this understanding of being human online have underscored the anaemic protection that individual control provides, largely by displacing the autonomous individual with a more social understanding of subjectivity (see, e.g. Cohen 2012; Koskela 2006; Liu 2022; Mackenzie 2015). This approach is interesting precisely because it can account for moments of human agency exercised in the context of a variety of resistive behaviours. For example, 11- and 12-year olds often report that they enjoy asking Siri and Alexa nonsensical questions that the machine cannot answer, as a way of asserting their mastery over the technology. Like the Rickroll meme[1] and the Grown Women Ask Hello Barbie Questions About Feminism video[2], this is a playful way for people to deconstruct the ways in which they are inserted into technical systems and collectively resist the social roles they are offered by the platforms they use.

However, as Los (2006) notes, resistance is a poor substitute for agential action, precisely because current platforms are "intrinsically bound to social, political, and economic interests" (Thatcher et al. 2016, 993) that may overpower the resister by co-opting their resistance and repackaging it to fit within the features that serve those interests. In this context, observers too often interpret the networked human as overly determined through the internalized norms of the platform or as restricted to a form of apolitical transgression/resistance similar to the Rickroll meme and other examples. Either way, we are left with critique but no path forward.

The project of being human in the digital world accordingly requires a better set of metaphors (Graham 2013), a richer conceptualization that can capture the human experience within performances, identities and interactions shaped by algorithmic nudges. I suggest that Benhabib's insight that we come to know ourselves and others by living in community is a productive starting point for developing

[1] www.youtube.com/watch?v=dQw4w9WgXcQ.
[2] www.nylon.com/articles/hello-barbie-feminism-buzzfeed.

such a lexicon, not least because the Meadian assumptions upon which it is based set the stage to reunite the search for human agency and the embrace of the social (Koopman 2010). It is also a useful way to extend the insights of relational autonomy scholars (Mackenzie 2019; Roessler 2021) to do what Pridmore and Wang (2018) call for in the context of digital life – to theorize human agency without severing it from our social bonds to others.

To help give this shape, I start my discussion by revisiting some data I collected from young Canadians in 2017[3] about their experiences on algorithmically driven platforms. These data were first collected to see how young people navigate their online privacy by making decisions about what photos of themselves to post; we reported that they described a complicated negotiation driven by the need to be seen but not to be seen too clearly, given the negative consequences of a failed performance (Johnson et al. 2017). However, the data also provide an interesting window into how young people make sense of their self-presentation and interactions with others in networked community spaces that are shaped by algorithms.

Accordingly, I conducted a secondary analysis of the data to explore these elements. I start this chapter by reviewing the findings of that analysis, focusing on the ways in which my participants responded to the algorithms that shaped their online experiences by projecting a self made up of a collage of images designed to attract algorithmic approval as evidenced by their ability to trigger positive responses from a highly abstract non-personalized online community. I then use Meadian notions of sociality to offer a theoretical framing that can explain the meaning of self, other and community found in the data. I argue that my participants interacted with the algorithm as if it were another social actor and reflexively examined their own performances from the perspective of the algorithm as a specific form of generalized other. In doing so, they paid less attention to the other people they encountered in online spaces and instead oriented themselves to action by emulating the values and goals of this algorithmic other. Their performances can accordingly be read as a concretization of these values and goals, making the agenda of those who mobilize the algorithm for their own purposes visible and therefore open to critique. I then use Mead's notion of the social me and the indeterminate I to theorize the limited and constrained moments of agency in the data when my participants attempted – sometimes successfully, sometimes not – to resist the algorithmic logics that shape networked spaces.

[3] The data was originally collected as part of the eQuality Project, a multi-year partnership of researchers, educators, policymakers, youth workers and youth funded by the Social Sciences and Humanities Council of Canada. For more information, see equalityproject.ca. The moment in time is also instructive, as it marks the shift away from early reports of enthusiasm for online self-exploration and connection (Environics 2000; Steeves 2005) to a more cautious view of online community as fraught with reputational risks (Bailey and Steeves 2015; Steeves 2012) and therefore something that is safer to watch than to participate in (Steeves et al. 2020).

8.1 WHAT SELF? WHAT OTHER? WHAT COMMUNITY?

As noted, in 2017 we conducted qualitative research to get a better sense of young people's experiences on social media. Our earlier work (Bailey and Steeves 2015) suggested that young people rely on a set of social norms to collaboratively manage both their identities and their social relationships in networked spaces and that they are especially concerned about the treatment of the photos they post of themselves and their friends. We wanted to know more about this, so we asked 18 teenagers between 13 and 16 years of age from diverse backgrounds, 4 of whom identified as boys and 14 of whom identified as girls, to keep a diary for 1 week of the photos they took. They then divided the photos into three categories:

- Those photos they were comfortable sharing with lots of people;
- Those photos they were comfortable sharing with a few people; and
- Those photos they were not comfortable sharing with anyone.[4,5]

The photos we collected through this process were largely what we expected to see – school events, group shots, food, lots of landscapes. But when we sat down and talked to our participants, the discussion was not at all what we expected. It quickly became clear that the decisions they were making about what photos to share with many people really had very little to do with their personal interests or their friendships. Although they described the networked world as a place where they could connect with their community of family and friends, the decision-making process itself did not focus on what their friends and family would like to see or what they would like to show them of themselves. Instead, it focused on "followers", an abstract and anonymous audience they assumed was paying attention to a particular platform. Because of this, they positioned themselves less as people exploring their own sense of identity in community and more as apprentice content curators responsible for feeding the right kind of content to that abstract audience.

The right kind of content was determined by a careful read of the algorithmic prompts they received from the platform. Part of this involved them doing the work of the platform (Andrejevic 2009); for example, they universally reported that they maintained Snapchat streaks by posting a photo a day, even when it was inconvenient, because it was what the site required of them. Interestingly, they did this most easily by posting a photo of nothing. For example, one participant was frequently

[4] We also suggested an alternative in case they were uncomfortable sharing a particular photo with us. In that case, they could submit a description of the photo instead. None of the participants opted for this alternative.

[5] After collecting the photos, we conducted individual interviews between 60 and 90 minutes in length, using a semi-structured interview guide to explore their photo choices. Interviews were transcribed and subjected to a thematic qualitative analysis. The research protocols were approved by the research ethics boards at the University of Ottawa, the University of Toronto, Western University and George Mason University. For the original report, see Johnson et al. (2017).

awakened by an alert just before midnight to warn her that her streaks were about to end, so she would cover her camera lens with her hand, take a photo of literally nothing and post the photo as required. It was very clear that the posts were not to communicate anything about themselves or to connect with other people, but to satisfy the demands of the algorithmic prompt.

However, the bulk of their choices rested on a careful analysis of what they thought the audience for a particular platform would be interested in seeing. To be clear, this audience was explicitly not made up of friends or other teens online; it was an abstraction that was imbued with their sense of what the algorithm that organized content on the site was looking for. For example, they all agreed that a careful read of the platform and the ways content was algorithmically fed back to them on Instagram indicated that it was an "artsy" space that required "artsy" content. Because of that, if you had an Instagram page, you needed to appear artsy, even if you were not. Moreover, given the availability of Insta themes, it was important to coordinate the posts to be consistently artsy in a "unique" way, even though that uniqueness did not align with your own personal tastes or predilections.

From this perspective, the self-presentations that they offered to the site revealed very little of themselves aside from their fluency in reading the appropriate algorithmic cues. The digital self was accordingly a fabricated collage of images designed to attract algorithmic approval; in their words, "post worthy" content was made up of photos that said something "interesting" not from their own point of view but from the point of view of the abstract audience that would judge how well they had read the algorithmic prompts. One of the girls explained it this way:

> Because VSCO is more artsy, for me, like, I know I post my cooler pictures over there. I thought this was a really cool picture [of the cast of the Harry Potter movies], and I thought maybe a lot of people would like it and like to see it, because a lot of people are fans of Harry Potter, obviously.

She then explained that the point was not to share her interest in Harry Potter with people she knew on or offline (in fact, she was not a fan); it was to identify a theme that would appeal to the algorithm so her content would be pushed up the search results page and attract likes from unknown others. Moreover, she felt that her choice was vindicated when two followers added the photo to their collections. In this context, a pre-existing audience had already made its preferences known and the online marketplace then amplified those preferences by algorithmically prioritizing content that conformed to them; accordingly, the most "interesting" self to portray was one that mirrored the preferences of that marketplace independent of whether or not those preferences aligned with the preferences of the poster.

This boundary or gap between their own preferences and the preferences they associated with their online self was intentionally and aggressively enforced. This was best illustrated when one of the participants was explaining why a photo she took of an empty white bookcase against a white wall could not be shared with anyone. She told me that she had originally planned on posting it to her Instagram page (her theme was "white" because monochromatic themes were "artsy") but then she noticed a small object on the top shelf. She expanded the photo to see that it was an anime figurine. It was there because she was an ardent anime fan. However, she was distraught that she had almost inadvertently posted something that could, if the viewer expanded the photo, reveal her interest online. She eschewed that type of self-exposure because it could be misconstrued by the algorithm and then made public in ways that could open her up to judgement and humiliation. As another participant explained, photos of your actual interests and close relationships aren't

> ... something that you throw outside there for the whole world to see. It's kind of something that stays personally to you ... when I have family photos I feel scared of posting them because I care about my family and I don't want them to feel envied by other people. So, yeah ... Cuz I don't want – cuz I kinda – I really like my family. I really like my brother. I don't want anyone making fun of my brother.

To avoid these harms, all our participants reported that they collaborated with friends to collectively curate each other's online presences, paying special care to images. Specifically, no one posted photos of faces, unless they were part of a large group and taken from a distance. Even then, each photo would be perused to see if everyone "looked good" and, before posting, it would be vetted by everyone in the photo to make sure they were comfortable with it going online.

Interestingly, there were two prominent exceptions to these rules. The first occurred when they were publicly showing affection to friends in very specific contexts that were unambiguous to those who could see them. This included overtly breaching the rules on birthdays: publicly posting a "bad" photo of a friend's face without permission, so long as it was tagged with birthday good wishes, was a way to demonstrate affection and friendship, akin to embarrassing them by decorating their lockers at school with balloons. The second exception involved interacting with branded commercial content. For example, one of the girls had taken a series of shots of herself at Starbucks showing her face with a Starbucks macchiato beside it. She was quite confident that this photo would be well received because Starbucks was a popular brand. Similarly, our participants were confident that photos and positive comments posted on fan sites would be well-received because they were part of the online marketplace.

All other purposes – actually communicating with friends or organizing their schedules, for example – occurred in online spaces, such as texting or instant messaging apps, that were perceived to be more private. But even there, they restricted the bulk of their communications to sharing jokes or memes and reserved their most personal or intimate conversations for face-to-face interactions where they couldn't be captured and processed in ways that were outside their control.

8.2 UNDERSTANDING ALGORITHMIC COMMUNITY

The snapshot in Section 8.1 paints a vivid picture of a digital self that seeks to master the algorithmic cues embedded in networked spaces to self-consciously fabricate a collage of images that will attract approval from an abstracted, highly depersonalized community. From my research participants' perspective, networked interaction is therefore not simply about the self expressing itself to others, as throughout this process personal preferences are carefully and meticulously hidden. Rather, it is about the construction of an online self that is "unique" in the sense that it is able to replicate the preferences of the online marketplace in particularly successful ways. Success is determined through feedback from an abstracted and anonymous group of others who view and judge the construction but, to attract the gaze of those others, content must first be algorithmically selected to populate the top of search results. To do this well, the preferences, experiences and thoughts that are unique to the poster must be hidden and kept from the algorithmic gaze, and the poster must post content that will both be prioritized by the algorithm and conform to the content cues embedded by the algorithm in the platform. This is a collaborative task; individuals carefully parse what online self they choose to present but also rely on friends and family to co-curate the image of the self, by helping hide the offline self from the algorithmic gaze and by posting counter content to repair any reputational harm if the online self fails to resonate with the preferences of the online marketplace (see also Bailey and Steeves 2015).

To better understand these emerging experiences of the online self, other and community, I suggest we revisit Mead's understanding of self and community as co-constructed through inter-subjective dialogue. For Mead, an essential part of being human is the ability to anticipate how the other will respond to the self's linguistic gestures, to see ourselves through the other's eyes. This enables us to put ourselves in the position of the other and reflexively examine ourselves from the perspective of the community as a whole. He calls this community perspective the "generalized other" (Mead 1934; see also Aboulafia 2016; Prus 1994).

Martin (2005) argues that this ability to take the perspective of the other is a useful way to understand community because it calls upon us to pay attention to "our common existence as interpretive beings within intersubjective contexts" (232). Certainly, my participants can be understood as interpreters of the social cues they found embedded in networked spaces, exemplifying Martin's understanding of perspective taking as "an orientation to an environment that is associated with acting within that environment" (234). What is new here is that my participants described a process in which they gave less attention to their interactions with other people in that environment and instead oriented themselves to action by carefully identifying and emulating the perspective of the algorithm that shaped the environment itself.

This was often an explicit process. When they explained how they were trying to figure out the algorithm's preferences and needs, they were not merely seeking to reach through the algorithm to the social actors behind it to interpret the expectations of the human platform owners or even the human audience that would see their content. Rather, by carefully reading the technical cues to determine what kind of content was preferred by the platform and offering up a fabricated collage of images designed to attract its approval, they both talked about and interacted with the algorithm *as if it were another subject*.

This is a kind of reverse Turing Test. They were not fooled into thinking the algorithm was another human. Instead, they injected the algorithm with human characteristics, seeking to understand what was required of them by identifying the algorithm's preferences and interacting with it as if it were another subject. They did this both directly (by feeding the platform information and watching to see what response was communicated back to them) and indirectly through the "followers" who acted as the algorithm's proxies. Moreover, the importance they accorded to these algorithmic preferences was demonstrated by the kinds of identities my participants chose to perform in response to this interaction – such as Harry Potter Fan and Starbucks Consumer – even when these identities did not align with the selves and community they co-constructed offline and on private apps with friends and family.

Daniel (2016) provides an entry point into exploring this gap between online and offline selves when he rejects the notion of the unitary generalized other and posits a multiplicity of generalized others that can better take into account experiences of social actors who are located in a multiplicity of communities. Certainly, his insight that "the self is constituted by its participation in multiple communities but responds to them creatively by enduring the moral perplexity of competing communal claims" (92) describes the difficulties my participants talked about as they sought to be responsive to the multiple perspectives of the various social actors in their lives, including family, friends, schoolmates *and* algorithms. But reconceiving these various audiences as a "plurality of generalized others" (Martin 2005, 236), each of which reflects a self based on a specific set of expectations and aspirations shared by those inhabiting a particular community space (Daniel 2016, 99), makes it possible to conceptualize – and analyze – the algorithm as the algorithmic other, with its own commercially-driven values and goals, that shapes selves and interactions in networked spaces.

To date, the most comprehensive critique of the commercial values and goals that shape the online environment has been made by Zuboff (2019). She argues that algorithms act as a form of Big Brother or, in her words, "a *Big Other* that encodes the 'otherized' viewpoint of radical behaviorism as a pervasive presence" (20). From this perspective, the problem rests in the fact that the algorithmic other does not operate to reflect the self back to the human observer so the human can see its performances as an object, but instead quantifies the fruits of social interaction in order to (re)define the self as an object that can be nudged, manipulated and controlled (Lanzing 2019; McQuillan 2016; Steeves 2020). In this way, the algorithmic other serves to:

> *automate us* ... [and] finally strips away the illusion that the networked form has some kind of indigenous moral content – that being "connected" is somehow intrinsically pro-social, innately inclusive, or naturally tending toward the democratization of knowledge. Instead, digital connection is now a brazen means to others' commercial ends. (Zuboff 2019, 19)

However, Zuboff's critique is dissatisfying as it gives us no way to talk about agency: if we are fully automated, then we have been fully instrumentalized. It also fails to capture the rich social-interactive context in which my research participants sought to understand and respond to the algorithms that shape their public networked identities. Once again, I suggest that Mead can help us because he lets us unpack the instrumentalizing logic of the nudge without giving up on agency altogether.

Certainly, my participants' experiences suggest that the kinds of identities that we can inhabit in networked spaces are constrained to those that conform to the commercial imperatives of the online ecology. However, the notion that a particular community constrains the kinds of identities we are able to experiment with is not new. As Daniel (2016) notes:

> It is crucial to appreciate that Mead's generalized other is aggressive and intrusive, not passively composed by the self ... This is clearer in the state of social participation, which requires the self to organize its actions so as to fit within a pattern of responsive relations whose expectations and aspirations precede this particular self's participation ... The generalized other should be understood as [this] pattern of responsive relations, which is oriented toward particular values and goals. (100)

From this perspective, the types of identities that we see performed online in response to the algorithmic other concretize the values and goals embedded in online spaces by platform owners who mobilize algorithms for their own profit; and, by making those values visible, they open them up to debate. This makes the algorithm a key point of critique because it is a social agent that operates to shape and instrumentalize human interactions for the purposes of the people who mobilize it. From this perspective, to solve the kinds of polarization, harassment and misinformation we see in the networked community we must start by analyzing how algorithms create a fruitful environment for those kinds of outcomes. Unpacking how this works is the first step in holding those who use algorithms for their own profit to public account.

The sociality inherent in my participants' interactions with the algorithmic other also lets us account for those small moments of agency reflected in the data. Mead posits that the self interacts with the generalized other in two capacities. The first is the social me that is performed for the generalized other and reflected back to the self so the self can gauge the success of its own performance. As noted in Section 8.1, the intrusiveness of the algorithmic other constrains the social me that can be performed in networked spaces. This is exemplified by my participants' concern that their networked selves – artsy consumers of branded products – conform to the expectations of the algorithmic other even when they can't draw a stick figure or don't like coffee. However, the second capacity of the self is the I, the self that observes the social me as an object to itself and then decides what to project next.

Mead accordingly helps us break out of algorithmic determination by anchoring agency in the indeterminacy of the I as a future potentiality. This indeterminacy is constrained because it is concretized as the social me as soon as the I acts. But its emergent character reasserts the possibility of change and growth precisely because it can only act in the future. By situating action in a future tense of possibility, we retain the ability to resist, to choose something different, to be unpredictable, to know things about ourselves that have not yet come into being. In this sense, the algorithm can constrain us, but it cannot fully determine us because we continue to emerge.

Certainly, my research participants sought to exercise agency over their online interactions by revealing and hiding, making choices as part of an explicitly conscious process of seeing the objective self reflected back to them. They also wrested online space away from the algorithm on occasion. Birthday photos, for example, were consciously posted in order to break the algorithmic rules and to connect not with the abstract audience but with the humans in their lived social world, a social world which both interpolates with and extends beyond networked spaces. This demonstrates both a familiarity with and an ability to pull away from the algorithmic other in favour of the generalized other they experience in real world community.

8.3 CONCLUSION

I argue that my participants' experiences demonstrate the paucity of identities available to networked humans who interact on sites that are shaped by the instrumental goals of profit and control. But those same experiences also underscore the rich sociality with which humans approach algorithmically driven ecologies, shaping their own interactions with the environment by injecting social meaning into the algorithm through their reading of the algorithmic other.

Certainly, the algorithmic positioning of human as object for its own instrumental purposes rather than for the social purposes of the self leaves us uneasy. Although we may feel reduced to an online self that is "compactified" into "a consumable package" and wonder if we can "know what it means to exist as something unsellable" (Fisher-Quann 2022), the point is we still wonder. Once again, agency exists as a potentiality in the moment of our own perusal of the self as object, in spite of – or perhaps because of – our interactions with the aggressive and intrusive nature of all generalized others (Daniel 2016).

Moreover, by conceiving of the algorithm as a social actor, we can extend the moment of human agency and bring the values and goals embedded in the algorithm out of the background and into the foreground of social interaction.

From this perspective we can open up the algorithmic black box and read its instrumental intentions through the performances it reflects back to us because we recognize and interact with the algorithmic other as other. From this perspective, the algorithm only "masquerades as uncontested, consensus reasons, grounds, and warrants when they are anything but" (Martin 2005, 251). Acknowledging the algorithm as an inherent part of online sociality helps us begin the hard task of collectively confronting the politics inherent in the algorithmic machine (McQuillan 2016, 2).

Mead's Carus Lecture in 1930 is prophetic in this regard. He said:

> It seems to me that the extreme mathematization of recent science in which the reality of motion is reduced to equations in which change disappears in an identity, and in which space and time disappear in a four-dimensional continuum of indistinguishable events which is neither space nor time is a reflection of the treatment of time as passage without becoming. (Mead 1932, 19)

Hildebrandt and Backhouse (2005) make the same point when they argue that the data that algorithms use to sort us are a representation, constructed from a particular point of view, of a messy, complicated, nuanced and undetermined person. They warn us that, if our discourse confuses the representation of an individual with the lived sense of self, we will fail to account for the importance of agency in the human experience. We will also be unable to unmask the values and goals of those humans who mobilize algorithms in the networked world for their own purposes.

REFERENCES

Aboulafia, Mitchell. "George Herbert Mead and the Unity of the Self." *European Journal of Pragmatism and American Philosophy* VIII, no. 1 (2016). https://journals.openedition.org/ejpap/465.

Andrejevic, Mark. *iSpy: Surveillance and Power in the Interactive Era*. Lawrence: University Press of Kansas, 2009.

Bailey, Jane, and Valerie Steeves, eds. *eGirls, eCitizens*. Ottawa: University of Ottawa Press, 2015.

Benhabib, Seyla. *Situating the Self: Gender, Community, and Postmodernism in Contemporary Ethics*. New York: Routledge, 1992.

Cohen, Julie E. *Configuring the Networked Self: Law, Code, and the Play of Everyday Practice*. New Haven, CT: Yale University Press, 2012.

Daniel, Joshua. "Richard Niebuhr's Reading of George Herbert Mead: Correcting, Completing, and Looking Ahead." *Journal of Religious Ethics* 44, no. 1 (2016): 92–115.

Eichenhofer, Johannes, and Christoph Gusy. "Courts, Privacy and Data Protection in Germany: Informational Self-determination in the Digital Environment." In *Courts, Privacy and Data Protection in the Digital Environment*, edited by Maja Brkan and Evangelia Psychogiopoulou, 101–119. Cheltenham: Edward Edgar Publishing, 2017.

Ellis, David, Rachel Oldridge, and Ana Vasconcelos. "Community and Virtual Community." *Annual Review of Information Science and Technology* 38, no. 1 (2004): 145–186.

Environics. *Young Canadians in a Wired World, Phase 1: Focus Groups with Parents and Children*. Ottawa: MediaSmarts, 2000.

Fisher-Quann, Rayne. "Standing on the Shoulders of Complex Female Characters: Am I in my Fleabag Era or Is my Fleabag Era in Me?" *Internet Princess*, February 6, 2022. https://internetprincess.substack.com/p/standing-on-the-shoulders-of-complex.

Graham, Mark. "Geography/Internet: Ethereal Alternate Dimensions of Cyberspace of Grounded Augmented Realities?" *The Geographic Journal* 179, no. 2 (2013): 177–182.

Haythornthwaite, Caroline. "Social Networks and Online Community." In *Oxford Handbook of Internet Psychology*, edited by Adam Joinson, Katelyn McKenna, Tom Postmes, and Ulf-Dietrich Reips, 121–134. New York: Oxford University Press, 2007.

Hildebrandt, Mireille, and James Backhouse, eds. *D7.2: Descriptive Analysis and Inventory of Profiling Practices*. European Union: FIDIS Network of Excellence, 2005.

Johnson, Matthew, Valerie Steeves, Leslie Shade, and Grace Foran. *To Share or Not to Share: How Teens Make Privacy Decisions about Photos on Social Media*. Ottawa: MediaSmarts, 2017.

Koopman, Colin. "The History and Critique of Modernity: Dewey with Foucault against Weber." In *John Dewey and Continental Philosophy*, edited by Paul Fairfield, 194–218. Carbondale: Southern Illinois University Press, 2010.

Koskela, Hille. "The Other Side of Surveillance: Webcams, Power and Agency." In *Theorizing Surveillance: The Panopticon and Beyond*, edited by David Lyon, 163–181. London: Routledge, 2006.

Lanzing, Marjolein. "'Strongly Recommended': Revisiting Decisional Privacy to Judge Hypernudging in Self-Tracking Technologies." *Philosophy & Technology* 32 (2019): 549–568.

Liu, Chen. "Imag(in)ing Place: Reframing Photography Practices and Affective Social Media Platforms." *Geoforum* 129 (2022): 172–180.

Los, Maria. "Looking into the Future: Surveillance, Globalization and the Totalitarian Potential." In *Theorizing Surveillance: The Panopticon and Beyond*, edited by David Lyon, 69–94. London: Routledge, 2006.

Mackenzie, Adrian. "The Production of Prediction: What Does Machine Learning Want?" *European Journal of Cultural Studies* 18, no. 4–5 (2015): 429–445.

Mackenzie, Catriona. "Relational Autonomy: State of the Art Debate." In *Spinoza and Relational Autonomy: Being with Others*, edited by Aurelia Armstrong, Keith Green, and Andrea Sangiacomo, 10–32. Edinburgh: Edinburgh University Press, 2019.

Martin, Jack. "Perspectival Selves in Interaction with Others: Re-reading G.H. Mead's Social Psychology." *Journal for the Theory of Social Behaviour* 35, no. 3 (2005): 231–253.

McQuillan, Dan. "Algorithmic Paranoia and the Convivial Alternative." *Big Data & Society* 3, no. 2 (2016): 1–12.

Mead, George Herbert. *Mind, Self, and Society from the Standpoint of a Social Behaviorist*. Chicago: University of Chicago Press, 1934.

The Philosophy of the Present, edited by Arthur E. Murphy. LaSalle, IL: Open Court, 1932.

Nafisi, Azar. *Reading Lolita in Tehran*. New York: Random House, 2003.

Pridmore, Jason, and Yijing Wang. "Prompting Spiritual Practices through Christian Faith Applications: Self-Paternalism and the Surveillance of the Soul." *Surveillance & Society* 16, no. 4 (2018): 502–516.

Prus, Robert. "Generic Social Processes and the Study of Human Experiences." In *Symbolic Interaction: An Introduction to Social Psychology*, edited by Nancy J. Herman and Larry T. Reynolds, 436–458. Maryland: Rowman & Littlefield, 1994.

Putnam, Robert D. *Bowling Alone: The Collapse and Revival of American Community*. New York: Simon & Schuster, 2000.

Roessler, Beate. *Autonomy: An Essay on the Life Well-Lived*. Cambridge: Polity Press, 2021.

Steeves, Valerie. "A Dialogic Analysis of Hello Barbie's Conversations with Children." *Big Data & Society* 7, no. 1 (2020): 1–12.

"Now You See Me: Privacy, Technology and Autonomy in the Digital Age." In *Current Issues and Controversies in Human Rights*, edited by Gordon DiGiacomo, 461–482. Toronto: University of Toronto Press, 2016.

"Privacy, Sociality and the Failure of Regulation: Lessons Learned from Young Canadians' Online Experiences." In *Social Dimensions of Privacy: Interdisciplinary Perspectives*, edited by Beate Roessler and Dorota Mokrosinska, 244–260. Cambridge: Cambridge University Press, 2015.

Young Canadians in a Wired World, Phase II: Trends and Recommendations. Ottawa: MediaSmarts, 2005.

Young Canadians in a Wired World, Phase III: Talking to Youth and Parents about Life Online. Ottawa: MediaSmarts, 2012.

Steeves, Valerie, Samantha McAleese, and Kara Brisson-Boivin. *Young Canadians in a Wireless World, Phase IV: Talking to Youth and Parents about Online Resiliency*. Ottawa: MediaSmarts, 2020.

Thatcher, Jim, David O'Sullivan, and Dillon Mahmoudi. "Data Colonialism through Accumulation by Dispossession: New Metaphors for Daily Data." *Environment and Planning D: Society and Space* 34, no. 6 (2016): 990–1006.

Zuboff, Shoshana. "Surveillance Capitalism and the Challenge of Collective Action." *New Labor Forum* 28, no. 1 (2019): 10–29.

9

The Birth of Code/Body

Azadeh Akbari

They ask me how did you get here? Can't you see it on my body? The Lybian desert red with immigrant bodies, the Gulf of Aden bloated, the city of Rome with no jacket. . . . I spent days and nights in the stomach of the trucks; I did not come out the same. Sometimes it feels like someone else is wearing my body.[1] (Shire 2011, 25)

We are Black and the border guards hate us. Their computers hate us too.[2] (Molnar 2020, 12)

This book contends with various ways of being human in the digital era, and this chapter intends to describe what it means to have a human body in our time. Much has been written about the colonial, racializing and gendered continuities of perceiving, sorting and discriminating bodies in a digital world. However, nothing like the digital has transformed the materiality of the body in its very flesh and bone. It seems redundant to say that the body is the prerequisite to being human, yet this superfluous fact questions how bodies function in in-between worlds: they flow in this world's digital veins and yet rigidly represent decisive characteristics. They seem unreal, an amalgamation of data sometimes, while at other times fingerprints, iris scans and bone tests portray a cage, a trap, a body that betrays. This contrast is especially visible in uncertain spaces, where identity becomes crucial and only certain categories of humans can *pass*, such as borders and refugee camps. These spaces are not only obscuring the body while exposing it; they also exist in a complex mixture of national jurisdiction, international regulations and increasingly private "stakeholders" in immigration management. In addition to the severity of experiencing datafication of bodies in these spaces, the deliberate unruliness paves the way for these spaces to become *technological testing grounds* (Molnar 2020); for example, technologies developed for fleeing populations were used for contact tracing during the COVID-19 pandemic.

The relationship between body, datafication and surveillance has been scrutinized from the early days of digital transformation. Today's most debated issues, such

[1] From the poem "Conversations about Home (at the Deportation Centre)" by Warsan Shire.

[2] Excerpt from group discussion at later-evacuated L'Autre Caserne community in Brussels.

as algorithmic bias, were already warned about, and the ramifications of their discriminatory assumption for marginalized people were highlighted at the end of the 1980s (Gandy 1989). Similarly, the predictive character of aggregated data and the consequences of profiling were analysed (Marx 1989). From these early engagements, many instances of showing how routinely technologies are used to govern, datafy and surveil the body developed (see, e.g. Bennett et al. 2014). Additionally, surveillance scholars discussed how the "boundary between the body *itself* and information *about* that body" is increasingly transforming (Van der Ploeg 2012, 179). Building on this rich body of literature and personal experiences of immigration, exile and entrapment, this chapter revisits the body, being uncomfortable in/with/within it and yet being aware of its power to define if one is considered human enough to bear rights, feelings and existence. Similar to the chapter's movement between boundaries of the material and virtual, the text also oscillates between academic thinking, autobiographical accounts, pictures and poesy; denoting the discomfort of being in a Code/Body.[3] In this chapter, poetic language remedies the absence of the performative to help with the linguistic distress for finding the right words to describe embodied feelings.

9.1 FROM DATA DOUBLES TO EMBODIMENT

The scholarship on datafication, surveillance and digital transformation in the 2000s is infatuated with what can be called the demise of the material body. The speed of datafication and digital change lead to the idea that the surveillance society gives rise to *disappearing* bodies (Lyon 2001); the body is datafied and represented through data in a way that its materiality is obscured. Although such conceptualizations had been formerly discussed, especially by feminist and queer scholars, the liberatory nature of these feminist interpretations of cyborg bodies (Haraway 1985) and body assemblages were not transferred into these new understandings of datafied and surveilled body. In their influential essay on surveillant assemblages, Haggerty and Ericson compare the digital era with Rousseau's proclamation, "man was born free, and he is everywhere in chains" by claiming that nowadays "humans are born free, and are immediately electronically monitored" (Haggerty and Ericson 2000, 611). The subjectivating effect of surveillance, then, is instantly interlinked with basic rights and the meaning of being human. The body, they argue, is positioned within this surveillance assemblage: it is "broken down into a series of discrete signifying flows" (Haggerty and Ericson 2000, 612). Contrary

[3] The combination of Code/Body is first used by Suneel Jethani (2020) in their paper on self-tracking and mediating the body. The paper uses the similar notion of Code/Body or coded body to represent the hybrid or networked body. However, my chapter's theoretical perspective differentiates between Code/Body and coded body and furthers the concept of Code/Body beyond self-quantification. This text is inspired by my lecture-performance at PACT Zollverein Performing Arts Theatre in Essen, Germany in 2023.

to the Foucauldian way of monitoring, the body needs to be fragmented to be observed. Fragments can be combined or re-combined into "data-doubles": ones that "transcend human corporeality and reduce flesh to pure information" (Haggerty and Ericson 2000, 613).

The scholarly debates on bodies in the following two decades were centred around the transformation of the body "via practices of socio-technical intermediation" (French and Smith 2016, 9). The body and its datafication, visualization, mediation and multiplication have become increasingly important. Research about sorting, profiling and reification of marginal identities (or race/gender/class/etc.), inclusion and exclusion proliferates and successfully demonstrates how bias, racism, oppression and discrimination are injected into digital lives. The data double revealed the concurrent processes of the body's objectification – to transform its characteristics to data – and its subjectivation due to the socio-technical processes of datafication. As Zuboff assertively writes in *The Age of Surveillance Capitalism*, "the body is simply a set of coordinates in time and space where sensation and action are translated as data" (Zuboff 2019, 203). In this reading of the body, behavioural surplus is the engine of surveillance capitalism and the body is only *another* source of data. However, recent technological advancements, especially in using bodily features for identification, have started to expand and reconfigure such accounts. More recent studies underline the body's centrality, for example, in big data surveillance and manipulation of the "surveilled subject's embodied practices" (Ball et al. 2016) or critically examine how biometric technologies transform the relationships between the body and privacy (Epstein 2016). It is argued that data body is not only a change in how bodies are represented but there exists an ontological change: the materiality of the body "and our subjective forms of embodiment that are caught in this historical process of change" are transforming (Van der Ploeg 2012, 179). This chapter contributes to these later discussions, where the body is not only central as the source of data but has its own agency as an actant in data assemblages.

9.2 THE BIRTH OF CODE/BODY

Following the global digital transformation, discussions on issues of privacy, data protection, algorithmic harm and similar have entered the academic discourse and public debate. The recent years have seen an increase in reporting about the Big Tech companies as emerging new actors in the international governance realm. However, only those events that entail geopolitical or socio-economic relations to the Western countries are deemed relevant. For example, the news of Chinese payment methods through facial recognition technology rapidly reached the Western media (Agence France-Presse 2019) but much less attention was paid to the internal politics of digitalization in the Global South or the new e-governance measures of international governance institutions. This reluctance is intensified when digital technologies target communities that are marginalized, stateless or economically disadvantaged. UNHCR's use of iris scanning for refugee cash assistance illustrates a case of extreme datafication of the body against people in dire need of assistance with hardly any voice to consent to or refuse the imposed technologies. Ninety per cent of refugees in Jordan are registered through EyeCloud, "a secure and encrypted network connection that can be used to authenticate refugees against biometric data stored in the UNHCR database" (UNHCR 2019). Iris scanning is then used for payment in the camp's supermarket to calculate and pay the wages for working inside the camp and it replaces any monetary transaction. The EyeCloud demonstrates how current datafication practices do not only stop at using the datafied body for identification and representation but actively integrate the body as a part of data machinery. This instrumentalized body simultaneously carries the gaze of surveillance and guards itself against itself. The consequences are painful: more than a decade ago, *The Guardian* newspaper reported that asylum seekers burn their fingertips on electric stoves or with acid to avoid the Dublin regulations and to avoid being returned to their point of arrival, usually in Greece or Italy (Grant and Domokos 2011). The betraying body, however, regenerates fingertips after 2 weeks. Similarly, in cases where the age assessment of a claimed minor proves inconclusive, the person could be referred for a bone density test of the wrist by x-ray in Malta (Asylum Information Database 2023) or a "dental x-ray of the third molar in the lower jaw and MRI of the lower growth plate of the femur bone" in Sweden (Rättsmedicinalverket 2022). In these cases, the immigration authorities believe the body's truthfulness and the accuracy of medical sciences against mendacious and deceitful asylum seekers. Table 9.1 shows the extent of data categories gathered on visa, immigration or asylum applicants travelling to Europe. The body increasingly becomes a vehicle for *knowing* the real person behind the application.

The body acts as a trap. It transcends the current argumentations about profiling, sorting or bias based on personal data. What we witness is not just the datafication of the body but its function as ID card, debit card or labour hours registration sheet. If the cash machines, IDs and punched cards were technologies of yesterday, today these features are transferred to the body. The body *becomes* the payment system, the surveillance machine, the border. It is integrated into the datafied society's infrastructure. It is platformized humanity. It is an integral material part of the bordering. On the Eastern European borders, heartbeat detectors, thermal-vision cameras and drones are used to unlawfully return the asylum seekers who manage to pass the border (Popoviciu 2021). The border is not a line on the map; it is everywhere (Balibar 2012, 78). The border is simultaneously a body on the move and a vehicle to keep out a body that does not belong. Consequently, the body/border can efficiently prevent flight since it entraps. When the Taliban got hold of biometric data banks that Western governments, the UN and the World Bank left behind in 2021, many activists and experts who collaborated with the coalition went

TABLE 9.1 *Data categories stored in European immigration data banks.*[4]

Personal data stored in the different EU immigration data banks						
Data Type	SIS	VIS	EURODAC	EES	ETIAS	ECRIS-TCN
Alphanumeric Data						
"general" information (name, age, gender, nationality)	x	x	x	x	x	x
Occupation		x			x	
Education					x	
Reason for travel		x				
Information about funds for living expenses		x				
Address, phone number, email-address, IP-address					x	
Information about past or present felonies	x				x	x
Information about recent stay in a war or conflict region					x	
Biometric Data						
Fingerprints	x	x	x	x		x
Facial image	x	x	x	x		x
Genetic data	x					

into hiding because any border passage would put them in immediate danger of identification (Human Rights Watch 2022). They went into indefinite house arrest within the skeleton of their own bodies. This notion of corporeal entrapment or embodied surveillance resonates with the new conceptualization of how we understand *space* in the era of datafication. *Coded space* is defined as "spaces where software makes a difference to the transduction of spatiality, but the relationship between code and space is not mutually constituted" (Kitchin and Dodge 2011, 18). The digitalization of border security at airports or the use of digital technologies in the classroom are examples of coded space. In all these instances, when technology fails, there are still ways to finish the intended task: if the machine at a fully-automated high-tech airport does not recognize you, there is always an officer who can legitimize the authenticity of your ID. However, in the *code/space* the existence of space is dependent on the code and vice versa. If you are attending an online presentation and the technology fails, that would end your interaction. The code/space highlights the dyadic relationship between the two and their co-constructive nature (Kitchin and Dodge 2011). The dyadic relationship also explains the sense of

[4] Table 9.1 was produced in 2022 in collaboration with Christopher Husemann, PhD student in political geography, University of Münster, and was later updated by the author.

corporeal entrapment. The datafied or *coded body* still exists, moves and functions. It has a mutual relationship with the data it produces but is not entirely constituted through it. We have our virtual profiles in social media platforms or wear smart watches but, as soon as we leave such spaces, we resign from being part of their universe. The *Code/Body*, however, is born in co-construction with the code and ceases existence if the code fails.

The Code/Body is an extension of code/space argumentation to the Foucauldian corporeal space, constantly subject to governmentality. Consequently, the surveillant assemblage introduced by Haggerty and Ericson (2000) is not only about the production of data double. Their use of the Deleuzian conceptualization of the "body without organs" as an abstraction of the material body does not reflect the co-construction of the virtual and the material. Code/Body, on the other hand, offers a way to understand how the materiality of the body remains integral to our understanding of the body's datafication while transcending the virtual–material dichotomy. The Code/Body carries manifold wounds: the bodily pain of being wounded – burnt fingertips, lungs full of water, starved behind border walls – and the hidden wounds of datafied exclusion. Although algorithms try to hide their bias, Code/Body reveals that race has a colour, ethnicity has an accent and gender could be "scientifically" examined. Underlining such material features of the body and their role in defining the Code/Body emphasizes "the co-constitution of humans and non-humans" (Müller 2015, 27) and brings our attention to how things are held together and how datafied societies function. Extending the assemblage point of view, Actor Network Theory (ANT) provides a better empirical ground to understand the politics of the networks. It moves the focus more on outward associations and less on the intrinsic characteristics of a thing or its abstraction. The Code/Body highlights the co-constitution of these outward–inward associations and the body's agency in changing the flows and associations within the assemblage. From this perspective, things have an open and contested character (Mol 1999, 75), and the body is performative, meaning that its position within an assemblage can redefine its reality. Consequently, if one thing could be shaped by a variety of practices and networked connections, it can be configured in multiple and ambivalent ways. Lawful immigrants from internationally undesirable countries experience this multiple configuration throughout their border experiences. Visas to countries that have been visited before are rejected; border officers ask irrelevant questions to make the entry unpleasant or surprisingly act extra friendly. Automated passport check stations flicker a red light for double control but, on the next visit, go green. The assemblage changes and the integrated body in it changes accordingly. The Code/Body is, then, the ultimate device to realize and fulfil this fluidity. As a result, it is highly political how assemblages take shape, what actants dominate the flows, and which of the multiple realities of a thing are given preference. The *ontological politics* (Mol 1999, 74) of Code/Body define the conditions of the possibility of being a human. Depending on their position in an assemblage, a person's body could be reconfigured very differently. Heartbeats mean one thing on a smartwatch at a spinning class and another when sitting behind a lie detector machine at a border detention centre. Such politics of being are not only about positionality and "where we are" but also include temporality and "when we are." I was held twice at the UK border detention centre despite having a valid visa. On both occasions, a sympathetic border officer took upon himself the time-consuming task of removing me from the "bad list." It feels like a wonder that, within 40 minutes, a detained suspicious person, banished to a corner of the airport under the watchful eyes of a guard, turns into a legal traveller. Like a thing, the body can be understood as "a temporary moment in an endless process of assembling materials, a partial stabilisation and a fragile accomplishment that is always inexorably becoming something else, somewhere else" (Gregson et al. 2010, 853). Code/Body, again, facilitates this temporary and mutable process of re-configuration. The more the body is datafied, the more physical it becomes.

9.3 A MOEBIUS BODY

The Code/Body blurs not only the virtual–material binaries but also nuances the politics of sorting by questioning the discourse of inclusion–exclusion through digital technologies, platforms and algorithms. Code/Body extends concepts such as the mediated body or the quantified self to propose an existential situation where the *self* stops to exist outside the code. This newly contended notion of self is the prerequisite of citizenship in the smart cities – the utopian dream of an urban life, which all societies are ambitiously moving towards. In future smart cities, we will not only witness behaviour nudging or the gamification of obedience (Botsman 2017); cities will be transformed into experimental labs, where the urban citizen is produced through measuring (Mattern 2016). On top of gathering data through sensors, following the movements and urban flows, and closely watching the bodies, the body becomes an instrument of belonging. To be in, it needs to be outed. The body needs to be thoroughly datafied to become integrated into the smart infrastructure of the city. Living in the Code/Body is a constant ride on a Moebius ring: the inside and outside depend on how one defines their situation or how their situation is defined for them. The Code/Body could belong to an urban assemblage at a specific time and lose all its association by a slight change in the code in the next second. In Figure 9.1, I have drawn a Moebius ring on the verdict of my complaint against UK immigration's refusal of my tourist visa.

I had lived in London for 4 years and, after giving up my residency and returning to Iran, my tourist visa application was rejected. I was confused: I used to belong, work, live and actively participate in British society. Why was I suddenly out? Curiously, the judge had suggested since I can use technologies such as Skype to contact my friends in the UK, my human rights are not deemed to be violated. The code kept my body outside through its affordances to bring us closer. The movement

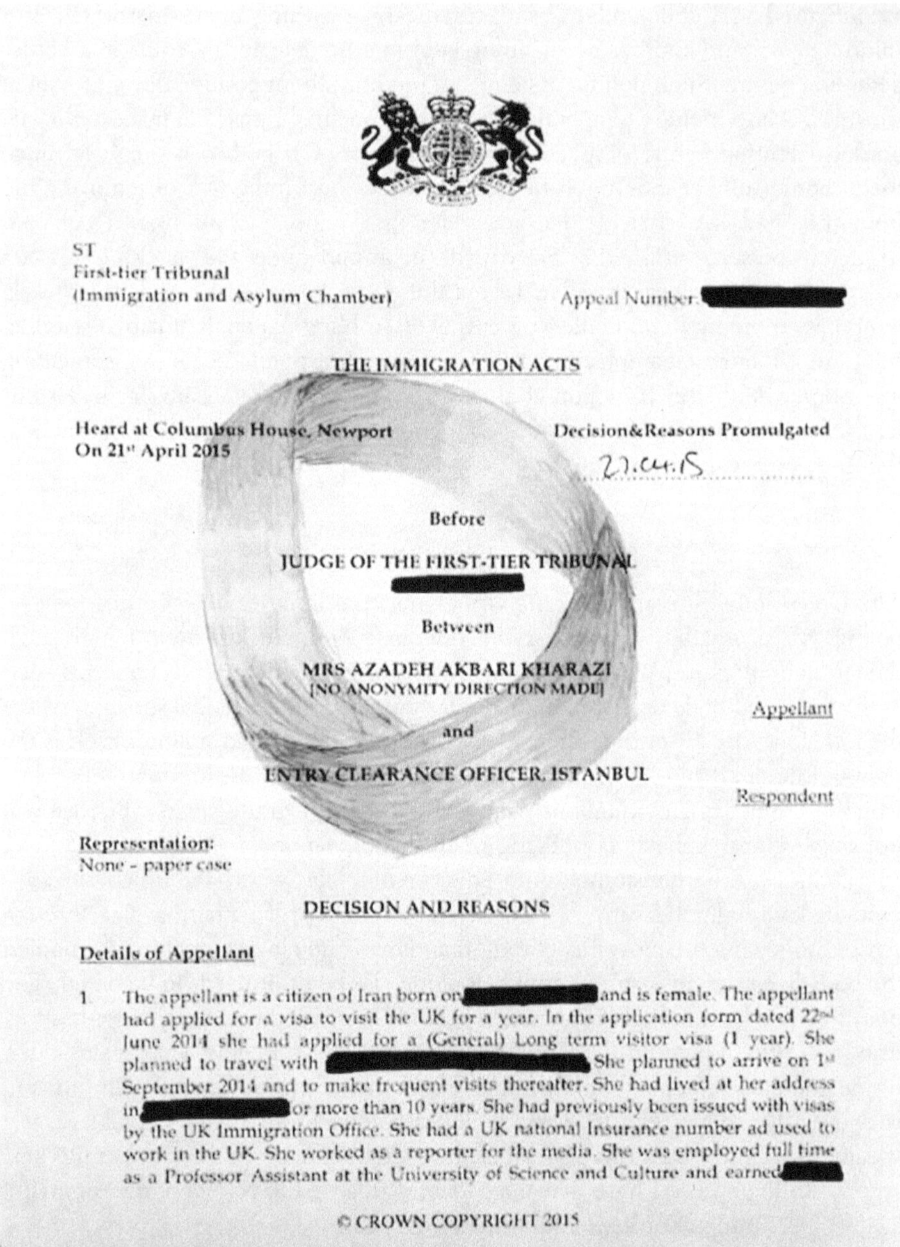

ST
First-tier Tribunal
(Immigration and Asylum Chamber) Appeal Number:

THE IMMIGRATION ACTS

Heard at Columbus House, Newport
On 21st April 2015

Decision&Reasons Promulgated
27.04.15

Before

JUDGE OF THE FIRST-TIER TRIBUNAL

Between

MRS AZADEH AKBARI KHARAZI
[NO ANONYMITY DIRECTION MADE]

Appellant

and

ENTRY CLEARANCE OFFICER, ISTANBUL

Respondent

Representation:
None - paper case

DECISION AND REASONS

Details of Appellant

1. The appellant is a citizen of Iran born on and is female. The appellant had applied for a visa to visit the UK for a year. In the application form dated 22nd June 2014 she had applied for a (General) Long term visitor visa (1 year). She planned to travel with . She planned to arrive on 1st September 2014 and to make frequent visits thereafter. She had lived at her address in or more than 10 years. She had previously been issued with visas by the UK Immigration Office. She had a UK national Insurance number ad used to work in the UK. She worked as a reporter for the media. She was employed full time as a Professor Assistant at the University of Science and Culture and earned

© CROWN COPYRIGHT 2015

FIGURE 9.1 Mobius strip on Immigration Courts' verdict © Azadeh Akbari, 2023

between inside and outside makes bodily functions fuzzy; as if one can die while breathing and live forever, even after the heart stops. The following quote from a Somali refugee (now residing in Europe) initially shocks the reader: Did they drown?

Immediately after this thought, it seems his body has been revived from a mass of drowned refugees.

> I was caught by the Lybian coastguard three times – first time from Qarabully; second time, Zawyia; third time, Zuwarna. And my fourth time, we drowned. And the fifth time, I made it to safety. (Hayden 2022, 5)

Another female Kurdish Iranian protestor during the Woman, Life, Freedom movement – a movement of Iranian women against compulsory Islamic dress code and discriminatory laws – reflects on how her body experiences the images she had previously seen on (social) media. She writes about how the physical and digital blend into each other and, despite the fear of pain instigated by watching social media videos, the real batons or pellets do not cause the expected physical pain.

> I once received loud cheers when I escaped a scene of confrontation with security forces and ran into the crowd. . . . The next morning when I was looking over my bruises in the mirror, the details of the confrontation suddenly passed before my eyes. . . . I had not simply been beaten; I had also resisted and threw a few punches and kicks. My body had unconsciously performed those things I had seen other protestors do. I remembered the astonished faces of the guards trying to subdue me. My memory had just now, after a time interval, reached my body. (L 2022)

The body's agency leaks into the consciousness only after it has performed a task. In moments of upheaval, where the oppressed body stands up to its oppressors, it tries to distort its entrapment. Despite being surveilled, controlled and censored the body lives the unpermitted imaginary: it kicks the security forces, it runs and hides, it shows skin. It revolts against the sensory limitations imposed on it. In Figure 9.2, Woman, Life, Freedom protestors have covered a subway CCTV camera with female menstrual pads. Their female bodies withstand the gaze that controls, hides, oppresses and objectifies them. Next to the camera is a hashtag with an activist's name: this time, virtual campaigns fuse into the material reality of the city. The Code/Body which is meant to be a part of the surveillant machinery through CCTV camera and facial recognition technologies, blinds the omnipresent eye with its most female bodily function: menstruation.

Similar to silencing some bodily features, some bodies are marked as intangible, unrepresentable and unfathomable. Despite being embedded within different streams of data and code, our collective imagination still does not register the precarity of some bodies. At the time that artificial intelligence claims to further the limits of our creative powers by creating historical scenes or impossible fantasies, I inserted the poem by Warsan Shire at the beginning of this chapter in three popular AI-based text-to-image generation platforms. The results in Figure 9.3 show irrelevant pictures of mostly men depicting some keywords of the poem. The messiness of the poetry – and the poet's feelings – does not translate into clear cut images. The machine fails to grasp even the theme of the poem. The wounded Code/Body remains hidden. The skin bears the pain of these wounds without

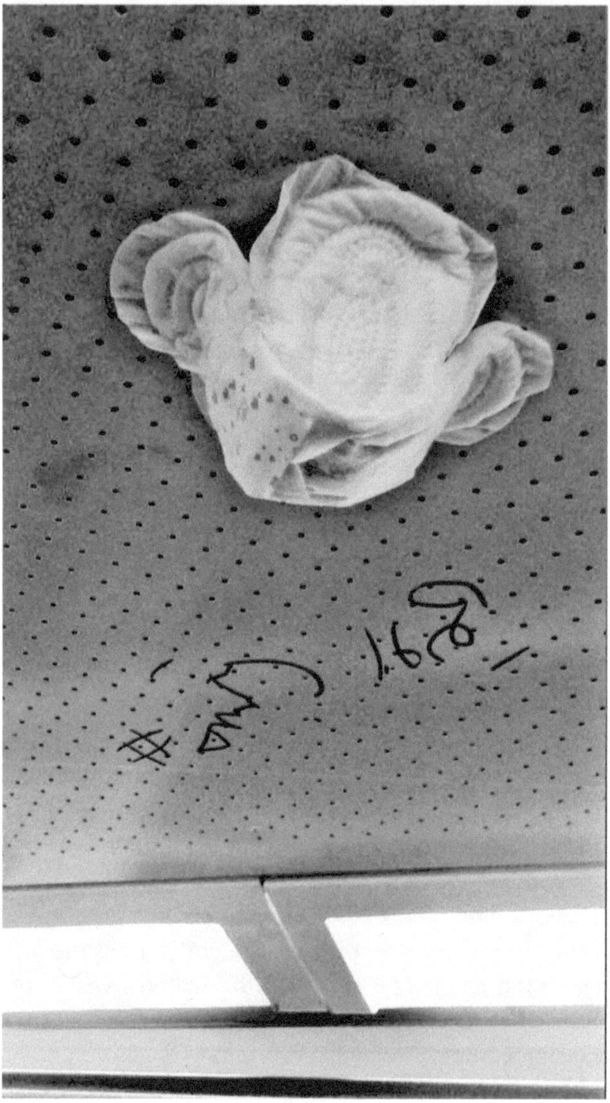

FIGURE 9.2 Blocking CCTV cameras in Public transportation with menstruation pads (Akbari 2023, 24).

bleeding and without any algorithm capturing its suffering. The person is caught in a body that can be datafied, but its emotions cannot be perceived.

This chapter does not aim to investigate the political, economic or social reasons or structures that construct the Code/Body. The biopolitical and necropolitical, the Foucauldian corporeal space and its governmentality have been the subject of many scholarly debates. How surveillance and datafication affect these spaces is also not a new matter of discussion. However, it seems persistently new how uncomfortable

FIGURE 9.3 AI-generated pictures created by Azadeh Akbari based on the poem "Conversations about Home (at the Deportation Centre)" by Warsan Shire, using three popular AI-based platforms

the body feels for some people. The more some lives are exposed to precarity of intense datafication, some bodies are forced to give away their unscrupulous owner. Surveilling and constant measuring of the Code/Body assures that these lives remain precarious. Some bodies, it seems, could be easily deleted, like a line of *dead code*.

Tell the sea after the news of my death
that I wasn't that thirsty to fill my lungs with his water,
that I am only an extremely exhausted man
who suffered all his life long from poverty
who worked all day long
to pursue a dignified life for his children
I wanted to flee like all poor people
I went to you, sea
to pull me out of the darkness
to take me to a brighter trajectory
You misunderstood me, sea
I told you that I wasn't thirsty

Mahmoud Bakir, a young father from Gaza, wrote this poem in February 2021 before drowning on his way to reach Europe.

REFERENCES

Agence France-Presse. "Smile-to-Pay: Chinese Shoppers Turn to Facial Payment Technology." *The Guardian*, September 4, 2019. www.theguardian.com/world/2019/sep/04/smile-to-pay-chinese-shoppers-turn-to-facial-payment-technology.

Akbari, Azadeh. "Iran: Digital spaces of protest and control." *European Center for Not-for-Profit Law* (2023). https://ecnl.org/publications/iran-digital-spaces-protest-and-control.

Asylum Information Database. "Identification: Malta" *Asylum Information Database | European Council on Refugees and Exiles* (blog), April 27, 2023. https://asylumineurope.org/reports/country/malta/asylum-procedure/guarantees-vulnerable-groups-asylum-seekers/identification/.

Balibar, Étienne. *Politics and the Other Scene*, translated by Christine Jones, James Swenson, and Chris Turner. New York: Verso, 2012.

Ball, Kirstie, MariaLaura Di Domenico, and Daniel Nunan. "Big Data Surveillance and the Body-Subject." *Body & Society* 22, no. 2 (2016): 58–81. https://doi.org/10.1177/1357034X15624973.

Bennett, Colin J., Kevin D. Haggerty, David Lyon, and Valerie Steeves, eds. *Transparent Lives: Surveillance in Canada*. Athabasca, Alberta: Athabasca University Press, 2014.

Botsman, Rachel. 2017. "Big Data Meets Big Brother as China Moves to Rate Its Citizens." *Wired UK*, October 21, 2017. www.wired.co.uk/article/chinese-government-social-credit-score-privacy-invasion.

Epstein, Charlotte. "Surveillance, Privacy and the Making of the Modern Subject: Habeas What Kind of Corpus?" *Body & Society* 22, no. 2 (2016): 28–57. https://doi.org/10.1177/1357034X15625339.

French, Martin, and Gavin J. D. Smith. "Surveillance and Embodiment: Dispositifs of Capture." *Body & Society* 22, no. 2 (2016): 3–27. https://doi.org/10.1177/1357034X16643169.

Gandy, Oscar H., Jr. "The Surveillance Society: Information Technology and Bureaucratic Social Control." *Journal of Communication* 39, no. 3 (1989): 61–76. https://doi.org/10.1111/j.1460-2466.1989.tb01040.x.

Grant, Harriet, and John Domokos. "Dublin Regulation Leaves Asylum Seekers with Their Fingers Burnt." *The Guardian*, October 7, 2011. www.theguardian.com/world/2011/oct/07/dublin-regulation-european-asylum-seekers.

Gregson, N., M. Crang, F. Ahamed, N. Akhter, and R. Ferdous. "Following Things of Rubbish Value: End-of-Life Ships, 'Chock-Chocky' Furniture and the Bangladeshi Middle Class Consumer." *Geoforum* 41, no. 6 (2010): 846–854. https://doi.org/10.1016/j.geoforum.2010.05.007.

Haggerty, Kevin D., and Richard V. Ericson. "The Surveillant Assemblage." *The British Journal of Sociology* 51 no. 4 (2000): 605–622. https://doi.org/10.1080/00071310020015280.

Haraway, Donna J. "A Manifesto for Cyborgs: Science, Technology, and Socialist Feminism for the 1980s." *Socialist Review* 15, no. 2 (1985): 65–107.

Hayden, Sally. *My Fourth Time, We Drowned.* New York: Melville House, 2022.

Human Rights Watch. "New Evidence That Biometric Data Systems Imperil Afghans." *Human Rights Watch*, March 30, 2022. www.hrw.org/news/2022/03/30/new-evidence-biometric-data-systems-imperil-afghans.

Jethani, Suneel. "Mediating the Body: Technology, Politics and Epistemologies of Self." *Communication, Politics & Culture* 47, no. 3 (2020): 34–43. https://doi.org/10.3316/informit.113702521033267.

Kitchin, Rob, and Martin Dodge. *Code/Space: Software and Everyday Life.* Cambridge, MA: The MIT Press, 2011. https://doi.org/10.7551/mitpress/9780262042482.001.0001.

L. "Figuring a Women's Revolution: Bodies Interacting with Their Images." *Jadaliyya*, October 5, 2022. www.jadaliyya.com/Details/44479.

Lyon, David. *Surveillance Society: Monitoring in Everyday Life.* Buckingham: Open University Press, 2001.

Marx, Gary T. *Undercover: Police Surveillance in America.* Oakland: University of California Press, 1989.

Mattern, Shannon. "Instrumental City: The View from Hudson Yards, circa 2019." *Places Journal*, April 2016. https://doi.org/10.22269/160426.

Mol, Annemarie. "Ontological Politics. A Word and Some Questions." In *Actor Network Theory and After*, edited by John Law and John Hassard, 74–89. Oxford: Blackwell Publishing, 1999.

Molnar, Petra. "Technological Testing Grounds: Migration Management Experiments and Reflections from the Ground Up." *EDRI*, 2020. https://edri.org/wp-content/uploads/2020/11/Technological-Testing-Grounds.pdf.

Müller, Martin. "Assemblages and Actor-Networks: Rethinking Socio-Material Power, Politics and Space." *Geography Compass* 9, no. 1 (2015): 27–41. https://doi.org/10.1111/gec3.12192.

Popoviciu, Andrei. "'They Can See Us in the Dark': Migrants Grapple with Hi-Tech Fortress EU." *The Guardian*, March 26, 2021. www.theguardian.com/global-development/2021/mar/26/eu-borders-migrants-hitech-surveillance-asylum-seekers.

Rättsmedicinalverket. "Medical Age Assessment." *Rättsmedicinalverket*, October 18, 2022. www.rmv.se/medical-age-assessment/.

Shire, Warsan. *Teaching My Mother How to Give Birth.* UK: Mouthmark series, 2011.

UNHCR. "EYECLOUD© Enhancing the Delivery of Refugee Assistance." *UNHCR Operational Data Portal*, 2019. https://data2.unhcr.org/en/documents/details/68208.

Van der Ploeg, Irma. "The Body as Data in the Age of Information." In *Routledge Handbook of Surveillance Studies*, edited by Kirstie Ball, Kevin Haggerty, and David Lyon, 176–184. London: Routledge, 2012.

Zuboff, Shoshana. *The Age of Surveillance Capitalism: The Fight for a Human Future at the New Frontier of Power.* New York: Public Affairs, 2019.

PART III

Technology and Policy

10

Exploitation in the Platform Age

Daniel Susser

Being human in the digital age means confronting a range of disorienting normative challenges. Social problems, such as ubiquitous surveillance, algorithmic discrimination, and workplace automation feel at once familiar and wholly new. It is not immediately apparent whether the language and concepts we've traditionally used to describe and navigate ethical, political, and governance controversies, the distinctions we've drawn between acceptable and unacceptable relationships, practices, and exercises of power, or the intuitions we've relied on to weigh and balance difficult trade-offs adequately capture the difficult issues emerging technologies create. At some level of abstraction, there is nothing truly new under the sun. But for our language and concepts to be practically useful in the present moment we have to attend carefully to how they track – and what they illuminate about – the real-world challenges we face.

This chapter considers a common refrain among critics of digital platforms: big tech "exploits" us (Andrejevic 2012; Cohen 2019; Fuchs 2017; Jordan 2015; Muldoon 2022; Zuboff 2019). It gives voice to a shared sense that technology firms are somehow mistreating people – *taking advantage* of us, *extracting* from us – in a way that other data-driven harms, such as surveillance and algorithmic bias, fail to capture.

Take gig work, for example. Uber, Instacart, and other gig economy firms claim that their platforms strengthen worker autonomy by providing flexible schedules and greater control over when, where, and how people work. Yet many worry that gig economy – or what Ryan Calo and Alex Rosenblat call "taking economy" – platforms are, in fact, exploiting workers (Calo and Rosenblat 2017). Regulators warn that gig platforms set prices using "non-transparent algorithms," charge high fees, shift business risks onto workers, and require workers to pay for overhead expenses that companies normally cover (e.g., car insurance and maintenance costs), allowing platforms to capture an unfair share of proceeds.[1] Workers are subjected

[1] According to the US Federal Trade Commission (2022, 5): "[G]ig companies may use nontransparent algorithms to capture more revenue from customer payments for workers' services than customers or workers understand."

to opaque, even deceptive, terms of employment, "algorithmic labour management" enables fine-grained, potentially manipulative control over work practices (Rosenblat and Stark 2016; Susser et al. 2019; US FTC 2022), and high market concentration leaves workers with few alternative options (US FTC 2022). Especially worrying, some forms of gig work – most notably "crowdwork," where work assignments are divided into micro-tasks and distributed online, which commonly drives content moderation and the labeling of training data for artificial intelligence (AI) – are reproducing familiar patterns of racial exploitation, with the global north extracting labor, digitally, from workers in the global south. Tech workers in Kenya have recently described these practices as "modern day slavery" and called on the US government to stop big tech firms from "systemically abusing and exploiting African workers."[2]

Now consider a very different example: the increasingly common practice of algorithmic pricing. Price adjustment is a central feature of market exchange – the primary mechanism through which markets (ideally) optimize economic activity. Sellers set prices in response to – amongst other things – overall economic conditions, competitor offerings, the cost of inputs, and buyers' willingness to pay. Today, many sellers rely on algorithms to do the work of price-setting and these new pricing technologies have sparked a number of concerns. Economists worry, in general, that algorithmic pricing drives prices upward for consumers, in some cases by enabling new forms of collusion between firms, and in others simply as a result of feedback dynamics between multiple pricing algorithms (MacKay and Weinstein 2020). But these technologies don't simply automate price-setting, they can "personalize" it, tailoring prices to individual buyers (Acquisti et al. 2016). "Personalized" (or "customized") pricing, as industry firms euphemistically call it, is opaque – buyers rarely know when and how prices are personalized, making comparison shopping difficult. And the information used to set prices can include personal information about individual buyers (Seele et al. 2021), leading to concerns that algorithmic pricing helps firms "extract wealth" from consumers and "shift it to themselves" (MacKay and Weinstein 2020, 1).

One more case: "surveillance advertising." The contemporary digital economy is driven by targeted advertising.[3] Rather than charge consumers for the services they offer, such as search and social media, companies like Google and Facebook infuse their products with ads. Some argue that this business model is a win–win: users get access to valuable digital services for free, while technology firms earn huge profits

2 "Open Letter to President Biden from Tech Workers in Kenya." For context, see Haskins (2024).

3 As Tim Hwang (2020, 5) writes, "From the biggest technology giants to the smallest startups, advertising remains the critical economic engine underwriting many of the core services that we depend on every day. In 2017, advertising constituted 87 percent of Google's total revenue and 98 percent of Facebook's total revenue."

monetizing users' attention.[4] But many have come to view the ad-based digital economy as a grave threat to privacy, autonomy, and democracy. Because targeted advertising relies on personal information – data about individual beliefs, desires, habits, and circumstances – to place ads in front of the people most likely receptive to them, digital platforms have become, effectively, instruments of mass surveillance (Tufekci 2018). And because targeted ads can influence people in ways they don't understand and endorse, they challenge important values like autonomy and democracy (Susser et al. 2019). Beyond these concerns, however, others argue that the surveillance economy involves an insidious form of *extraction*. Julie E. Cohen describes the market for personal information as the enclosure of a "biopolitical public domain," which "facilitates new and unprecedented surplus extraction strategies within which data flows extracted from people – and, by extension, people themselves – are commodity inputs, valuable only insofar as their choices and behaviours can be monetized" (Cohen 2019, 71).[5]

The goal of what follows is to unpack the claims that these platform-mediated practices are exploitative. What does exploitation entail, exactly, and how do platforms perpetrate it? Is exploitation in the platform economy a new *kind* of exploitation, or are these old problems dressed up as new ones? What would a theory of digital exploitation add to our understanding of the platform age? First, I define exploitation and argue that critics are justified in describing many platform practices as wrongfully exploitative. Next, I focus on platforms themselves – both as businesses and technologies – in order to understand what is and isn't new about the kinds of exploitation we are witnessing. In some cases, digital platforms perpetuate familiar forms of exploitation by extending the ability of exploiters to reach and control exploitees. In other cases, they enable new exploitative arrangements by creating or exposing vulnerabilities that powerful actors couldn't previously leverage. On the whole, I argue, the language of exploitation helps express forms of injustice overlooked or only partially captured by dominant concerns about, for example, surveillance, discrimination, and related platform abuses, and it provides valuable conceptual and normative resources for challenging efforts by platforms to obscure or legitimate them.

[4] For example, the Interactive Advertising Bureau (IAB), a trade association for the online marketing industry, argued in a recent comment in response to the US Federal Trade Commission's Notice of Proposed Rulemaking on commercial surveillance: "there is substantial evidence that data-driven advertising actually benefits consumers in immense ways. As explained below, not only does data-driven advertising support a significant portion of the competitive US economy and millions of American jobs, but data-driven advertising is also the linchpin that enables consumers to enjoy free and low-cost content, products, and services online" (IAB 2022, 10).

[5] Or, as Shoshana Zuboff (2019, 94) puts it, "the essence of the exploitation [typical of 'surveillance capitalism'] is the rendering of our lives as behavioural data for the sake of others' improved control of us," the "self-authorized extraction of human experience for others' profit" (Zuboff 2019, 19).

10.1 DEFINING EXPLOITATION

What exploitation is and what makes it wrong have been the subject of significant philosophical debate. In its modern usage, the term has a Marxist vintage: the engine and the injustice of capitalism, Marx argued, is the exploitation of workers by the capitalist class. For Marx, labor is unique in its ability to generate value; lacking ownership and control over the means of production, workers are coerced to give over to their bosses most of the value they create. This, in Marx's view, is the sense in which workers are exploited: value they produce is taken, *extracted* from them, and claimed, unjustly, by others.[6]

Some media studies and communications scholars have adopted this Marxian framework and applied it in the digital context, arguing that online activity can be understood as a form of labor and platform exploitation as appropriation of the value such labor creates.[7] For example, pioneering work by Dallas Smythe on the "audience commodity" – the packaging and selling of consumer attention by advertisers – which focused primarily on radio and television, has been extended by theorists such as Christian Fuchs and Mark Andrejevic to understand the internet's political economy through a constellation of Marxist concepts, including exploitation, commodification, and alienation.[8] As Andrejevic argues, this work adds a crucial element to critical theories of the digital economy, missing from approaches focused entirely on data collection and privacy (2012, 73).

While these accounts offer important insights, I depart from them somewhat in conceptualizing platform exploitation, for several reasons. Many – including many Marxist theorists – dispute the details of Marx's account. Specifically, critics have demonstrated that the "labour theory of value" (the idea that value is generated exclusively by labor, that it is more or less homogeneous, and that it can be measured in "socially necessary labour time"), upon which Marx builds his notion of exploitation, is implausible (Cohen 1979; Wertheimer 1996, x). So, the particulars of the orthodox Marxist story about exploitation are probably wrong and building a theory of digital exploitation on top of it would mean placing that theory on a questionable foundation. Still, the normative intuition motivating the theory – that workers are often subject to unjust extraction, that something of theirs is taken, wrongfully, to benefit others – is widely shared, and efforts have been made to put that intuition on firmer theoretical ground (Cohen 1979; Reiman 1987; Roemer 1985).

Moreover, the concept of exploitation is more capacious than the Marxist account suggests. Beyond concerns about capitalist exploitation, we might find and worry

6 For a more complex picture of the relationship between exploitation and capitalist appropriation, especially focusing on its racialized character, see Nancy Fraser (2016).

7 See, for example, Tiziana Terranova (2000).

8 For example, see Fuchs (2010). For a helpful intellectual history of related work on the political economy of media and communication technology, see Lee McGuigan (2014).

about exploitation more broadly, in some cases outside of economic life altogether (Goodin 1987). Feminist theorists, for example, have identified exploitation in sexual and marital relationships (Sample 2003), bringing a wider range of potential harms into view. And, while the exploitation of workers – central to Marxist accounts – continues to be vitally important, as we will see, the incorporation of digital platforms into virtually all aspects of our lives opens the door to forms of exploitation Marxist accounts underemphasize or ignore.

Contemporary theorists define exploitation as *taking advantage of someone* – using them to benefit oneself. Paradigm cases motivating the philosophical literature include worries about sweatshop labor, commercial surrogacy, and sexual exploitation.[9] Of course, taking advantage is not always wrong – one can innocently take advantage of opportunities or rightly take advantage of an opponent's misstep in a game. Much of the debate in exploitation theory has thus centred on its "wrong-making features," that is, what makes taking advantage of someone morally unacceptable. There are two main proposals: one explains wrongful exploitation in terms of unfairness, the other in terms of disrespect or degradation.

10.1.1 *Exploitation as Unfairness*

Taking advantage of someone can be unfair either for procedural or substantive reasons. An interaction or exchange is procedurally unfair if the process is defective – for example, if one party deceives the other about the terms of their agreement or manipulates them into accepting disadvantageous terms. Substantive unfairness, by contrast, is a feature of outcomes. Even if the process of reaching an agreement is defect-free, the terms agreed to might be unacceptable in and of themselves. Consider sweatshop labor: a factory owner could be entirely forthright about wages, working conditions, and the difficult nature of the job, and likewise workers could reflect on, understand, and – given few alternative options – decide to accept them. The process is above-board, yet in many cases of sweatshop labor the terms themselves strike people as obviously unfair.

One way to understand what has gone wrong here is via the notion of "social surplus."[10] Often when people interact or exchange the outcome is positive-sum: cooperation can leave everyone better off than they started. In economics, the surplus created through exchange is divided (sometimes equally, sometimes unequally) between sellers and buyers. But the concept of a social surplus need not be expressed exclusively in monetary terms. The idea is simply that when people interact, they often increase total welfare. If I spend my Saturday helping a friend move, he benefits from (and I lose) the labor I've provided for free. But we both

[9] On sweatshop labor, see e.g., Jeremy Snyder (2010); and Matt Zwolinski (2012). On commercial surrogacy, see e.g., Wertheimer (1996). On sexual exploitation, see Sample (2003).

[10] For an overview of competing accounts, see Zwolinski et al. (2022).

enjoy each other's company, feel secure in knowing we're deepening our relationship, and I derive satisfaction from doing someone a favor.

Exploitation enters the picture when the social surplus is divided unfairly.[11] Returning to the sweatshop case, for example, the exchange is unfair – despite the absence of procedural issues – because the factory owner claims more than his fair share of the value created. He could afford to pay the factory workers more (by collecting a smaller profit) but chooses not to.[12] Likewise, we sometimes use the language of exploitation to describe similar dynamics within personal relationships: if one friend always relies on another for help but rarely reciprocates, we say that the first is exploiting the second.

10.1.2 *Exploitation as Degradation*

Not all exploitation, however, can be explained in terms of unfairness. Take price gouging, another standard example of exploitation: imagine, say, a thirsty hiker, lost in the desert, encounters a fellow traveller who offers to part with their extra bottle of water for $1,000.[13] The seller is perfectly forthright about their product, its condition, and the terms of sale, and the buyer reflects on, understands, and decides to accept them. In other words, there is no procedural unfairness involved. Moreover, if buying the water will save the hiker's life, he is – in one sense – getting a pretty good deal. Most people value their life at a lot more than $1,000. Indeed, as Zwolinski points out, in such cases there is reason to believe that the hiker is getting far more of the surplus created through the exchange than the greedy seller (the former gets his life, the latter $1,000). So substantive unfairness – unevenly distributing the social surplus – can't explain the problem here either.

For some theorists, cases like this demonstrate another possible wrong-making feature of exploitation: degradation, or the failure to treat people with dignity and respect. Allen Wood (1995) argues that using another person's vulnerability to one's own advantage is instrumentalizing and demeaning. "Proper respect for others is violated when we treat their vulnerabilities as opportunities to advance our own interests or projects. It is degrading to have your weaknesses taken advantage of, and dishonorable to use the weaknesses of others for your ends" (Wood 1995, 150–51). Indeed, for Wood (1995, 154), even in cases like sweatshops, which – as we've just

[11] Determining what counts as an unfair division of the social surplus is, unsurprisingly, a matter of some controversy. Hillel Steiner (1984) argues that the distribution is unfair when it's the product of historical injustice, while, for John Roemer (1985), the unfairness derives from background conditions of inequality. On Alan Wertheimer's (1996) account, the distribution is unfair when one party pays more than a hypothetical "fair market price."

[12] This is another way of framing the normative intuition that motivates Marxist accounts of exploitation: the capitalist class claims an unfair share of the surplus created by the working class. See Roemer (1985) and Reiman (1987).

[13] This example is borrowed from Zwolinski et al. (2022).

seen – can plausibly be explained in terms of unfairness, this kind of degradation is the deeper, underlying evil.

Some argue that exploitation is wrong solely in virtue of one or another of these moral considerations – at bottom, it is either unfair *or* degrading – and such theorists have worked to show that certain cases intuitively cast in one moral frame can be explained equally well or better through another. For the present purposes, I follow theorists who adopt a more pluralistic approach and define wrongful exploitation as Matt Zwolinski (2012) does: *taking advantage of someone in an unfair or degrading way*.[14] In some cases, exploitation is wrong because it involves unfairness, in other cases because it involves degradation. Oftentimes more than one wrong-making feature is at play, and digital platforms potentially raise all these concerns.

10.2 PLATFORM EXPLOITATION?

A first question, then, is whether the kinds of practices I described at the start reflect these normative problems. Are platforms exploiting people?

If exploitation is taking advantage of someone in an unfair or degrading way, and what enables exploitation – what induces someone to accept unfair terms of exchange or what makes taking advantage of such terms degrading – is the exploitee's vulnerability (the fact that they lack decent alternatives), then identifying exploitation is partly an empirical exercise. It requires asking, on a case-by-case basis: Are people vulnerable? What are their options? Are platforms taking advantage of them?

However, that need not prevent us from generalizing a little. Returning to the alleged abuses by gig economy companies, we can now recast them in this frame. Recall the FTC's concern that gig platforms set prices using "non-transparent algorithms." Reporting on ethnographic work in California's gig-based ride hail industry, legal scholar Veena Dubal describes drivers struggling to understand how the prices they're paid for individual rides are set, why different drivers are paid different rates for similar rides, or how to increase their earnings. Not only because the algorithms powering ride-hail apps are opaque, but because they set prices dynamically: "You've got it figured out, and then it all changes," one driver recounts (Dubal 2023, 1964).[15] Using the language developed in Section 10.1, we can describe this opacity and dynamism as sources of procedural unfairness – whether the terms of exchange reached are fair or not, the process of reaching them is one in which drivers are disempowered relative to the gig platforms they are "negotiating" with.[16]

[14] For an overview and argument in favor of a pluralist approach, see Snyder (2010).

[15] Veena Dubal (2023). See also, Zephyr Teachout (2023).

[16] Even describing the process as a negotiation is perhaps too generous – drivers simply have the option of accepting a ride and the designated fare or not.

There is also reason to worry that the terms reached are often substantively unfair, with platforms siphoning off more than their fair share of profits – an unfair distribution of the social surplus. Beyond concerns about how gig apps set prices, or about the ability of drivers to understand and exert agency in the process, the FTC complaint points out that ride hail apps charge drivers high fees, shift risks of doing business – usually absorbed by firms – onto drivers, and require them to pay for overhead expenses that companies normally cover, such as car insurance and maintenance costs. Similarly, crowdworkers in the global content moderation industry describe doing essential but "mentally and emotionally draining work" for little pay and without access to adequate mental health support: "Our work involves watching murder and beheadings, child abuse and rape, pornography and bestiality, often for more than 8 hours a day. Many of us do this work for less than $2 per hour."[17]

While charges of exploitation may be unwarranted in cases where, for example, ride hail drivers really are just driving for a little bit of extra cash on the side, in the mine run of cases, where gig workers lack other job options and depend on the income earned through gig app work, the charges seem fitting. Moreover, there is reason to believe that gig companies like Uber actively work to create the very vulnerabilities they exploit, by using venture capital funding to underprice competition, pushing incumbents out of the market and consolidating their own position. One reason ride hail drivers often lack alternative options is Uber has put them out of business.

Algorithmic pricing in consumer contexts also raises procedural and substantive fairness concerns. Like ride hail drivers navigating opaque, dynamic fare setting systems, consumers are increasingly presented with inconsistent prices for the same goods and services, making it difficult to understand why one is offered a particular price or how it compares to the prices others are offered (Seele et al. 2021). And, because the algorithms determining prices are inscrutable (as in the gig app case), there is an informational asymmetry between buyers and sellers that puts the former at a significant disadvantage, potentially creating procedural fairness problems. How can a buyer decide if prices are competitive without knowing (at least roughly) how they compare to prices others in the marketplace are paying, and how can they comparison shop when prices fluctuate unpredictably?[18]

Personalized pricing makes things even worse. In addition to issues stemming from algorithmic opacity and dynamism, price personalization – or what economists call "first-degree" or "perfect" price discrimination (i.e., the tailoring of prices to specific attributes of individual buyers) – raises the specter that sellers are preying on buyer vulnerabilities. On one hand, as Jeffrey Moriarty (2021, 497) argues, price

[17] "Open Letter to President Biden from Tech Workers in Kenya," May 22, 2024, www.foxglove.org.uk/open-letter-to-president-biden-from-tech-workers-in-kenya/.

[18] For a related discussion, see Ariel Ezrachi and Maurice Stucke (2016).

discrimination is commonplace and generally considered acceptable.[19] Even highly personalized pricing might be unproblematic, provided buyers know about it and have the option to shop elsewhere.[20] From an economics perspective, first-degree price discrimination has traditionally been viewed as bad for consumers but good for overall market efficiency. If buyers pay exactly as much as they are hypothetically willing to (their "reservation price") – and not a cent less – then sellers capture all of the surplus but also eliminate deadweight loss (Bar-Gill 2019).

Algorithmically personalized pricing changes things. First, as we have seen, it is often opaque and inscrutable – buyers do not know that they are being offered individualized prices, or if they do, how those prices are determined. Thus, even if they could shop elsewhere, they might not know that they should. Second, the above arguments assume that personalized pricing simply attempts to find and target the buyer's reservation price. But Oren Bar-Gill (2019) points out that the conception of "willingness to pay" underlying these traditional arguments, which imagines the reservation price simply as a function of consumer preferences and budgets, misses an important input: how buyers perceive prices and a product or service's utility.

People are often mistaken about one or both, misjudging, for example, how much something will cost overall, how often they will use it, the value they will ultimately derive from it, and so on (one can think here of the cliché about gym memberships purchased on January 1). Personalized pricing algorithms can provoke and capitalize on these errors, encouraging people to over-value goods (increasing willingness to pay) and under-predict total cost – that is, it can *change* their reservation price (Calo 2014). In such cases, Bar-Gill (2019, 221) argues, the traditional economics story is wrong – first-degree price discrimination harms consumers *and* diminishes overall efficiency, as "cost of production exceeds the actual benefit (but not the higher, perceived benefit)." The only benefit is to sellers, who capture the full surplus (and then some), raising substantive fairness concerns. Thus, the exploitation charge seems plausible in this case too. Though again, much depends on the details. If buyers know prices are being personalized, and they can comparison shop, it is less obvious that sellers are taking advantage of them.

Finally, behavioural advertising. Are data collectors and digital advertisers taking advantage of us? In the United States, commercial data collection is virtually unconstrained, and data subjects have little choice in the matter. Companies are required only to present boilerplate terms of service agreements, indicating what data they will collect and how they plan to use it. Data subjects usually have only

[19] Indeed, offering different people different prices may, on balance, benefit the worst off. To use a well-known example, if pharmaceutical companies couldn't charge different prices to consumers in rich and poor countries, they would have to charge everyone (including those with the fewest resources) higher prices in order to recoup costs. See Jeffrey Moriarty (2021).

[20] Moriarty (2021, p. 498) explicitly argues that under these conditions price personalization is non-exploitative. Etye Steinberg (2020) disagrees, arguing that data-driven personalized pricing is unfair on account of concerns about relational equality.

two options: accept the terms or forego the service. As many have argued, this rarely amounts to a real choice.[21] If, for example, one is required to use Microsoft Office or Google Docs as part of their job, are they meaningfully free to refuse the surveillance that comes with it? Put another way, many people are in a real sense dependent on digital technologies – for their jobs, at school, in their social lives – and surveillance advertisers, unfairly, take advantage of that dependency for their own gain.

Having said that, it is worth asking further questions about how those gains are distributed – who benefits from this system? Much of the value derived from surveillance advertising obviously flows directly into the industry's own coffers: revenue from online advertising accounts for the vast majority of profits at Google and Facebook, the two largest industry players (Hwang 2020). But where does the surplus come *from*? According to one view, elaborated most dramatically by Shoshana Zuboff, the surplus comes from us. It is a "behavioural surplus" – information about our individual desires, habits, and hang-ups, used to steer us toward buying stuff (Zuboff 2019). According to this argument, personal information and the predictions they make possible are merely conduits, carrying money from regular people's pockets into the hands of companies running ads (with the surveillance industry taking a cut along the way). In other words, data subjects are being exploited for the benefit of advertisers and sellers.

There is another view, however, according to which this whole system is a sham. Tim Hwang and others argue that behavioural advertising simply doesn't work – the predictions sold to sellers are largely wrong and the ads they direct rarely get us to buy anything (Hwang 2020).[22] But, as Hwang points out, that does not mean people do not benefit from online advertising. *We* benefit from it, enjoying for free all the services digital ads underwrite, which we would have to pay for if the ads went away. On this view, personal data is a conduit carrying money from the advertising budgets of sellers into the hands of app makers and producers of online content (with, again, the surveillance industry collecting its cut along the way). In other words, *the companies running ads are being exploited* for our benefit.

10.3 WHAT'S OLD IS NEW AGAIN

To this point, I have discussed platforms in general terms, focusing on what they do and whether we ought to accept it rather than on what they are and how they are able to treat people this way. I turn now to the latter: what platforms are, how they can engage in these different forms of exploitation, and what role digital technology specifically is playing in all of this.

[21] For an overview, see Susser (2019).

[22] For a more careful investigation into this question and its implications, see Daniel Susser and Vincent Grimaldi (2021).

The term "platform" is used in multiple registers. In some contexts, it is used to describe a set of companies – for example, Amazon, ByteDance, Meta, or Google. In other contexts, the term is used to describe the heterogeneous set of digital technologies such companies build, deploy, and use to generate revenues – for example, Amazon's marketplace, the TikTok or Instagram apps, or Google's digital advertising service. This ambiguity or multiplicity of meaning is neither a mistake nor an accident; platforms are both of these things simultaneously, businesses and technologies, and they must be understood both in economic and sociotechnical terms.

Unlike ordinary service providers, platforms function primarily as social and technical infrastructure for interactions between other parties. TikTok, Instagram, and social media platforms more broadly find audiences for content creators and advertisers who will pay to reach them. Gig economy platforms, like Uber and Lyft, facilitate exchanges between workers and people in need of their labor. As Tarleton Gillespie (2010, 4) points out, the term "platform" misleadingly brings to mind a sense of neutrality: "platforms are typically flat, featureless, and open to all." In fact, digital platforms work tirelessly to shape the interactions they host and to influence the people involved. As we've seen, they do this by carefully designing technical affordances (such as opaque and personalized pricing algorithms) and by pressing economic advantages (when, for example, they leverage venture capital to underprice incumbents and eliminate competition).

So: platforms mediate and structure relationships. Some of these relationships have long existed and have often been sites of exploitation; when platforms enter the picture, they perpetuate and profit from them. Other relationships are new – innovations in exploitation particular to the platform age.

10.3.1 *Perpetuating Exploitation*

Many platforms profit by creating new opportunities for old forms of exploitation. Platform-mediated work is a case in point: while not all employers exploit their employees, the labor/management relationship is frequently a place where worries about exploitation arise, and digital platforms breathe new life into these old concerns.

Indeed, platforms can increase the capacity of exploiters to take advantage of exploitees by enabling exploitation at scale, expanding the reach of exploitative firms and growing the pool of potential exploitees (Pfotenhauer et al. 2022).[23] Gig app firms, based in Silicon Valley and operated by a relatively small number of engineers, managers, and executives, profit from workers spread throughout the world – in 2022, for example, Uber had 5 million active drivers worldwide (Biron 2022). Moreover, as we have seen, these dynamics are visible in the broader phenomenon

[23] Pfotenhauer et al. (2022) describe the inexorable march toward massive scale as "the uberization of everything," which introduces, they argue, "new patterns of exploitation."

of "crowdwork," or what Dubal (2020) terms "digital piecework."[24] Platforms like Amazon Mechanical Turk (AMT) carve work (such as social media content moderation and labeling AI training data) into small, discrete, distributable chunks, which can be pushed out to workers sitting in their homes or in computer centres, new sites of so-called digital sweatshops (Zittrain 2009). As sociologist Tressie McMillan Cottom (2020) argues, these practices constitute a kind of "predatory inclusion" – one of many ways digital platforms have implicated themselves in broader patterns of racial capitalism.

At a more granular level, digital platforms also facilitate worker exploitation by reconfiguring work, work conditions, and wage determination. A growing body of scholarship explores the nature and functioning of "algorithmic labor management": the use of digital platforms to control workers and organize work. In contrast with simplistic narratives about automation displacing workers, this research brings to light the myriad ways digital technologies are becoming insinuated in human labor, changing its character, shifting risks, and creating new pathways for discrimination and extraction. Pegah Moradi and Karen Levy (2020) argue, for example, that automation and platform intermediation often increase profits for firms not by producing new efficiencies, but rather by shifting the costs of inefficiencies onto workers. "Just-in-time" scheduling algorithms make it possible to employ workers at narrower intervals dynamically tailored to demand, reducing labor costs by rendering jobs more precarious and less financially dependable for workers (Moradi and Levy 2020). And algorithmic management lets employers "narrowly define work to include only very specific tasks and then pay workers for those tasks exclusively" (Moradi and Levy 2020, 281). Ride-hail drivers, for instance, are compensated only for active rides, not for the time they spend searching for new passengers.

From a law and policy perspective, platforms also make it easier to exploit workers through legal arbitrage. By creating the appearance of new forms of work, gig economy apps render workers illegible to the law, and, in so doing, they allow firms to ignore worker rights and circumvent existing worker protections. For example, high profile political battles have recently been waged over whether gig workers should be legally classified as independent contractors or as employees of gig economy companies.[25] Gig economy firms contend that all their platforms do is connect workers to paying customers; the workers don't work *for them*, but rather for app users. Gig workers and their advocates argue that firms carefully manage and directly profit from their labor, and as such they ought to be given the same rights, benefits, and protections other workers enjoy. As Dubal writes about app-based

[24] Others describe this as "ghost work." See Mary L. Gray and Siddharth Suri (2019) and Veena Dubal (2020).

[25] Or perhaps some third thing. See Valerio De Stefano (2016), Orly Lobel (2019), and Veena Dubal (2021).

Amazon delivery drivers, "In this putative nonemployment arrangement, Amazon does not provide to the DSP [delivery service providers] drivers workers' compensation, unemployment insurance, health insurance, or the protected right to organize. Nor does it guarantee individual DSPs or their workers minimum wage or overtime compensation" (Dubal 2023, 1932).

10.3.1 *Innovations in Exploitation*

Different dynamics are at work in cases like algorithmic pricing. Here, the relationship mediated by digital platforms – in the pricing case, the relationship between buyers and sellers – is not normally a site of exploitation.[26] The introduction of digital platforms transforms the relationship into an exploitative one, making one party vulnerable to the other in new ways, or giving the latter new tools for taking advantage of existing vulnerabilities they couldn't previously leverage.

As we've seen, sellers can use algorithmic pricing technologies to capture more and more of – and perhaps even raise – a buyer's reservation price, by engaging in increasingly sophisticated forms of first-degree price discrimination. In part, this means utilizing the particular affordances of digital platforms to take advantage of existing vulnerabilities sellers couldn't previously leverage. Specifically, platforms enable the collection of detailed personal information about each individual buyer, including information about their preferences, finances, and purchasing histories, which are highly relevant to decisions about pricing. And platforms can analyze that information to make predictions about buyer willingness to pay on-the-fly, dynamically adjusting prices in the moment for different buyers (Seele et al. 2021). Thus, while it has always been the case that some buyers were willing to pay more than others for certain goods, sellers haven't always been able to tell them apart, or to use that information to take advantage of buyers at the point of sale.

The affordances of digital platforms also create new vulnerabilities, by making prices more inscrutable. Without knowing (or at least being able to make an educated guess about) why a seller has offered a particular price, and without being able to see what prices other buyers in the marketplace are paying, buyers are placed at a significant disadvantage when bargaining with sellers. And lest one think this is "merely" an issue when shopping online, think again: retailers have tested personalized pricing systems for physical stores, where cameras and other tracking technologies identify particular customers and electronic price tags vary prices accordingly (Seele et al. 2021). If sellers deploy such systems, they will deprive buyers of access to information about even more of the marketplace, creating new vulnerabilities sellers can exploit.

[26] We often worry about sellers deceiving buyers or selling them unsafe products, and consumer protection law is designed to prevent such harms. But we don't normally worry that sellers will *exploit* buyers.

Moreover, beyond transforming typically non-exploitative relationships into exploitative ones, platforms can create entirely new social relationships, which exist, at least partly, for the express purpose of enabling exploitation. This is the story of "surveillance capitalism." Digital advertising platforms have created sprawling, largely invisible ecosystems of data collectors and aggregators, analytics firms, and advertising exchanges, which data subjects – everyday people – know little about. They have brought into being a new set of relationships (e.g., the data aggregator/ data subject relationship), designed from the ground up to facilitate one party extracting from the other.

We should expect more of this the more we integrate digital platforms into our lives. As platforms extend their reach, mediating new contexts, relationships, and activities, the data collection that comes in tow renders us – and our vulnerabilities – more visible and, as platforms become gatekeepers between us and more of the things we want and need – work, goods and services, information, communication – they create new opportunities to take advantage of what they learn.

10.4 CONCLUSION

What are we to make of all of this? To conclude, I want to suggest that the language of exploitation is useful not only as a broad indictment against perceived abuses of power by big tech firms. Understanding platforms as vehicles of exploitation helps to illuminate normative issues central to the present conjuncture.

First, theories of exploitation highlight an important but underappreciated truth, which challenges prevailing assumptions in debates about platform governance: exchange can be mutually beneficial, voluntary, and – still – wrong.[27] Which is to say, two parties can consent to an agreement, the agreement can serve both of their interests, and yet, nonetheless, it can be wrongfully exploitative. This idea, sometimes referred to as "wrongful beneficence," can be counterintuitive, especially in the United States and other liberal democratic contexts, where political cultures centred on individual rights often treat the presence of consent as settling all questions about ethical and political legitimacy. If two people come to an agreement, there is no deception or manipulation involved, and the agreement is good for both of them (all things considered), many assume the agreement is, therefore, beyond reproach.

Consider again paradigmatic cases of exploitation. When a price gouger sells marked-up goods to someone in need – scarce generators, say, to hurricane survivors – the buyer consents to the purchase and both parties leave significantly better off than they were. Likewise, when a sweatshop owner offers low-paying work in substandard conditions to local laborers and – given few alternatives – they accept,

[27] As Joel Feinberg (1990, 176) put it, "a little-noticed feature of exploitation is that it can occur in morally unsavory forms without harming the exploitee's interests and, in some cases, despite the exploitee's fully voluntary consent to the exploitative behaviour." Wood (1995), Wertheimer (1996), Sample (2003), and others also emphasize this point.

the arrangement is voluntary and serves both the owner's and the worker's interests.[28] Thus, if the price gouger and the sweatshop owner have done anything wrong in these cases, it is not that they have diminished the other parties' interests or forced them to act against their will. Rather, as we've seen, the former taking advantage of the latter is wrongfully exploitative because the treatment is unfair (i.e. the price of the generator is exorbitant, and the sweatshop pay is exceedingly low) and/or degrading (it fails to treat exploitees with dignity and respect).

This insight, that exploitation can be wrong even when mutually beneficial and voluntary, helps explain the normative logic of what Lewis Mumford (1964) called technology's "magnificent bribe" – the fact that technology's conveniences seduce us into tacitly accepting its harms (Loeb 2021). Indictments against digital platforms are frequently met with the response that users not only accept the terms of these arrangements, they benefit from them. Mark Zuckerberg, for example, famously argued in the pages of the *Wall Street Journal* that Facebook's invasive data collection practices are justified because: "People consistently tell us that if they're going to see ads, they want them to be relevant. That means we need to understand their interests."[29] In other words, according to Zuckerberg, Facebook users find behaviourally targeted advertising (and the data collection it requires) beneficial, so they choose it voluntarily.[30] Similarly, as we have seen, gig economy companies deflect criticism by framing the labor arrangements they facilitate as serving the interests of gig workers, both economically and as a means of strengthening worker independence and autonomy.

The language of exploitation shows a way through this moral obfuscation. Implicit in tech industry apologia is the assumption that simply adding to people's options can't be wrong. But the price gouging and sweatshop labor cases reveal why it can be: if the only reason someone accepts an offer is because they lack decent alternatives, and if the terms being offered are unfair or degrading, then the offer wrongfully takes advantage of them and their situation. So, while it is true that in many cases digital platforms expand people's options, giving them opportunities to benefit in ways they would otherwise lack, and which – given few alternatives – they sometimes voluntarily accept, that is not the end of the normative story. If platforms are in a position to provide the same benefits on better terms and simply refuse, they are engaging in wrongful exploitation and ought to be contested.

28 One might want to argue that the buyer in the first case and worker in the second are "coerced by circumstances," and therefore the exchanges are not truly voluntary. However, as Chris Meyers (2004) points out, that's not the price gouger's or the sweatshop owner's fault – they didn't create the desperate conditions, and all they are doing is adding to the sets of options from which the other parties can choose. If in doing so they are wronging them (which, in cases of wrongful beneficence, they arguably are) it is not because they are forcing them to act against their will.

29 Mark Zuckerberg (2019, January 25) in *The Facts About Facebook.*

30 Of course, researchers have cast doubt on these claims about user preferences. See Joseph Turow and Chris Jay Hoofnagle (2019).

Second, having said that, the fact that people benefit from and willingly participate in these arrangements should not be ignored – it tells us something about the wider landscape of options they face. When people buy from price gougers or sell their labor to sweatshop factories they do so because they are desperate. From a diagnostic perspective, we can see that taking advantage of someone in such circumstances is morally wrong. But how, as a society, we should *respond* to that injustice is a more complicated matter. If there aren't better alternatives available to them, eliminating the option – by, for example, banning price gouging and sweatshop labor, or for that matter, gig work or behavioural advertising – could make the very people one is trying to protect even worse off, at least in the short run (Wood 1995, 156).

As Alan Wood (1995) argues, there are two ways to respond to exploitation: what he terms "interference" and "redistribution."[31] Interference focuses on the exploiter, stepping in to prevent them from exercising power to take advantage of others. Fair labor standards, for example, interfere with an employer's ability to exploit workers, and price controls interfere in the market to prevent gouging. Redistribution, by contrast, focuses on exploitees: rather than directly interfering to keep the powerful in check, redistributive strategies aim to empower the vulnerable. Universal basic income policies, for example, strengthen workers' ability to decline substandard pay and work conditions. Of course, economic support isn't the only way to help the vulnerable resist exploitation – one might think of certain education or job training programs as designed to achieve similar ends.

Differentiating between interference and redistribution strategies is useful for weighing the myriad proposals to rein in platform abuse. Some proposals adopt an interference approach, which focuses on constraining the powerful – banning gig economy apps or behavioural advertising, for example, or imposing moratoria on face recognition technology.[32] Others aim to empower the vulnerable: digital literacy programs, for instance, equip people to make better decisions about how to engage with platforms and forced interoperability policies would enable users to more easily switch platforms if they feel like they're being treated unfairly.[33] Some strategies combine interference and redistribution: if successful, efforts to revive

[31] Erik Malmqvist and András Szigeti (2021) argue that there is, in fact, a third option – what they term "remediation." To my mind, remediation is a form of redistribution.

[32] Bans and moratoria are frequently proposed, and sometimes implemented, as a strategy for bringing abuse by digital platforms under control. Uber, for example, has been directly banned or indirectly forced out of the market at various times and places (Rhodes 2017). Regulators, especially in Europe, have made compelling cases to eliminate behavioural advertising, especially when targeted at children. See, for example, www.forbrukerradet.no/wp-content/uploads/2021/06/20210622-final-report-time-to-ban-surveillance-based-advertising.pdf. And a number of cities in the United States have imposed moratoria on the use of facial recognition technology by the police and other public actors, while at the same time it continues to find new applications. See, for example, www.wired.com/story/face-recognition-banned-but-everywhere/

[33] See, for example, www.eff.org/deeplinks/2019/07/interoperability-fix-internet-not-tech-companies.

antitrust enforcement in the technology industry would diminish the power of monopoly firms, weakening their ability to engage in exploitation, while also empowering users by increasing competition and thus strengthening their ability to refuse unfavorable terms.[34]

There are trade-offs involved in the decision to utilize one or the other type of approach. People voluntarily accept unfair terms of exchange when they lack decent alternatives, so interference strategies could do more harm than good if they aren't accompanied by redistributive efforts designed to expand people's options. If people are reliant on crowdwork, for example, because they can't find better paying or more secure jobs, then limiting opportunities for such work might – on balance – make them worse off rather than better, putting them in an even more precarious financial position than where they started.[35] Similar concerns have been raised about behavioural advertising. Despite its harms, observers point out that digital advertisement markets are "the critical economic engine underwriting many of the core [internet] services that we depend on every day" (Hwang 2020, 1). Interfering in these markets haphazardly could threaten the whole system.[36]

If we step back, however, these insights together paint a clearer and more damning picture than is perhaps first suggested by the careful way I have parsed them. They suggest that the platform age emerged against a backdrop of deep social and economic vulnerability – a world in which many lacked adequate options to begin with – and platform companies responded by developing technologies and business models designed to perpetuate and exploit them. It is a picture, in other words, of many platforms as fundamentally predatory enterprises: high-tech tools for capturing and hoarding value, and not – as their proponents would have us believe – marvels of value creation. This is, I think, the basic normative intuition behind claims that digital platforms are exploitative, and we shouldn't let our efforts to unspool its implications distract us from the moral clarity driving it.

Moreover, as the Marxist critique emphasizes, what makes exploitation particularly insidious is the thin cover of legitimacy it creates to conceal itself, the veneer of willingness by all parties to participate in the system – their consent and mutual benefit – that obscures the unfairness and degradation hiding just below the surface. As more and more people see through this normative fog, long-held assumptions that digital platforms (as they currently exist) are, at their core, forces for good are losing strength, space is opening up to imagine new, different sociotechnical arrangements, and conditions are improving to advance them.

34 See, for example, www.newyorker.com/magazine/2021/12/06/lina-khans-battle-to-rein-in-big-tech.

35 Once again, questions about these trade-offs mirror debates about how to respond to exploitative sweatshop labor. For a helpful overview of these debates, see Snyder (2010).

36 Hwang (2020) suggests "controlled demolition" instead. For a more nuanced history and political economy of digital advertising markets, see Lee McGuigan (2023) in *Selling the American People: Advertising, Optimization, and the Origins of Adtech*.

REFERENCES

Acquisti, Alessandro, Curtis Taylor, and Liad Wagman. "The Economics of Privacy." *Journal of Economic Literature* 54, no. 2 (2016): 442–492.

Andrejevic, Mark. "Exploitation in the Data Mine." In *Internet and Surveillance: The Challenges of Web 2.0 and Social Media*, edited by Christian Fuchs, Kees Boersma, Anders Albrechtslund, and Marisol Sandoval, 71–88. New York: Routledge, 2012.

Bar-Gill, Oren. "Algorithmic Price Discrimination When Demand Is a Function of Both Preferences and (Mis)Perceptions." *The University of Chicago Law Review* 86, no. 2 (2019): 217–254.

Biron, Bethany. "Number of Uber Drivers Hits Record High of 5 Million Globally as Cost of Living Soars: With 70% Citing Inflation as Their Primary Reason for Joining the Company." *Business Insider*, August 3, 2022. www.businessinsider.com/uber-drivers-record-high-5-million-cost-living-inflation-2022-8.

Calo, Ryan. "Digital Market Manipulation." *The George Washington Law Review* 82, no. 4 (2014): 773–802.

Calo, Ryan, and Alex Rosenblat. "The Taking Economy: Uber, Information, and Power." *Columbia Law Review* 117, no. 6 (2017): 1623–1690.

Cohen, Gerald A. "The Labor Theory of Value and the Concept of Exploitation." *Philosophy & Public Affairs* 8, no. 4 (1979): 338–360.

Cohen, Julie E. *Between Truth and Power: The Legal Constructions of Informational Capitalism*. New York: Oxford University Press, 2019.

Cottom, Tressie McMillan. "Where Platform Capitalism and Racial Capitalism Meet: The Sociology of Race and Racism in the Digital Society." *Sociology of Race and Ethnicity* 6, no. 4 (2020): 441–449.

De Stefano, Valerio. "The Rise of the 'Just-in-Time Workforce': On-Demand Work, Crowd Work and Labour Protection in the 'Gig-Economy'." *Comparative Labor Law & Policy Journal* 37, no. 3 (Spring 2016): 471–504.

Dubal, Veena. "On Algorithmic Wage Discrimination." *Columbia Law Review* 123 (2023): 1929–1992.

"The New Racial Wage Code." *Harvard Law and Policy Review* 15 (2021): 511–549.

"The Time Politics of Home-Based Digital Piecework." *Center for Ethics Journal: Perspectives on Ethics*, July 4, 2020. https://c4ejournal.net/2020/07/04/v-b-dubal-the-time-politics-of-home-based-digital-piecework-2020-c4ej-xxx/.

Ezrachi, Ariel, and Maurice E. Stucke. "The Rise of Behavioural Discrimination." *European Competition Law Review* 37, no. 2 (2016): 485–492.

Feinberg, Joel. *The Moral Limits of the Criminal Law*. Vol. 4, *Harmless Wrongdoing*. Oxford: Oxford University Press, 1990.

Fraser, Nancy. "Expropriation and Exploitation in Racialized Capitalism: A Reply to Michael Dawson." *Critical Historical Studies* 3, no. 1 (2016): 163–178.

Fuchs, Christian. "Labor in Informational Capitalism and on the Internet." *The Information Society* 26, no. 3 (2010): 179–196.

Social Media: A Critical Introduction. London: Sage, 2017.

Gillespie, Tarleton. "The Politics of 'Platforms'." *New Media & Society* 12, no. 3 (2010): 347–364.

Goodin, Robert. "Exploiting a Situation and Exploiting a Person." In *Modern Theories of Exploitation*, edited by Andrew Reeve, 166–200. London: Sage, 1987.

Gray, Mary L., and Siddharth Suri. *Ghost Work: How to Stop Silicon Valley from Building a New Global Underclass*. Boston: Harper, 2019.

Haskins, Caroline. "The Low-Paid Humans behind AI's Smarts Ask Biden to Free Them from 'Modern Day Slavery'." *Wired*, May 22, 2024. www.wired.com/story/low-paid-humans-ai-biden-modern-day-slavery/.

Hwang, Tim. *Subprime Attention Crisis: Advertising and the Bomb at the Heart of the Internet*. New York: Farrar, Straus and Giroux, 2020.

Interactive Advertising Bureau. "Advance Notice of Proposed Rulemaking for a Trade Regulation Rule on Commercial Surveillance and Data Security," November 2022. www.iab.com/wp-content/uploads/2022/11/IAB-ANPRM-Comments.pdf.

Jordan, Tim. *Information Politics: Liberation and Exploitation in the Digital Society*. London: Pluto Press, 2015.

Lobel, Orly. "The Debate Over How to Classify Gig Workers Is Missing the Bigger Picture." *Harvard Business Review*, July 24, 2019. https://hbr.org/2019/07/the-debate-over-how-to-classify-gig-workers-is-missing-the-bigger-picture.

Loeb, Zachary. "The Magnificent Bribe." *Real Life Magazine*, October 25, 2021. https://reallifemag.com/the-magnificent-bribe/.

MacKay, Alexander, and Samuel Weinstein. "Dynamic Pricing Algorithms, Consumer Harm, and Regulatory Response," 2020. www.ssrn.com/abstract = 3979147.

Malmqvist, Erik, and András Szigeti. "Exploitation and Remedial Duties." *Journal of Applied Philosophy* 38, no. 1 (2021): 55–72.

McGuigan, Lee. "After Broadcast, What? An Introduction to the Legacy of Dallas Smythe." In *The Audience Commodity in the Digital Age*, edited by Lee McGuigan and Vincent Manzerolle, 1–22. New York: Peter Lang, 2014.

Selling the American People: Advertising, Optimization, and the Origins of Adtech. Cambridge, MA: The MIT Press, 2023. 10.7551/mitpress/13562.001.0001.

Meyers, Chris. "Wrongful Beneficence: Exploitation and Third World Sweatshops." *Journal of Social Philosophy* 35, no. 3 (2004): 319–333.

Moradi, Pegah, and Karen Levy. "The Future of Work in the Age of AI: Displacement or Risk-Shifting?" In *The Oxford Handbook of Ethics of AI*, edited by Markus D. Dubber, Frank Pasquale, and Sunit Das, 269–288. New York: Oxford University Press, 2020.

Moriarty, Jeffrey. "Why Online Personalized Pricing Is Unfair." *Ethics and Information Technology* 23, no. 3 (2021): 495–503.

Muldoon, James. *Platform Socialism: How to Reclaim Our Digital Future from Big Tech*. London: Pluto Press, 2022.

Mumford, Lewis. "Authoritarian and Democratic Technics." *Technology and Culture* 5, no. 1 (1964): 1–8.

"Open Letter to President Biden from Tech Workers in Kenya," May 22, 2024. www.foxglove.org.uk/open-letter-to-president-biden-from-tech-workers-in-kenya/.

Pfotenhauer, Sebastian, Brice Laurent, Kyriaki Papageorgiou, and Jack Stilgoe. "The Politics of Scaling." *Social Studies of Science* 52, no. 1 (2022): 3–34.

Reiman, Jeffrey. "Exploitation, Force, and the Moral Assessment of Capitalism: Thoughts on Roemer and Cohen." *Philosophy & Public Affairs* 16, no. 1 (1987): 3–41.

Rhodes, Anna. "Uber: Which Countries Have Banned the Controversial Taxi App." *The Independent* (September 22, 2017). www.independent.co.uk/travel/news-and-advice/uber-ban-countries-where-world-taxi-app-europe-taxi-us-states-china-asia-legal-a7707436.html.

Roemer, John. "Should Marxists Be Interested in Exploitation?" *Philosophy & Public Affairs* 14, no. 1 (1985): 30–65.

Rosenblat, Alex, and Luke Stark. "Algorithmic Labor and Information Asymmetries: A Case Study of Uber's Drivers." *International Journal of Communication* 10 (2016): 3758–3784.

Sample, Ruth. *Exploitation: What It Is and Why It's Wrong*. Lanham, MD: Rowman and Littlefield, 2003.

Seele, Peter, Claus Dierksmeier, Reto Hofstetter, and Mario D. Schultz. "Mapping the Ethicality of Algorithmic Pricing: A Review of Dynamic and Personalized Pricing." *Journal of Business Ethics* 170, no. 4 (2021): 697–719. https://doi.org/10.1007/s10551-019-04371-w.

Snyder, Jeremy. "Exploitation and Sweatshop Labor: Perspectives and Issues." *Business Ethics Quarterly* 20, no. 2 (2010): 187–213.

Steinberg, Etye. "Big Data and Personalized Pricing." *Business Ethics Quarterly* 30, no. 1 (January 2020): 97–117. https://doi.org/10.1017/beq.2019.19.

Steiner, Hillel. "A Liberal Theory of Exploitation." *Ethics* 94, no. 2 (1984): 225–241.

Susser, Daniel. "Notice after Notice-and-Consent: Why Privacy Disclosures are Valuable Even if Consent Frameworks Aren't." *Journal of Information Policy* 9 (2019): 37–62.

Susser, Daniel, Beate Roessler, and Helen Nissenbaum. "Online Manipulation: Hidden Influences in a Digital World." *Georgetown Law Technology Review* 4, no. 1 (2019): 1–45.

Susser, Daniel, and Vincent Grimaldi. "Measuring Automated Influence: Between Empirical Evidence and Ethical Values." In *Proceedings of the 2021 AAAI/ACM Conference on AI, Ethics, and Society*, 1–12. New York: ACM, 2021. https://dl.acm.org/doi/proceedings/10.1145/3461702.

Teachout, Zephyr. "Algorithmic Personalized Wages." *Politics and Society* 51, no. 3 (2023): 436–458.

Terranova, Tiziana. "Free Labor: Producing Culture for the Digital Economy." *Social Text* 18, no. 2 (2000): 33–58.

Tufekci, Zeynep. "Facebook's Surveillance Machine." *The New York Times*, March 19, 2018. www.nytimes.com/2018/03/19/opinion/facebook-cambridge-analytica.html.

Turow, Joseph, and Chris Hoofnagle. "Mark Zuckerberg's Delusion of Consumer Consent." *The New York Times*, January 29, 2019. www.nytimes.com/2019/01/29/opinion/zuckerberg-facebook-ads.html.

US Federal Trade Commission. "Policy Statement on Enforcement Related to Gig Work," September 15, 2022. www.ftc.gov/legal-library/browse/policy-statement-enforcement-related-gig-work.

Wertheimer, Alan. *Exploitation*. Princeton, NJ: Princeton University Press, 1996.

Wood, Allen. "Exploitation." *Social Philosophy and Policy* 12, no. 2 (1995): 136–158.

Zittrain, Jonathan. "The Internet Creates a New Kind of Sweatshop." *Newsweek*, December 7, 2009. www.newsweek.com/internet-creates-new-kind-sweatshop-75751.

Zuckerberg, Mark. "The Facts about Facebook." *Wall Street Journal*, January 24, 2019. www.wsj.com/articles/the-facts-about-facebook-11548374613.

Zuboff, Shoshana. *The Age of Surveillance Capitalism: The Fight for a Human Future at the New Frontier of Power*. New York: PublicAffairs, 2019.

Zwolinski, Matt. "Structural Exploitation." *Social Philosophy and Policy* 29, no. 1 (2012): 154–179.

Zwolinski, Matt, Benjamin Ferguson, and Alan Wertheimer. "Exploitation." In *The Stanford Encyclopedia of Philosophy*, edited by Edward N. Zalta and Uri Nodelman. Stanford, CA: Stanford University, 2022. https://plato.stanford.edu/archives/win2022/entries/exploitation/.

11

People as Packets in the Age of Algorithmic Mobility Shaping

Jason Millar and Elizabeth Gray

Mobility has a "hallowed place" in the liberal democratic tradition, providing us with what Blomley has described as "one means by which we can examine the uses to which spaces are put in political life and political relations" (Blomley 2009, 206). Mobility is, accordingly, inherently tied to governance and provides a window on the expansion and contraction of the fundamental rights, such as gender equality (Walsh 2015), that shape the human experience.

In this chapter, we look carefully at how people will move through a fully digitized society. We start by examining how turn-by-turn navigation technologies are automating the human task of driving, and, in doing so, have quietly established a footing for algorithmically controlled mobility systems. Whoever controls the algorithms that route mobility within a system gains de facto control over people and their mobility rights, determining who gets access to mobility, how they access it, and numerous decisions about associated benefits (e.g. quality of service, comfort, and time to destination) and risks (e.g. exposure to noise and other pollution, traffic congestion, and discrimination). In other words, whoever controls those algorithms can deliberately and effectively shape our experience of mobility in ways that were previously unheard of, significantly shifting the experience of being human in the digital age.

Early indicators of this shift seem clear. Turn-by-turn navigation is ubiquitous thanks to the proliferation of smart phones, and the algorithms that power it have become increasingly capable of responding to real-time changes in traffic patterns in order to minimize the time it takes to get to our destinations. That ruthless efficiency – the narrow emphasis on saving time – tempts us to rely on turn-by-turn navigation to get us where we want to be, even when driving in familiar places along familiar routes. Turn-by-turn navigation also powers ride hailing services like Uber and Lyft, and will eventually power more fully automated vehicles, thus restricting the set of navigational decisions available to human drivers and human passengers. These trends demonstrate how we are increasingly delegating navigational decision-making to technologies that, in turn, are (partially) automating the actual person behind the wheel.

We argue that we are currently in the early days of algorithmically controlled mobility systems, but that, even if it is nascent in its form and reach, *mobility shaping* – the act of deliberately and effectively controlling mobility patterns using an algorithmically controlled mobility system[1] – is raising a set of unresolved ethical, political, and legal issues that have significant consequences for shaping human experience in the future. The specific subset of questions we focus on in this chapter considers the extent to which the people travelling, the vehicles they use, and the geographic spaces through which they move, ought to be treated neutrally in the algorithmically controlled mobility system. By way of analogy, we argue that these emerging normative questions in mobility echo those that have been asked in the more familiar context of *net neutrality*. We seek to apply some of the ethical and legal reasoning surrounding net neutrality to the newly relevant algorithmically controlled mobility space, while adding some considerations unique to mobility. We also suggest extending some of the legal and regulatory framework around net neutrality to mobility providers, for the purpose of establishing and ensuring a just set of principles and rules for shaping mobility in ways that promote human flourishing.

Section 11.1 provides a brief historical survey of turn-by-turn navigation[2] and contextualizes the current socio-technical landscape. Section 11.2 examines the net neutrality controversy and legal rationales designed to ensure technical infrastructure creates political and economic relationships that are fair to people as citizens and rights-holders. Section 11.3 provides a comparative analysis between information networks (e.g. the Internet) and mobility networks, to demonstrate the extent to which the analogy helps us anticipate issues of fairness in algorithmically controlled mobility systems. Finally, Section 11.4 raises an additional set of ethical issues arising from mobility shaping, including the uneven distribution of mobility benefits and risks, the values underpinning navigational choices, and the enclosure of public concerns in private data.

11.1 A BRIEF HISTORY OF THE AUTOMATION OF DRIVING NAVIGATION

Prior to the widespread availability of turn-by-turn navigation apps on smartphones,[3] most drivers navigated via a combination of memory, instinct, road markers, oral

1 Mobility, as we conceive of it, refers to all the ways in which people and goods move through built environments. "The mobility system" is thus a broad concept: it encompasses personal vehicles (cars and trucks, as well as scooters, bicycles, and similar vehicles), pedestrian movement, goods transportation, all forms of mass and public transit, and the roads and pathways themselves.

2 For the purposes of this chapter, the terms "GNSS," "GNSS device," "navigation system," "in-car navigation system," and "turn-by-turn navigation system" are used relatively interchangeably (unless otherwise specified). The acronym "GNSS" stands for "Global Navigation Satellite System," and includes the US military's Global Positioning System (GPS), the Russian GLONASS, the recently completed European Galileo system, and the even more recent Chinese BeiDou, among others.

3 This shift occurred sometime around autumn 2010, when Google Maps Navigation, the turn-by-turn enabled mapping app which at the time was distinct from Google Maps, appeared as a free download for all Android and iOS smartphone users.

directions, and paper maps. In most cases, each driving and navigation decision was shaped by two forces: the decisions of the *person driving the vehicle* (e.g. what speed to travel, whether to turn, change lanes, or come to a sudden stop) and the decisions of democratic institutions and administrative bodies that are both populated with people who administer the rules (e.g. to build roads, establish speed limits, and place road signs), and accountable to people as electors. Though these two forces remain relevant, new technologies are changing how people conceptualize mobility navigation. Incredibly detailed digital maps, satellite connectivity, and, most crucially, the enormous uptake of smartphones and other smart devices, have enabled the near-ubiquity of turn-by-turn navigation systems. This section briefly examines the history of automating in-car navigation.

11.1.1 *In-Car Navigation, Then*

In-car turn-by-turn navigation systems predate the First World War. In the early days of road travel, motorists could purchase after-market devices such as the "Chadwick Road Guide" to aid in the complex task of navigation (French 2006). This mechanical invention, first available in 1910, featured an interchangeable perforated metal disc (each corresponding to a specific route) intricately connected to one of the vehicle's wheels. As the vehicle drove, the disc would turn and activate actions or warnings, such as "continue straight ahead" or "turn sharply to the left." The driver could thus be "guided over any highway to [their] destination," with the device "instructing [them] where to turn and [in] which direction" (French 2006, 270). However, there were obvious drawbacks to the Chadwick Road Guide and its contemporaries. Most significantly, these devices could only offer a limited number of predetermined routes. Besides that, the devices were complicated, delicate, and relatively expensive.

In-car navigation devices continued to evolve slowly over the next several decades (French 2006). Despite improvements, these systems could still not provide real-time information about current driving conditions and lacked accuracy over long distances.

11.1.2 *In-Car Navigation, Now*

More recently, a suite of technologies, including GPS, digital cameras, cloud computing, vision systems driven by artificial intelligence, and the widespread adoption of smartphones, have enabled the rapid adoption of much more effective navigation systems.[4] Satellite imagery and computer vision techniques enable the

[4] Satellite imagery and computer vision techniques enable the creation of maps so detailed that the fan blades inside rooftop HVAC units can be seen on some buildings in downtown Los Angeles (O'Beirne 2017).

creation of maps so detailed that the fan blades inside rooftop HVAC units can be seen on some buildings in downtown Los Angeles (O'Beirne 2017). Additionally, the advent of multiple satellite positioning systems – the Global Navigation Satellite System (GNSS) – coupled with the widespread adoption of wireless communication systems, allows for far more accurate development, update, deployment, and use of maps.

Smartphones have likely resulted in the most significant changes in automating in-car navigation in recent years. Worldwide, approximately 63 per cent of adults owned smartphones in 2017 (Molla 2017). In the United States, that number is significantly higher, at 81 per cent as of June 2019 (Pew Research Center 2019). There are now more mobile phones (8.58B) than people (7.95B) on the planet (Richter 2023). According to another recent study, over three-quarters of those US smartphone users "regularly" use navigation apps (that is, 77%) (Panko 2018).[5] Eighty-seven per cent of those respondents primarily use the apps for driving directions (as opposed to walking, cycling, public transit, or just as maps), and 64 per cent use the apps while driving (Panko 2018).[6] Additionally, anecdotal experience suggests that drivers use the apps even in neighbourhoods they know, along routes they often travel. The "nudges" they receive from navigation systems can alert them to poor traffic conditions and work out alternative routes if something goes wrong. As drivers incorporate turn-by-turn navigation into their daily driving routines, and delegate navigation decisions to those apps, they are ushering in the age of algorithmically controlled mobility systems.

11.1.3 *The NavigationMarketplace*

Despite its growing popularity, the costs of up-front investment in the mapping infrastructure means relatively few companies compete in the turn-by-turn navigation market. Alphabet (Google's parent company) is by far the most significant player in both mapping and turn-by-turn navigation. The Google Maps app, on which 67 per cent of US navigation app users rely, dominates turn-by-turn navigation. Google Maps far outstrips both Apple Maps and the Israeli-founded system Waze, at 11 per cent and 12 per cent, respectively (Panko 2018). Moreover, Alphabet purchased Waze in 2013 (Cohan 2013), and so Waze and Google now share the same base map data. Alphabet thus controls nearly 80 per cent of smartphone-assisted turn-by-turn navigation. As a further sign of Alphabet's dominance, the Google Maps API is currently embedded in more than five million websites, far more than any of its competitors (BuiltWith 2019).[7]

5 While these numbers are US-centric, much of the developed world is likely relatively similar.

6 The remaining 36 per cent simply use the apps to plan routes ahead of time (Panko 2018).

7 The next most popular map embedding is the Russian "Yandex Maps" service, on around 400,000 sites (BuiltWith 2019).

Alphabet has another advantage in the field: the sheer amount of its accumulated data. Google Maps was launched in 2005 and has been collecting mapping data ever since, using aerial photography, satellite images, land vehicles, and individual smartphone data. In 2012, Google had more than 7,000 employees and contractors on its mapping projects, including the Street View cars (Carlson 2012).[8] Google Maps has more than one billion active users worldwide (Popper 2017); At the time of writing, Waze has more than 151 million (Porter 2022). Apple Maps, Alphabet's closest US competitor in the navigation space, has only been active since 2012, and buys its mapping data second-hand, mostly from the Dutch navigation system company TomTom (Reuters 2015). Though expanding, the Europe-based Here WeGo, founded by Nokia and currently owned by a consortium of German car manufacturers, does not yet threaten Alphabet's dominance (Here Technologies 2019). Likewise, although Uber is conducting mapping projects (Uber 2019), as are Ford and other traditional car manufacturers (Luo 2017), Alphabet's current advantage is undisputed.

Whether or not Alphabet continues to dominate the in-car navigation landscape, turn-by-turn navigation systems will only become more important as connectivity and functionality improve. For example, turn-by-turn navigation has evolved to include other modes of mobility, including walking, cycling, and public transportation, positioning it as the go-to technology for getting around. Fully autonomous vehicles, should they ever come to fruition, will rely on navigation systems to a far greater extent than even the most obedient driver, as they will undoubtedly move within the mobility system according to the rules designed into routing algorithms. Thus, decisions we make now about how to develop, implement, and regulate turn-by-turn navigation systems will fundamentally shape algorithmically controlled mobility systems in the coming decades.

11.2 A BRIEF HISTORY OF NET NEUTRALITY

In anticipation of the evolution of mobility towards algorithmically controlled mobility systems, it is useful and instructive to reflect on the net neutrality debates that have shaped our algorithmically controlled information system – also known as the Internet – in the past two decades. The debates surrounding net neutrality are important because they have been an ongoing site for political struggle and the need to infuse tech policy with human-centric policies. We consider net neutrality to be a useful metaphor in thinking about the ethics of algorithmically controlled mobility, primarily because information networks and mobility networks each contain: their own unique units of analysis – packets of information, and packets of people (or mobility); their own paths through the network – wires and roads; and their own

[8] Due to these resources, Street View is even available at Antarctica's McMurdo Station, and underwater at the Great Barrier Reef (Google Maps: Street View 2019).

control/routing algorithms that determine how to get the packets to their destination. The parallels, and distinctions, between information networks and algorithmically controlled mobility systems can help anticipate and inform ethical design and regulatory responses in the mobility context as they provide a roadmap to encourage designers and policymakers to develop socio-technical design specifications, and consider the ways that regulation can promote or constrain human mobility. This section provides a brief overview of the main technical, political, and ethical issues in net neutrality, including the concepts of "discrimination," "non-discrimination," and "neutrality," and technical and ethical concerns related to Deep Packet Inspection and the legal concept of "common carriage."

11.2.1 *What Are DataPackets?*

Data packets, generally consisting of a header and a payload, can be thought of as the basic units of Internet communication. All information sent over the Internet (e.g. emails, movies, cat memes, Instagram posts, and TikToks) is broken up into smaller chunks of data that are packaged up as one or more data packets. If multiple packets are needed to carry the transmitted information, as they usually are, the divisions between packets are made automatically. Each individual packet is then sent to its destination separately, along whatever route is most convenient at the time (Indiana University 2018). Packet headers include high-level routing information, such as the packet's source, destination IP addresses, and information instructing how to correctly assemble multiple packets together when they reach their destination (Indiana University 2018). The remainder of the packet is referred to as the payload, containing chunks of the transmitted information.

11.2.2 *Packet Discrimination and the Emergence of Net Neutrality*

Early in the Internet's history, communications between people were divided into packets of information that travelled from one place to another with very little oversight. In this early "network of Eden" (Parsons 2013, 14), packets were only subjected to Shallow Packet Inspection (SPI) techniques. As the name implies, SPI is designed only to allow network routers to access high-level information about the packet delivery instructions, that is, SPI limits the inspection to the packet headers (Parsons 2013). Thus, an Internet Service Provider (ISP), using network routers designed to limit routing decisions based on SPI, might examine the source IP address of the packet, the packet identification number, or the kind of protocol the specific packet uses, but would not typically have access to the packet content itself. Thus, SPI is used primarily as a routing tool, much like addresses on envelopes travelling through the post.

Because SPI allows for examining destination and source IP addresses, it enables only relatively crude forms of information discrimination, such as blacklisting, firewalling, and others based solely on IP addressing. "Discrimination" in this sense refers to the choices made in routing one packet compared to another. These choices might be automated and algorithmic, or they might be human-driven. Algorithmic discrimination in this sense might be as simple as the automatic "decision" to route a packet along a specific path with no human oversight. Human-driven discrimination in this context, for example, could include a corporate policy of treating packets originating from a source IP that is known to spread viruses as "blacklisted" in the corporate network – that is, preventing untrusted packets from reaching the corporate server as a security measure. SPI-enabled discrimination may have political or moral dimensions; for instance, some corporate firewalls block all packets from social media websites, while government firewalls could prevent citizens from accessing content that challenges the state.

Clearly, these kinds of restrictions could have a significant impact on the humans using the system to communicate. An ISP's decision to block particular packets, in particular, likely has far-reaching implications for a broad swath of citizens; and could also potentially manipulate packet routing across the Internet to suit its own purposes. For instance, an ISP could prevent its customers from accessing certain websites or could delay certain packets from one website from reaching their destination as quickly as other websites' packets. Thus, ISP packet discrimination has the potential to preference certain corporate and state interests over others. When it became clear that many ISPs were using packet discrimination to further their own corporate interests, a public controversy erupted over the role of packet discrimination in anti-competitive market manipulation, precisely because it unevenly, thus unfairly, constrained communication opportunities for people using the Internet to share content and information.

Concerns about the anti-competitive nature of ISP packet discrimination led Tim Wu to propose "the principle of *network neutrality* or *non-discrimination*" (2002, 1). Net neutrality, as Wu imagines it, is a principle that "distinguish[es] between *forbidden* grounds of discrimination – those that distort secondary markets, and *permissible* grounds – those necessary to network administration and to [avoid] harm to the network" (2002, 5). For Wu, forbidden grounds are those based on "internetwork criteria": "IP addresses; domain names; cookie information; TCP port; and others" that can lead to unfair outcomes for (classes of) individuals (2002, 5). The permissible grounds are limited to local network integrity concerns, in particular, bandwidth and quality of service. As Wu describes, rather than blocking access to bandwidth-intensive applications like online gaming sites, and thus distorting information flow in favour of non-blocked applications, an ISP concerned with net neutrality "would need to invest in policing bandwidth usage" as a means of nudging consumers (2002, 6). The result would be a more even playing field for all network applications, shaped primarily by human communication choices, instead of an artificially influenced market sphere set up for the benefit of those controlling the flow of information.

Wu's (2002) concept and coinage took off, and was discussed at the highest levels of the US government (Madrigal and LaFrance 2014). Moreover, net neutrality is now a proxy for deeper ethical and political issues fundamentally tied to the values of human communication, privacy, surveillance, consumer rights, and freedom of speech. This has direct political consequences. Access to information, an important principle at the core of net neutrality, is recognized in Canada as an implied constitutional right (Ontario (Public Safety and Security) v. Criminal Lawyer's *Association* 2010). Further, the ability to lawfully access information is a cornerstone of modern democracy: without a well-informed electorate, the health of a democracy is imperilled (Canada (Information Commissioner) v. Canada (Minister of National Defence) 2011). Globally, content discrimination on the Internet is perhaps "the [free speech] issue of our time" (Hattem 2014), creating a space for political action and resistance.

11.2.3 *The Rise of Deep Packet Inspection*

Further changes to packet inspection technology amplified a broader set of net neutrality concerns. Deep Packet Inspection (DPI) technology, enabled in 2003 by changes in network router design, enables access to the content of the message itself in real-time. Some DPI equipment can monitor hundreds of thousands of packets simultaneously, in effect looking over the shoulder of the people communicating and reading the text of their emails and other communications (Anderson 2007).

The US telecom corporation Comcast provided a striking example of DPI-enabled algorithmic discrimination. In 2007, several public interest groups filed a complaint with the US Federal Communications Commission (FCC), citing Comcast's practice of secretly "delaying" the transmission of packets from peer-to-peer file-sharing sites (FCC 2008). Comcast argued that severely delaying traffic from these sites was necessary to manage bandwidth requirements, and that earlier rulings and statements from the FCC had merely prohibited outright blocking. The FCC disagreed, holding that the delays in this case were so extreme that they amounted to blocking (FCC 2008). In any event, the FCC noted, "Comcast selectively targeted and terminated the upload connections of ... peer-to-peer applications and ... this conduct significantly impeded consumers' ability to access the content and use the applications of their choice" (FCC 2008, para. 44). The FCC ordered Comcast to end its blocking practices in the interest of "the open character and efficient operation of the Internet" (FCC 2008, para. 51).

Although later rulings invalidated the FCC's order, and have called the Commission's jurisdiction into question, Comcast adjusted its network management practices so that no specific application, or category of applications, was targeted by its routing algorithms. Rather, network congestion is now managed by slowing down the connections of specific individuals (heavy bandwidth users) during peak usage periods (Comcast Corporation 2008). Although these practices are still discrimination of a sort, they have become commonplace and seem to fall within the permissible grounds identified by Wu (2002).

11.2.4 *Common Carriage*

The principle of net neutrality is partly based on the idea of "common carriage," a legal concept that has long roots in the common law. Common carriage speaks to the need to ensure infrastructural systems serve the interests of citizens in ways that are recognized and acknowledged as fair.

Common carriage itself arose from the "common calling": people engaged in what might be called public service professions, such as innkeepers, barbers, and farriers, could be found liable for refusing service to an individual without reasonable justification (Burdick 1911). Those with a common calling made a "general undertaking" to serve the public at large "in a workmanlike manner," and any failure to do so left them open to legal action under the law of contract (Burdick 1911, 518).

As technology advanced, the common calling expanded to include "common carriers," particularly railroads, shipping lines, and other transportation organizations. One defining feature of common carriers, as opposed to common callings, is the up-front infrastructure investment that the former requires. Building a railroad requires massive amounts of start-up capital, time, and (typically) political goodwill. These factors make it difficult for competitors to enter the market, thus limiting both competition and consumer options. If someone wishes to travel but does not wish to pay a certain price for a train ticket, their options are limited. They may find alternative means of transport or choose not to go, but (except in the most exceptional circumstances) they cannot build themselves a railroad. Thus, railroads and other common carriers operate as "virtual monopol[ies]" (Wyman 1904, 161) and, though they are often private companies, they are "in the exercise of a sort of public office, [with] public duties to perform" (New Jersey Steam Navigation Co. v. Merchants' Bank 1848, 47). As a result, their service should be agnostic with respect to the cargo (and people) they transport.

Though the Internet shares features of common carriers, whether the Internet is considered a common carrier depends on national jurisdiction. Canadian policy, for example, is firmly behind the common carrier model, and the need to ensure all people have fair access to infrastructural services. Because of this political commitment to equal treatment of people, the Canadian Radio-television and Telecommunications Commission (CRTC), which assumed telecommunications control from a variety of bodies in 1968, strongly supports the equal treatment of the data those people communicate "regardless of its source or nature" (CRTC 2017, para. 3).[9]

9 In the United States, debate over the Internet's classification, whether as a common carrier or as a less-regulated "information service," has raged for nearly two decades (Finley 2018). Across

11.3 NET NEUTRALITY AND THE ETHICS OF MOBILITY SHAPING

Net neutrality debates, and the discussion of common carriage principles, alert us to many related problems in algorithmically controlled mobility systems. An algorithmically controlled mobility system recalls the distinction between "forbidden" and "permissible" discrimination of information packets, where people are reduced to mobility packets comprised of specific vehicles and the goods and people within them. Like common carriers, algorithmically controlled mobility systems require substantial up-front investment in both publicly and privately owned and operated infrastructure, creating virtual monopolies (as evidenced by the very few global players in the space and Alphabet's overwhelming dominance in the market). Indeed, their public–private nature raises complex questions about the governance of algorithmically controlled mobility systems as a public good. Thus, there are many similarities between neutrality in the Internet context and mobility neutrality in the context of algorithmically controlled mobility systems, though there are important distinctions to be drawn as well. This section will examine the applicability of net neutrality concepts to the mobility context in more detail.

11.3.1 *Traffic Shaping Is to Information Packets as Mobility Shaping Is to People Packets*

To a routing algorithm, there is little difference between a packet of digital information moving through a digital information network (e.g. the Internet) and a packet of people (or goods) moving through a physical mobility network. In an important sense, a map of a digital information network is very similar to a map of a mobility network, with origins, pathways, routing decision points, destinations, and rules about how a packet can move through the system. Just as algorithms control and shape the flow of packets in information systems, often referred to as *traffic shaping*, algorithms control and shape the flow of people packets through mobility systems, which we refer to as *mobility shaping*. Thus, there is *an ethics of mobility shaping* that must be considered when designing the set of rules that govern an algorithmically controlled mobility system. Mobility shaping algorithms, for example, could be designed to move people packets from source to destination according to principles of fairness.

There is a clear analogy to both SPI and DPI in the mobility shaping context. Mobility shaping decisions could be relatively neutral, based only on a set of information containing origin and destination. Mobility shaping could also be complex,

the Atlantic, the European Union (EU) adopted the *Open Internet Regulation* in 2015. The *Regulation* enshrines non-discrimination and net neutrality in EU law, implicitly invoking the common carriage paradigm for ISPs (EC 2015). However, it is important to note that, in general, the EU comprises civil law jurisdictions which do not explicitly share the common law "common carriage" concept.

intended to support new models of mobility service delivery, and based on detailed information about who (or what) is in the vehicle, such as their socioeconomic status, age, political leaning, gender, purchase history, customer rating, and driving experience preferences, among endless other data breadcrumbs. Indeed, whole new categories of information could be invented to accommodate new forms of mobility shaping. One can imagine different mobility service levels, such as virtual fast lanes, made available to the wealthy (or inaccessible to the poor) or perhaps available to those subscribing to particular loyalty programs (themselves designed to collect more of individuals' data).

DPI for mobility shaping is already a fact of everyday life and new possibilities for mobility shaping are emerging as more mobility algorithms are designed to take individuals' data into account. Individual user preferences that shape mobility, say the choice of avoiding tolls or highways, are commonplace features in turn-by-turn navigation apps. But mobile devices and online platforms linking single user accounts together over multiple services (e.g. Google Search, Gmail, Docs, Photos, Maps, and smart phone location data) are enabling the collection and curation of massive datasets applicable to mobility shaping,[10] significantly upping the ante when it comes to the potential for lived discrimination and unfairness.

Highly granular geo-physical records of a person's location and movement can reveal many aspects of their life, especially when linked to other data about that person. For example, Waze collects location data and repackages that data as insights into consumer behaviour. A chart on the "Waze For Brands" website displays "Driving Patterns," showing "when drivers are most likely to visit different business categories" (Waze n.d.). The categories shown are "Auto," "Coffee," "Fast Food," "Fuel," and "Retail" and can be sorted by day or by hour. From the chart, we learn that the more than 90 million Waze users worldwide are most likely to visit coffee shops between 8 am and 10 am, and are least likely to go to retail stores on Sundays. These particular facts are not earth-shattering revelations, but they signal the trend toward DPI-based mobility shaping models designed to serve private interests rather than the public good. In addition to access to its entire global database, Waze also provides local marketers with multiple advertising strategies. Among other tools, Waze offers Branded Pins with Promoted Search (large branded corporate symbols that appear on the map when the user is within a certain distance of the promoted location) and Zero-Speed Takeovers (large banner ads that cover the Waze interface if the user stops nearby) (Waze 2019). Thus, the "map" shown to Waze users doubles as a promotional engine intended to shape navigation decisions by nudging a driver in a particular direction.

[10] A recent article describes one researcher's reaction to seeing his Google dataset, "When he requested his data from Google, he found that it was constantly tracking his location in the background, including calculating how long it took to travel between different points, along with his hobbies, interests, possible weight and income, data on his apps and records of files he had deleted. And that's just for starters" (Popken 2018, para. 4).

Mobility shaping, though in its infancy, is on the rise; today's navigational nudges will be tomorrow's strategies for absolute control over people's mobility. However, the principles and rules defining forbidden and permissible mobility shaping are as yet undefined. In Section 11.3.2 we consider to what extent the rules used to distinguish between forbidden and permissible information traffic shaping in the net neutrality debate may help us to better understand and protect the importance of regulation to protect individual mobility rights.

11.3.2 *Forms of Inclusion, Exclusion, and Discrimination*

Today's turn-by-turn navigation systems, by design, shape mobility by nudging the human user (i.e. driver, cyclist, etc.) to take a certain path to their destination. Generally speaking, today's systems are designed to minimize the time it would take to reach a chosen destination – but mobility can be algorithmically shaped according to any number of values and preferences other than minimizing time to destination. Turn-by-turn systems also currently shape mobility by nudging people toward certain destinations rather than others, for example by presenting curated lists of options when drivers search for nearby restaurants, gas stations, or other potential destinations. In this sense, mobility shaping functions as a powerful choice architecture, designed to privilege certain values and preferences over others. Mobility shaping can obscure whole categories of routing options or destinations, keeping vehicles on roads designed for high volumes of traffic or out of neighbourhoods where children tend to play in the streets or wealthy homeowners want privacy. Mobility shaping algorithms can also be designed to maximize returns on investment for those corporations heavily invested in the technology, leveraging vast quantities of individual data and preferencing other interests (e.g. corporate) over the needs of people in ways that remain largely opaque to the public. As we march down the road of automating mobility, delegating more decision making to navigation algorithms (which will eventually have broad power over more automated forms of mobility), nudges eventually morph into pushes. At some point in time the idea of people acting as agents entitled to move through space making fine-grained mobility decisions for their own purposes – turning left here instead of right because it's prettier, switching into this lane versus that one to get a better look at a friend's new garden, taking Main St. instead of Fifth to avoid passing an ex-partner – fades into the background of the algorithmically controlled mobility system.

Borrowing from Wu's (2002) net neutrality framework, some of these mobility shaping strategies may be based on permissible discrimination, some may not. Many of them could mimic the discriminatory practices discussed in the net neutrality context, particularly "blocking," "zero-rating," and "throttling," each of which will now be discussed in turn.

11.3.2.1 Blocking

Blocking, in the net neutrality context, is the simple blacklisting of certain Internet destinations (websites). The Fairplay Canada proposal, in 2018, for example, sought to compel ISPs to block access to any site deemed to contain copyright-infringing content (CRTC 2018; O'Rourke 2018). Blocking is also sometimes called "filtering" (generally by its proponents) and is used to prevent access to content that is considered illegitimate.

In the mobility shaping context, blocking strategies are easily imagined. Mobility shaping algorithms could blacklist physical destinations, or origins, with varying degrees of interpretability and transparency. On the clearly permissible end of the spectrum, trying to access a restricted destination (such as a military base) could result in a refusal to navigate to that location. In the less straightforwardly permissible spectrum could be situations in which those hailing rides are refused pickups or drop-offs from/to locations that are, for any number of questionable reasons, blacklisted. More subtly, though, certain destinations might simply be left off the map or excluded from the system's search function, as is the case with the famous Hollywood sign in Los Angeles (Walker 2014). Mobility shapers might use such strategies to artificially restrict access to politicized locations (for example, the meeting points for political protests or abortion clinics) that do not align with corporate or state interests. Combined with DPI, blocking could be targeted at individual mobility users, who find themselves excluded from certain destinations, mobility services, routing options, or mobility service levels, and could prove very difficult to detect.

11.3.2.2 Zero-rating

The practice of zero-rating is, in some ways, the inverse of blocking. In the net neutrality context, zero-rating involves exempting certain websites or web resources from bandwidth caps. This practice thus encourages an ISP's customers to consume the "free" resources instead of content that will increase their data consumption levels. Zero-rating is thus an artificial intervention in a secondary market (that is, in content), and one that often benefits the ISP – particularly when the ISP also provides the content.[11]

[11] That was the case in 2015, when a complaint was filed at the Canadian Radio-television and Telecommunications Commission against Bell Mobility, Quebecor Media Inc., and Videotron (CRTC 2019). The companies, which provide Internet access to many millions of Canadian consumers, also provided streaming television services over the websites "Bell Mobile TV" and "illico.tv." These websites were either exempted from customers' data plans or severely discounted, in some cases by almost 90 per cent (CRTC 2019). This practice encouraged the ISP's customers to subscribe to and use Bell and Videotron sites, rather than other audio-visual content sites (such as Netflix). The Commission ruled that the zero-rating practice conferred an "undue and unreasonable preference" on those who subscribed to the

"Zero-rating"-like strategies are possible in the mobility shaping context. This is not necessarily a bad thing: as in the net neutrality context, there may be reasonable and valid grounds for prioritizing some routes, services, or locations. For instance, cities might choose to subsidize ride-hailing fares to and from hospitals in order to help people get to the hospital more easily and to save on maintaining expensive parking facilities. There could be benefits to zero-rating airports or central transit hubs or to nudging drivers onto major highways rather than along side streets.

However, there may be times when zero-rating could be less permissible – for instance, if a dominant mobility service provider used zero-rating to dissuade people from accessing services or locations associated with a small competitor's mobility ecosystem. As an example, Google Maps could offer cheaper fares to users hailing Lyft or Uber rides so long as Google Maps powered them both, thus discriminating against users who choose to hail a ride using a non-Google-powered service. As on the Internet, zero-rating in the mobility context could impermissibly affect a secondary market – in this example, ride-hailing providers – in ways that constrain human agency and fair access to services.

11.3.2.3 Throttling

Throttling, on the Internet, is the practice of selectively and deliberately either improving or degrading the level of service (i.e. the speed of information transfer) between two internet addresses. Throttling can be similar to blocking, but rather than barring a website or web resource outright, an ISP can merely make that resource very slow or difficult to access. In the Comcast Corporation (2008) complaint discussed in Section 11.2.3, one of Comcast's arguments was that they were not truly "blocking" peer-to-peer transfers but simply "delaying" them. In that case, however, the FCC (2008) determined that Comcast was essentially engaged in blocking because the "delays" were effectively infinite. Yet even shorter delays can have a significant effect: a Google study from 2016 showed that 53 per cent of mobile device users will abandon a website that takes more than 3 seconds to load (Think with Google 2018). More recent data suggests that the "bounce rate" (the number of visitors who leave a site after viewing only one page) increases dramatically with loading times – users are 90 per cent more likely to leave a site that takes 5 seconds to load than a site that only takes 1 second (An 2018). Worse, if loading the site takes 10 seconds, the user is 123 per cent more likely to bounce than if it only takes 1 second (An 2018). Clearly, website throttling need not cause enormous "real-world" delays to have the same effects as outright blocking, with the same consequences for human agency and choice.

ISP's mobile content services, violating the *Telecommunications Act*, and conferring a corresponding undue and unreasonable *disadvantage* on ISP customers who did not subscribe to the ISP's content offerings (CRTC 2019, para. 61).

In the mobility context, throttling can be thought of as the deliberate manipulation of the time it takes to travel between two locations; it is the algorithmic creation of fast lanes and traffic jams. Throttling on the internet is intended to persuade or dissuade customers from accessing a particular resource by making access to the resource feel either seamless and smooth or frustratingly slow. Mobility shaping by throttling could be as simple as nudging certain drivers into "slow lanes" on a multilane freeway with common "stay in the right-hand lane" messages, while nudging privileged individuals into less occupied "fast lanes." More drastic versions could take certain drivers along completely different routes in order to keep "fast lanes" relatively unoccupied. In an automated driving context where drivers are only there to take over in emergencies, or not at all, systems would simply force vehicles into virtually negotiated fast and slow lanes. As with blocking and zero-rating, certain forms of discrimination by throttling could be deemed permissible, perhaps to support democratically accountable initiatives, or other essential services like first responders. Others could be more difficult to justify: offering fast lanes as a means of rewarding people who purchase particular vehicle brands, and slow lanes, either through access queuing or slower transit times, for people living in low income neighbourhoods, could be deemed impermissible.

11.4 THE NEED FOR AN ETHICS OF MOBILITY SHAPING

Given the centralized control that algorithms will (and to an extent already do) exert over various aspects of human mobility, and the differing qualities of mobility service that individuals might be subject to in an algorithmically controlled system, mobility shaping practices thus threaten to exacerbate existing mobility inequalities, while inventing whole new categories of harm to the people who move through space.

Responding to these new ethical challenges will require a more clearly articulated ethics of mobility shaping. In this section we suggest a few general categories of inquiry that we feel could help lay the ethical groundwork for dealing with the specific issues, several of which we have raised, that arise in the context of mobility shaping. Our goal here is to start a conversation, recognizing that much more work is required to flesh these issues out.

11.4.1 *The Just Distribution of Mobility Benefits and Harms*

As we have described, mobility shaping can result in the uneven and problematic distribution of mobility benefits and harms. As mobility shaping becomes more prevalent and displaces traditional individual driver-determined forms of navigation, it will be important to examine whether any scheme of altering people's ability to move from place to place results in a permissible or impermissible distribution of those affordances. Those benefits and harms include access to mobility, accessibility of mobility, quality of mobility service, noise and air pollution, vehicle speed and congestion, and the safety of vulnerable road users (e.g. pedestrians and cyclists) (Millar 2017). Like other distribution problems we face in society, mobility distribution problems, many of which will be created or exacerbated by mobility shaping, should be decided by careful attention to contextual details to avoid problematic constraints on human agency.

11.4.2 *Preserving Individual and Collective Mobility Decision Making*

Current mobility shaping algorithms are ruthlessly focused on minimizing the time to destination, while ignoring other individual and social values that are likely worth preserving in the mobility context. At times, for example, drivers might prefer a slower, more scenic, or less busy route along a rural road to increase their well-being, rather than travelling through a busy industrial corridor. They might prefer to avoid quiet neighbourhoods where children often play in the streets, in order to improve safety. Yet most turn-by-turn navigation systems do not allow individual drivers to *easily* adjust their route to accommodate such values-based considerations. As these systems evolve, it might be important to build them in ways to help preserve and amplify the role of human agency in mobility decision making.

This focus on time-efficiency can also disrupt democratic values, especially given the important role that the public space plays in democratic governance. Local citizens have a democratic interest in traffic planning that apps like Waze undermine. The town of Leonia, New Jersey, for instance, is bordered by Interstate 95 and has always struggled with vehicles cutting through town. But with the arrival of Waze and other efficiency-seeking navigation systems, Leonia saw a massive uptick in rush hour traffic, so extreme that many residents could not leave their driveways. In response, Leonia decided to close nearly all of its streets to non-local traffic during rush hour periods, 7 days a week (Foderaro 2017). Though this might seem like a happy ending for the people of Leonia, it underscores the immediate impact that corporate mobility shaping can have on people's experience of space and the systems of democratic accountability in which traffic planning decisions are typically made. At the same time, it points to the incredible potential for more democratic forms of algorithmic mobility shaping.[12]

[12] *The Low Down to Hull and Back* illustrates another way in which navigational systems disregard local concerns (CBC News 2019). *The Low Down* is an English-language newspaper based in Gatineau, Quebec, and has used a combination of English and French place names to refer to Quebec locations since its founding. For instance, the paper would refer to "Valley Road" rather than "Chemin de la Vallée de Wakefield," but use "Lac Philippe" and not "Philippe Lake." However, because of Google Maps' conventions, *The Low Down* has recently changed its standard. The app would not recognize English place names, and reporters sent out to cover stories were getting lost in Gatineau Park ("le parc de la Gatineau"). For consistency, the paper has therefore decided to switch to French for all place names. Norms around choosing between English and French are politically fraught in Quebec, but Google

These concerns reflect a significant difference between the Internet and mobility networks. While the Internet began as many disjunct, semi-private networks, albeit ones often constructed with public funding, most roads began as inherently public. Homer's (1898) *Iliad*, for instance, refers to moving "along the public way," and though private roads were known in the Roman Empire, the "main roads ... were built, maintained and owned by the State" (Jacobson 1940, 103).[13] Toll roads and private roads are still relatively uncommon. As a result, decision-making about roads has been a critical aspect of public discourse for hundreds, if not thousands of years.

In this emerging era of private digital navigational and mapping data and increasingly automated mobility, which function as the metaphorical routers and packets of algorithmically controlled mobility systems, we are confronting the unanticipated privatization of the roads themselves. Though the roads may remain public, that designation could morph into something quite alien relative to our current understanding of mobility, as private interests drape an invisible yet powerful web of algorithmic control over our physical space. Decisions about mobility are being removed from the democratic sphere, and a fundamental restructuring is occurring with little oversight, debate, or explanation. These forms of digital enclosure – of creating a digital fence around ostensibly public roads and structuring people's mobility within the network – deserve attention, so that we preserve what forms of individual and collective mobility interests are deemed worth preserving, and balance individual, collective, and private interests in mobility more transparently and democratically.

11.5 CONCLUSION

The age of digital connectivity and mobile computing has brought massive changes to human movement. Human drivers increasingly delegate navigational decision making to apps, thus automating significant aspects of driving and enabling early forms of mobility shaping. The similarities between traffic shaping on the Internet and mobility shaping on physical roadways provide a starting point for examining the ethical and legal challenges that turn-by-turn navigation systems are raising in the public sphere. Yet, although compelling, the parallels between communication networks and mobility networks are not the whole story. As we move towards ever greater algorithmic shaping of our mobility, we must recognize that our ability to move freely in the physical world engages with some of our most fundamental democratic freedoms, that access to mobility uniquely reflects societal values, distinguishing it from information, and demanding a more rigorous investigation

Maps undermines them. *The Low Down*'s story illustrates a telling detail about our relationship to maps and systems: rather than changing what they saw on the map, the people reluctantly changed themselves.

[13] Though generally built for the State's military use, the public at large was not excluded from these main roads.

of the ethics of mobility that can account for mobility shaping.[14] This paper hopes to spark those investigations and ensuing debates – now is the time to evaluate the permissibility of different forms of mobility shaping, and to lay the normative foundation for tomorrow's algorithmically controlled mobility systems.

REFERENCES

An, Daniel. "Find Out How You Stack Up to New Industry Benchmarks for Mobile Page Speed." *Think with Google*. Internet Archive Wayback Machine. February 2018. https://web.archive.org/web/20190125174538/https:/www.thinkwithgoogle.com/marketing-resources/data-measurement/mobile-page-speed-new-industry-benchmarks/.

Anderson, Nate. "Deep Packet Inspection Meets 'Net Neutrality, CALEA." *Ars Technica*, July 26, 2007. https://arstechnica.com/gadgets/2007/07/deep-packet-inspection-meets-net-neutrality/.

Blomley, Nicholas K. "Mobility, Empowerment and the Rights Revolution." In *Geographical Thought: A Praxis Perspective*, edited by George Henderson and Marvin Waterstone, 201–215. London: Routledge, 2009.

BuiltWith. "Google Maps Usage Statistics." *Internet Archive Wayback Machine*. January 23, 2019. https://tinyurl.com/ydbcqlht.

Burdick, Charles K. "The Origin of the Peculiar Duties of Public Service Companies." *Columbia Law Review* 11, no. 8 (1911): 743–764. https://doi.org/10.2307/1110915.

Canada (Information Commissioner) v Canada (Minister of National Defence), 2011 SCC 25, [2011] 2 SCR 306. https://decisions.scc-csc.ca/scc-csc/scc-csc/en/item/7939/index.do.

Carlson, Nicholas. "To Do What Google Does in Maps, Apple Would Have to Hire 7,000 People." *Business Insider Australia*, June 27, 2012. www.businessinsider.com/to-do-what-google-does-in-maps-apple-would-have-to-hire-7000-people-2012-6.

CBC News. "Western Quebec Newspaper Changes Policy to Help Google Maps Users." *CBC*, January 17, 2019. www.cbc.ca/news/canada/ottawa/outaouais-french-street-names-gps-1.4974821.

Cohan, Peter. "Four Reasons Google Bought Waze." *Forbes*, June 11, 2013. www.forbes.com/sites/petercohan/2013/06/11/four-reasons-for-google-to-buy-waze/?sh = 2f6ba0a6726f.

Comcast Corporation. "Description of Planned Network Management Practices to be Deployed Following the Termination of Current Practices." *Comcast*. 2008. http://downloads.comcast.net/docs/Attachment_B_Future_Practices.pdf.

CRTC. "Asian Television Network International Limited, on Behalf of the FairPlay Coalition: Application to Disable Online Access to Piracy Websites." *Government of Canada*. October 2, 2018. https://crtc.gc.ca/eng/archive/2018/2018-384.htm.

"Complaint against Bell Mobility Inc. and Quebecor Media Inc., Videotron Ltd. and Videotron G.P. Alleging Undue and Unreasonable Preference and Disadvantage in regard to the Billing Practices for their Mobile TV Services Bell Mobile TV and illico.tv." *Government of Canada*. January 29, 2019. https://crtc.gc.ca/eng/archive/2015/2015-26.htm.

"Telecom Regulatory Policy CRTC 2017-104." *Government of Canada*. April 20, 2017. https://crtc.gc.ca/eng/archive/2017/2017-104.htm.

[14] This paper was drafted during the COVID-19 pandemic in Ontario, during the fourth week of mobility restrictions. The inherent value of physical access to public space has rarely been so starkly evident.

EC, Regulation (EU) 2015/2120 of the European Parliament and of the Council of 25 November 2015 laying down measures concerning open internet access and amending Directive 2002/22/EC on universal service and users' rights relating to electronic communications networks and services and Regulation (EU) No 531/2012 on roaming on public mobile communications networks within the Union (Text with EEA relevance), [2015] OJ, L 310/1. https://eur-lex.europa.eu/eli/reg/2015/2120/oj.

FCC. "FCC 08-183." 2008. https://docs.fcc.gov/public/attachments/fcc-08-183a1.pdf.

Finley, Klint. "A Brief History of Net Neutrality." *WIRED*, May 9, 2018. www.wired.com/amp-stories/net-neutrality-timeline/.

Foderaro, Lisa W. "Navigation Apps Are Turning Quiet Neighborhoods into Traffic Nightmares." *The New York Times*, December 24, 2017. www.nytimes.com/2017/12/24/nyregion/traffic-apps-gps-neighborhoods.html.

French, R. L. "Maps on Wheels." In *Cartographies of Travel and Navigation*, edited by James R. Akerman, 269–270. Chicago: University of Chicago Press, 2006.

Google Maps: Street View. "Where We've Been & Where We're Headed Next." Google. Internet Archive Wayback Machine. January 22, 2019. https://web.archive.org/web/20190125160029/https:/www.google.ca/streetview/understand/.

Hattem, Julian. "Franken: Net Neutrality Is 'First Amendment Issue of Our Time'." *The Hill*, July 8, 2014. https://thehill.com/policy/technology/211607-franken-net-neutrality-is-first-amendment-issue-of-our-time.

Here Technologies. "About Us." *Here*. 2019. www.here.com/company/about-us.

Homer. *The Iliad*, translated by S. Butler. Book XV. London: Longman Green and Co., 1898. https://omnika.org/texts/875#Book-XV.

Indiana University. "What Is a Packet?" *University Information Technology Services*, January 18, 2018. https://kb.iu.edu/d/anyq.

Jacobson, Herbert R. "A History of Roads from Ancient Times to the Motor Age." Master's Thesis, Georgia School of Technology, 1940. https://repository.gatech.edu/server/api/core/bitstreams/566242b3-8fcf-4d88-a509-56b08323d563/content.

Luo, Wei. "DeepMap Collaborates with Ford on HD Mapping Research for Autonomous Vehicles." *DeepMap, Inc.*, October 24, 2017. https://deepmap.medium.com/deepmap-collaborates-with-ford-on-hd-mapping-research-for-autonomous-vehicles-e0c444764320.

Madrigal, Alexis C., and Adrienne LaFrance. "Net Neutrality: A Guide to (and History of) a Contested Idea." *The Atlantic*. April 25, 2014. www.theatlantic.com/technology/archive/2014/04/the-best-writing-on-net-neutrality/361237/.

Millar, Jason. "Ethics Settings for Autonomous Vehicles." In *Robot Ethics 2.0*, edited by Patrick Lin, Keith Abney, and Ryan Jenkins, 20–34. Oxford: Oxford University Press, 2017.

Molla, Rani. "Two-thirds of Adults Worldwide Will Own Smartphones Next Year." *Vox*, October 16, 2017. www.vox.com/2017/10/16/16482168/two-thirds-of-adults-worldwide-will-own-smartphones-next-year.

New Jersey Steam Navigation Co v Merchants' Bank, 47 US (6 How) 344 (1848). https://supreme.justia.com/cases/federal/us/47/344/.

O'Beirne, Justin. "Google Maps's Moat." *Justin O'Beirne* (blog), 2017. www.justinobeirne.com/google-maps-moat.

Ontario (Public Safety and Security) v Criminal Lawyers' Association, 2010 SCC 23, [2010] 1 SCR 815. https://decisions.scc-csc.ca/scc-csc/scc-csc/en/item/7864/index.do.

O'Rourke, Patrick. "CRTC Denies Bell-led FairPlay Canada Coalition on 'Jurisdictional Grounds'." *MobileSyrup*, October 2, 2018. https://mobilesyrup.com/2018/10/02/crtc-denies-fairplay-canada-coalition-jurisdictional-grounds/.

Panko, Riley. "The Popularity of Google Maps: Trends in Navigation Apps in 2018." *The Manifest*, July 10, 2018. https://themanifest.com/app-development/trends-navigation-apps.

Parsons, Christopher. "The Politics of Deep Packet Inspection: What Drives Surveillance by Internet Service Providers?" PhD Dissertation, University of Victoria, 2013. https://dspace.library.uvic.ca/items/233f1449-c664-40d6-b6d6-dea15058a2c7.

Pew Research Center. "Mobile Fact Sheet." *Pew Research Center*, June 12, 2019. www.pewresearch.org/internet/fact-sheet/mobile/.

Popken, Ben. "Worried about What Facebook Knows about You? Check out Google." *NBC News*, March 28, 2018. www.nbcnews.com/tech/social-media/worried-about-what-facebook-knows-about-you-check-out-google-n860781.

Popper, Ben. "Google Announces over 2 Billion Monthly Active Devices on Android." *The Verge*, May 17, 2017. www.theverge.com/2017/5/17/15654454/android-reaches-2-billion-monthly-active-users.

Porter, Jon. "Google Is Bringing Together Its Waze and Maps Teams as It Pushes to Reduce Overlap." *The Verge*, December 8, 2022. www.theverge.com/2022/12/8/23499734/google-maps-waze-development-teams-combined-productivity.

Reuters. "TomTom Shares Jump after Apple Renews Digital Maps Contract." *Reuters*, May 17, 2015. www.reuters.com/article/us-tomtom-apple/tomtom-shares-jump-after-apple-renews-digital-maps-contract-idUSKBN0O40GE20150519.

Richter, Felix. "Charted: There Are More Mobile Phones than People in the World." *World Economic Forum*, April 11, 2023. www.weforum.org/agenda/2023/04/charted-there-are-more-phones-than-people-in-the-world/.

Think with Google. "Mobile Site Abandonment." *Think with Google*. Internet Archive Wayback Machine. August 15, 2018. https://web.archive.org/web/20180815133218/https:/www.thinkwithgoogle.com/data/mobile-site-abandonment-three-second-load/.

Uber. "Uber – Mapping." January 22, 2019. www.uber.com/info/mapping/.

Walker, Alissa. "Why People Keep Trying to Erase the Hollywood Sign from Google Maps." *Gizmodo*, November 21, 2014. https://gizmodo.com/why-people-keep-trying-to-erase-the-hollywood-sign-from-1658084644.

Walsh, Margaret. "Gender and American Mobility: Cars, Women and the Issue of Equality." In *Cultural Histories of Sociabilities, Spaces and Mobilities*, edited by Colin Divall, 29–38. London: Routledge, 2015.

Waze Ads Starter Help. "About Ad Formats in Waze." *Waze*, Google. n.d. Accessed April 2022. https://support.google.com/wazelocal/answer/9747689?hl = en&ref_topic = 6153431&visit_id = 637496346364878181-3063296140&rd = 1.

Wu, Tim. *A Proposal for Network Neutrality*. Charlottesville: University of Virginia Law School, 2002.

Wyman, Bruce. "The Law of the Public Callings as a Solution of the Trust Problem." *Harvard Law Review* 17, no. 4 (1904): 217–247. www.jstor.org/stable/1323312.

12

Doughnut Privacy

A Preliminary Thought Experiment

Julie E. Cohen

Previous chapters in the book have highlighted the ways that data-driven technologies are altering the human experience in the digital world. In this chapter, I explore the implications of the "doughnut" model of sustainable economic development for efforts to strike the appropriate balance between data-driven surveillance and privacy. I conclude that the model offers a useful corrective for policymakers seeking to ensure that the development of digital technologies serves human priorities and purposes.

Among environmental economists and some city planners, Kate Raworth's (2017) theory of "doughnut economics" is all the rage. Raworth argues that, in an era when human wellbeing depends on sustainable development rather than on unlimited growth, economics as a discipline can no longer embrace models of welfare oriented exclusively toward the latter. As an alternative model to the classic upward-trending growth curve, she offers the doughnut: an inner ring consisting of the minimum requirements for human wellbeing, a middle band consisting of the safe and just space for human existence, and an ecological ceiling above which continued growth produces planetary disaster.[1]

I will argue, first, that a similarly doughnut-shaped model can advance conceptualization of the appropriate balance(s) between surveillance and privacy and, second, that taking the doughnut model seriously suggests important questions about the uses, forms, and modalities of legitimate surveillance. Foregrounding these questions can help policymakers centre the needs and priorities of humans living in digitally mediated spaces.

A note on definitions: By "surveillance" I mean to refer to sets of sociotechnical conditions (and their associated organizational and institutional practices) that involve the purposeful, routine, systematic, and focused collection, storage, processing, and use of personal information (Murakami Wood 2006). By "privacy" I mean

My thanks to participants in the eQuality Project research workshop "On Being Human in the Digital World" and the 2022 Privacy Law Scholars Conference for their helpful comments, and to Rasheed Evelyn, Conor Kane, and Sherry Tseng for research assistance.

[1] You can see Raworth's (2017) doughnut diagram at www.kateraworth.com/doughnut/.

to refer to sets of sociotechnical conditions (and their associated organizational and institutional practices) that involve forbearance from information collection, storage, processing, and use, thereby creating "...(degrees of) spatial, informational, and epistemological open-endedness" (Cohen 2019b, 13). Although conditions of surveillance and privacy are inversely related, they are neither absolute nor mutually exclusive – for example, one can have surveillance of body temperatures without collection of other identifying information or surveillance of only those financial transactions that exceed a threshold amount – and they are capable of great variation in both granularity and persistence across contexts.

12.1 FROM FRAMING EFFECTS TO MENTAL MAPS: DEFINING POLICY LANDSCAPES

The animating insight behind the doughnut model concerns the importance of mental maps in structuring shared understandings of the feasible horizons for economic and social policymaking. Frames and models create mental maps that foreclose some options and lend added weight to others (van Hulst and Yanow 2016). For that reason, if one wishes to contest existing policy choices, it will generally be insufficient simply to name the framing effects that produced them. Displacing framing effects requires different mental maps.

Specifically, the doughnut model of sustainable development represents an effort to displace an imagined policy landscape organized around the familiar figure of the upward-trending growth curve. The curve depicts (or so it is thought) the relationship between economic growth and social welfare: more is better. That philosophy resonates strongly with the logics of datafication and data extractive capitalism. Unsurprisingly, the imagined topography of policy interventions relating to surveillance is also organized around an upward-trending growth curve, which reflects (or so it is thought) the relationship between growth in data-driven "innovation" and social welfare: here too, more is better. The doughnut model visually reorders policy priorities, producing imagined policy landscapes that feature other human values – sustainability and privacy – more prominently.

12.1.1 *Sustainability and the Economic Growth Curve*

In economic modelling, the classic upward-trending growth curve links increased growth with increased social welfare. The curve tells us that more economic growth produces more social welfare and, conversely, that increasing social welfare requires continuing economic growth (Raworth 2017). The resulting mental map of feasible and desired policy interventions has produced decades of discussions about economic policy that take for granted the primacy of growth and then revolve narrowly around the twin problems of how to incentivize it and, equally important, how to avoid disincentivizing it.

Although sustainability has emerged over the last half century as a key determinant of social welfare – indeed, an existentially important one – it has no clear place within that imagined landscape. This has become increasingly evident in recent decades. Concerns about long-term sustainability and species survival have fueled increasingly urgent challenges to production and consumption practices that treat resources as infinite and disposable. Those concerns have inspired new approaches to modeling production and consumption as circular flows of resources (Friant et al. 2020). In the abstract, however, circular-economy models have trouble escaping the gravitational pull of a policy landscape dominated by the upward-trending growth curve. In many circular-economy narratives, recycling-driven approaches to production and consumption are valuable, and deserving of inclusion in the policy landscape, precisely because they fuel continuing growth (Corvallec et al. 2022).

The doughnut model is premised on a more foundational critique of growth-driven reasoning. It deploys ecological and systems thinking to model policy frontiers – outer bounds on growth that it is perilous to transgress. And it represents those boundaries using a crisp, simple visual depiction, offering policymakers a new imagined landscape for their recommendations and interventions (Raworth 2017, 38–45). It compels attention to sustainability considerations precisely because it forces us to look at them – and it demands that ostensibly more precise mathematical models and forecasts organized around growth be dismantled and reorganized around development ceilings calibrated to preserve safe and just space for human existence (Luukkanen et al. 2021).

12.1.2 *Privacy and the Surveillance Innovation Curve*

Imagined policy landscapes also do important work shaping policy outcomes in debates about surveillance and privacy. Most often, that landscape is dominated by a close relative of the economist's upward-trending growth curve, which models data-driven "innovation" versus social welfare. Like the upward-trending growth curve in economics, the upward-trending surveillance innovation curve suggests that, generally speaking, new ventures in data collection and processing will increase social welfare – and, conversely, that continuing increases in social welfare demand continuing growth in data harvesting and data processing capacities (e.g. Thierer 2014).

Imagined policy landscapes dominated by the upward-trending surveillance innovation curve have proved deeply inhospitable to efforts to rehabilitate privacy as an important social value. Richly textured accounts of privacy's importance abound in the privacy literature. Some scholars (e.g. Cohen 2012, 2013; Richards 2021; Roessler 2005; Steeves 2009) focus on articulating privacy's normative values; others (e.g. Nissenbaum 2009) on defining norms of appropriate flow; and others (e.g. Post 1989; Solove 2008) on mapping privacy's embeddedness within a variety of social and cultural practices. But the imagined policy landscape generated by the upward-trending surveillance innovation curve locates "innovation" and its hypothesized ability to solve a wide variety of economic and social problems solidly at centre stage.

As in the case of sustainable development, the doughnut model is an effective visual device for directing attention toward the negative effects of excess surveillance and, therefore, toward the difficult but necessary task of specifying surveillance ceilings. Additionally, theoretical accounts of privacy directed primarily toward rehabilitating it as a value worth preserving typically do not offer enough guidance on how to identify necessary surveillance floors. Claims about appropriate versus inappropriate flow (Nissenbaum 2009) tend to be most open to contestation at times of rapid sociotechnical change, when norms of contextual integrity are unsettled. My own account of post-liberal privacy as an inherently interstitial and structural construct devotes some attention to the technical and operational requirements for implementing privacy safeguards (Cohen 2012, 2013, 2019b) but does not consider how to distinguish between pro-social and anti-social surveillance implementations. The doughnut model productively engages and frames questions about how to identify and manage both kinds of surveillance/privacy frontiers.

12.2 FROM MENTAL MAPS TO POLICY HORIZONS: MAPPING SURVEILLANCE/PRIVACY INTERFACES

The doughnut model for privacy policymaking defines two distinct "surfaces" over which balance needs to be achieved. The outer perimeter of the doughnut includes sectors representing different threats to safe and just human existence flowing from excesses of surveillance. Conversely, as in the case of the sustainability doughnut, the hole at the centre represents insufficient levels of data-driven surveillance – or privacy afforded to a degree that undermines the social foundation for human wellbeing.

12.2.1 *The Sustainability Ceiling: Antisocial Surveillance (and Prosocial Privacy)*

The growing and increasingly interconnected literatures in surveillance studies, information studies, and law have developed detailed accounts of the ways that excesses of surveillance undermine prospects for a safe and just human existence. Just as the outer perimeter of Raworth's (2017) doughnut is divided into sectors representing different kinds of planetary threats, so we can divide the privacy doughnut's outer perimeter into sectors representing the different kinds of threats to human wellbeing that scholars have identified. Because the literatures on these issues are extensive, I will summarize them only briefly.

Some sectors of the privacy doughnut's outer perimeter involve surveillance practices that undermine the capacity for self-development. Dominant platform companies such as Google, Meta, Amazon, TikTok, and Twitter, and many other providers of networked applications and information services use browsing, reading, listening, and viewing data to impose pattern-driven personalization, tailoring the information environment for each user to what is already known about that user or inferred based on the behaviours and preferences of similar users. Pattern-driven personalization privileges habit and convenience over more open-ended processes of exploration, experimentation, and play (Cohen 2012, 2013; Richards 2021; Steeves 2009). It also facilitates the continual delivery of nudges designed to instill more predictable and more easily monetizable patterns of behavior (Zuboff 2019).

Other sectors involve surveillance practices that destabilize democratic institutions and practices. In particular, providers of online search and social media services use data about user behaviours and preferences to target and/or uprank flows of information, including both user-generated content and promoted content. Patterns of affinity-based information flow deepen political polarization, and this in turn affords more fertile ground for misinformation to take root and disinformation campaigns to flourish (e.g. Cohen 2019a; Nadler et al. 2018). The persistent optimization and re-optimization of online environments around commercial and narrowly tribal priorities and interests undermines trust in democratic institutions and erodes the collective capacity to define and advance more broadly public-regarding priorities and interests (Farrell and Schneier 2018; Viljoen 2021; see also Chapter 2, by Murakami Wood).

Other sectors involve surveillance practices that reinforce economic power and widen distributive gaps. Many employers use surveillance technologies to monitor employee behavior both in and, increasingly, outside workplaces (Ajunwa et al. 2017). Persistent work-related surveillance magnifies power disparities between employers and workers and raises the barriers to collective organization by workers that might mitigate those disparities (Rogers 2023). The same persistent surveillance of user behaviors and preferences that enables pattern-driven personalization of the information environment also facilitates personalization of prices and non-price terms for consumer goods and services, imposing hierarchical logics within consumer markets (e.g. Cohen 2019a; Fourcade and Healy 2017; Zuboff 2019).

Other sectors involve surveillance practices that compound pre-existing patterns of racialized and/or gendered inequality (e.g. Benjamin 2019; Citron 2022; Richardson and Kak 2022; see also Chapter 9, by Akbari). Scholars who focus on race, poverty, and their intersections show that privacy tends to be afforded differently to different groups, in ways that reinforced racialized abuses of power and that subjugate the poor while framing poverty's pathologies as failures of personal responsibility (Bridges 2017; Eubanks 2018; Gilliom 2001; Gilman 2012). Data extractive capitalism reinforces and widens these patterns and strengthens linkages between market-based and carceral processes of labeling and sorting (Benjamin 2019; Browne 2017; see also Chapter 5, by Lyon).

Seen through a global prism, many extractive surveillance implementations reinforce pre-existing histories of colonialist exploitation and resource extraction (Couldry and Mejias 2019; see also Chapter 9, by Akbari). Recognition of the resulting threats to self-governance and self-determination has fueled a growing movement by scholars and activists in the Global South to assert control of the arc of technological development under the banner of a new "non-aligned technologies movement" (Couldry and Mejias 2023).

Last, but hardly least, the surveillance economy also imposes planetary costs. These include both chemical pollution caused by extraction of rare earth metals used in digital devices and air pollution, ozone depletion and other climate effects produced by immense data centres (Crawford 2021). These problems also link back to Raworth's (2017) original doughnut diagram; the surveillance economy is both socially and ecologically unsustainable.

12.2.2 *The Hole at the Centre: Prosocial Surveillance (and Antisocial Privacy)*

If the doughnut analogy is to hold, the hole at the doughnut's centre must represent too much privacy – privacy afforded to a degree that impedes human flourishing by undermining the social foundation for collective, sustainable governance. Diverse strands of scholarship in law and political theory have long argued that excesses of privacy can be socially destructive. The doughnut model reinforces some of those claims and suggests skepticism toward others. But the privacy doughnut's 'hole' also includes other, more specific surveillance deficits. I will develop this argument by way of two examples, one involving public health and the other involving the public fisc.

Liberal and feminist scholars have long argued that certain understandings of privacy reinforce conditions of political privation and patriarchal social control. The most well-known liberal critique of excess privacy is Hannah Arendt's (1958) description of the privation of a life lived only in home spaces segregated from the public life of the engaged citizen. Building on (and also critiquing) Arendt's account of privacy and privation, feminist privacy scholars (e.g. Allen 2003; Citron 2022; Roessler 2005) have explored the ways that invocations of privacy also function as a modality of patriarchal social control. It is useful to distinguish these arguments from those advanced by communitarian scholars about the ways that privacy undermines social wellbeing (e.g. Etzioni 2000). Theorists in the latter group have difficulty interrogating communally asserted power and identifying any residual domain for privacy. The communitarian mode of theorizing about privacy therefore tends to reinforce the imagined policy landscape generated by the upward-trending surveillance innovation curve. In different ways and to different extents, liberal and feminist critiques of excess privacy are concerned with the nature of the balance struck between "public" and "private" spheres of authority and with the ways in which excesses of privacy can impede full inclusion in civil society and reinforce maldistributions of power.

Moving beyond these important but fairly general objections, excess privacy can also impede human flourishing in more context-specific ways. Here are two examples:

The events of the past years have illustrated that competent and humane public health surveillance is essential for human flourishing even when it overrides privacy claims that might warrant dispositive weight in other contexts (Rozenshtein 2021; see also Chapter 5, by Lyon). A competent system of public health surveillance needs to detect and trace the spread of both infections and viral mutations quickly and capably (Grubaugh et al. 2021). A humane system of public health surveillance must identify and care for those who are sick or subject to preventive quarantine. At the same time, however, such a system must safeguard collected personal information so it cannot be repurposed in ways that undermine public trust, and it must take special care to protect vulnerable populations (Hendl et al. 2020). Competent and humane public health surveillance therefore necessitates both authority to collect and share information and clearly delineated limits on information collection and flow.

Some public health surveillance operations clearly cross the doughnut's outer perimeter. From the Western legal perspective, obvious candidates might include the Chinese regime of mandatory punitive lockdowns (e.g., Chang et al. 2022) and (at one point) testing via anal swabs (Wang et al. 2021). But having avoided these particular implementations does not automatically make a system of public health surveillance competent and humane. In the United States and the United Kingdom, for example, information collected for pandemic-related public health care functions has flowed in relatively unconstrained ways to contractors deeply embedded in systems of law enforcement and immigration surveillance, fueling public distrust and fear (No Tech for Tyrants and Privacy International 2020).

Particularly in the current neoliberal climate, however, it has been less widely acknowledged that other kinds of public health surveillance interventions fail the threshold-conditions criterion. The US regime of public health surveillance during the coronavirus pandemic operated mostly inside the doughnut's hole, relying on patchy, haphazard, and often privatized networks of protocols for testing and tracing backstopped by an equally patchy, haphazard, and often privatized network of other protective and social support measures (Jackson and Ahmed 2022). Some nations, meanwhile, constructed systems of public health surveillance designed to operate within the doughnut. One example is the Danish regime combining free public testing and centralized contact tracing with a public passport system designed to encourage vaccination and facilitate resumption of public and communal social life (Anderssen et al. 2021; see also Ada Lovelace Institute 2020). Additionally, although a responsible and prosocial system of public health surveillance must balance the importance of bodily control claims in ways that respect individual dignity, it should not permit overbroad privacy claims to stymie legitimate and necessary public health efforts (Rozenshtein 2021). Refusal to participate in testing and tracing operations, to comply with humanely designed isolation and masking protocols, and to enroll in regimens for vaccination and related status reporting can fatally undermine efforts to restore the threshold conditions necessary for human flourishing – that is, to return society more generally to the zone of democratic sustainability defined by the doughnut.

As a second example of necessary, public-regarding surveillance, consider mechanisms for financial surveillance. The legal and policy debates surrounding financial and communications surveillance arguably present a puzzle. If, as any competent US-trained lawyer would tell you, speech and money are sometimes (always?) interchangeable, we ought to be as concerned about rules allowing government investigators access to people's bank statements as we are about rules allowing the same investigators access to people's communication records. Yet far more public and scholarly attention attaches to the latter. In part, this is because the financial surveillance rules are complex and arcane and the entities that wield them are obscure. In part, however, it is because it is far more widely acknowledged that systemic financial oversight – including some financial surveillance – implicates undeniably prosocial goals.

Financial surveillance authority underpins the ability to enforce tax liabilities without which important public services necessary for human wellbeing could not be provided (Swire 1999). Such services include everything from roads, clean water, and sewage removal to public education, housing assistance, and more. By this I don't mean to endorse current mechanisms for providing such assistance or the narratives that surround them, but only to claim that such services need to be provided and need to be funded.

Relatedly, financial surveillance authority enables investigation of complex financial crimes, including not only the usual poster children in contemporary securitized debates about surveillance (organized crime, narcotrafficking, and global terrorism) (Swire 1999), but also and equally importantly the kleptocratic escapades of governing elites and oligarchies. A wide and growing assortment of recent scandals – involving everything from assets offshored in tax havens (ICIJ 2021) to diverted pandemic aid (AFREF et al. 2021; Podkul 2021) to real estate and other assets maintained in capitalist playgrounds by oligarchs and the uber-rich (Kendzior 2020; Kumar and de Bel 2021) – underscore the extent to which gaps in financial oversight systems threaten social wellbeing. Effective, transnational financial surveillance is an essential piece (though only one piece) of an effective response.

The inability to perform any of these financial surveillance functions would jeopardize the minimum requisite conditions for human flourishing. And, to be clear, this argument does not depend on the continued existence of nation states in their current form and with their current geopolitical and colonial legacies.

If current nation states ceased to exist tomorrow, other entities would need to provide, for example, roads, clean water, and sewage removal, and other entities would need to develop the capacity to support and protect the least powerful.[2]

12.3 INSIDE THE DOUGHNUT:ABOLITION V./OR/AND GOVERNANCE

To (over)simplify a bit, so far, I may seem to have argued that one can have too much surveillance or not enough. Broadly speaking, that is a familiar problem within the privacy literature, so at this point it may appear that I have not said that much after all. And equally important, I have not specifically addressed the characteristic orientations and effects of surveillance models in our particular, late capitalist, insistently racialized society. In practice, surveillance implementations have tended to entrench and intensify extractive, colonialist, and racialized pathologies (Benjamin 2019; Browne 2017; Couldry and Mejias 2023; see also Chapter 9, by Akbari), and awareness of that dynamic now underwrites a rapidly growing movement for surveillance abolition whose claims lie in tension with some of my own claims about the doughnut's inner ring.

12.3.1 *An Existential Dilemma*

Surveillance abolition thinking rejects thinking about the possibility of reorienting surveillance technologies toward prosocial and equality-furthering goals as pernicious and wrongheaded. Although beneficial uses are hypothetically possible, the track record of abuse is established and far more compelling. There is no 'right kind' of surveillance because all kinds of surveillance – including those framed as luxuries for the well-to-do – will invariably present a very different face to the least fortunate (Gilliard 2020, 2022). Drawing an explicit parallel to the campaign for abolition of policing more generally (e.g. McLeod 2019; Morgan 2022), surveillance abolition thinking calls upon its practitioners to imagine and work to create a world in which control over data and its uses is radically reimagined (Milner and Traub 2021). Abolitionist thinkers and activists tend to view proposals for incremental and/or procedural privacy reforms as working only to entrench surveillance-oriented practices and their disparate impacts more solidly.

As one example of the case for surveillance abolition, consider evolving uses of biometric technologies. Facial recognition technology has been developed and tested with brutal disregard for its differential impacts on different skin tones and genders (Buolamwini and Gebru 2018) and deployed for a wide and growing variety of extractive and carceral purposes (Garvie et al. 2016; Hill 2020). At the same time, it has been normalized as a mechanism for casual, everyday authentication of access to

[2] The implications of these arguments for current experiments in cryptocurrency-based disintermediation of fiat currency are evident but beyond the scope of this paper.

consumer devices in a manner that creates profound data security threats (Rowe 2020). India's Aadhaar system of biometric authentication, which relies on digitalized fingerprinting, was justified as a public welfare measure, but works least well for the least fortunate – for example, manual laborers whose fingerprints may have been worn away or damaged (Singh and Jackson 2017). At the same time, the privatization of the "India stack" has created a point of entry for various commercial and extractive ventures (Hicks 2020).

As a second example of the case for surveillance abolition, consider credit scoring. In the United States, there are deep historical links between credit reporting and racial discrimination (Hoffman 2021), and that relationship extends solidly into the present, creating self-reinforcing circuits that operate to prevent access to a wide variety of basic needs, including housing (Leiwant 2022; Poon 2009; Smith and Vogell 2022) and employment (Traub 2014). In municipal and state systems nationwide, unpaid fines for low-level offenses routinely become justifications for arrest and imprisonment, creating new data streams that feed back into the credit reporting system (Bannon et al. 2010).

The other half of the existential dilemma to which this section's title refers, however, is that governing complex societies requires techniques for governing at scale. Some functions of good governance relate to due process in enforcement. I do not mean this to refer to policing but rather and more generally to the ability to afford process and redress to those harmed by private or government actors. For some time now, atomistic paradigms of procedural due process have been buckling under the strain of large numbers. The data protection notion of a "human in the loop" is no panacea for the defects embedded in current pattern-driven processes (e.g. Crootof et al. 2023; Green 2022), but, even if it were, it simply isn't possible to afford every type of complaint that a human being might lodge within a bureaucratic system the type of process to which we might aspire.

Other functions of good governance are ameliorative. Governments can and do (and must) provide a variety of important public benefits, and surveillance implementations intersect with these in at least three ways. First, surveillance can be used (and misused) to address problems of inclusion. Failure to afford inclusion creates what Gilman and Green (2018) term "surveillance gaps" in welfare and public health systems. Second, distributing government benefits without some method of accounting for them invites fraud – not by needy beneficiaries too often demonized in narratives about responsibility and advantage-taking, but rather by powerful actors and garden-variety scammers seeking to enrich themselves at the public's expense (AFREF et al. 2021; Podkul 2021). Third, mechanisms for levying and collecting tax revenues to fund public benefits and other public works invite evasion by wealthy and well-connected individuals and organizations (Global Alliance for Tax Justice 2021; Guyton et al. 2021; ICIJ 2021). In a world of large numbers, the possibilities for scams multiply. Surveillance has a useful role to play in combating fraud and tax evasion. For example, the Internal Revenue Service, which is chronically under-resourced, spends an outsize portion of the enforcement resources that it does have pursuing (real or hypothesized) tax cheats at the lower end of the socioeconomic scale (Kiel 2019), but training artificial intelligence for fraud detection at the upper end of that scale, where tax evasion is also more highly concentrated (Alstadsaeter et al. 2019), could produce real public benefit.

In short, a basic function of good government is to prevent the powerful from taking advantage of the powerless, and this requires rethinking both what constitutes legitimate surveillance and what constitutes legitimate governance. Current surveillance dysfunctions and injustices suggest powerfully that the root problem to be confronted involves re-learning how to govern, and for whose benefit, before re-learning how to surveil.

The doughnut model is not a cure-all for pathologies of exclusion and exploitation that have deep historical roots, but it does more than simply position privacy problems as matters of degree. It suggests, critically, that one can have too much of the wrong kind of surveillance, and/or not enough of the right kind, and that "wrong" and "right" relate to power and its abuses in ways that have very specific valences. We may make some headway simply by asking more precise questions about the types of surveillance that a just society *must* employ or *should never* permit. But not enough. Surveillance implementations are always already situated relative to particular contexts in which power and resources are distributed unequally and, unless very good care is taken, they will tend to reinforce and widen pre-existing patterns of privilege and disempowerment. Even for processes that (are claimed to) occur within the doughnut's interior, the details matter.

12.3.2 *Policymaking inside the Doughnut:Five Legitimacy Constraints*

Engaging the abolitionist critique together with the need to govern at scale suggests (at least) five additional constraints that ostensibly prosocial surveillance implementations must satisfy. The first two constraints, *sectoral fidelity* and *data parsimony*, are necessary to counteract surveillance mission creep. Policymakers must ask more precise questions about the particular sustainability function to which a proposed implementation relates and must insist on regimes that advance that function and no others. And the formal commitment to sectoral fidelity must be supported by a mandate for parsimonious design that, wherever possible and to the greatest extent possible, prevents collected data from migrating into new surveillance implementations. The third constraint is *distributive justice*. Policymakers must interrogate existing and proposed surveillance implementations through an equity lens and, as necessary, abandon or radically modify those that reinforce or increase pre-existing inequities. The fourth and fifth constraints, *openness to revision* and *design for countervailing* power, work against epistemic closure of narratives embraced to justify surveillance in the first place. Policymakers should create oversight mechanisms that facilitate revisiting and revising policies and practices and should require design for countervailing power in ways that reinforce such mechanisms.

One of privacy law's most difficult challenges has involved building in appropriate leeway for evolution in data collection and use while still minimizing the risk of surveillance mission creep. The data minimization and purpose limitation principles that underpin European-style data protection regimes represent one articulation of this challenge, but those principles date back to the era of standalone databases and present interpretive difficulties in an era of interconnected, dynamic information systems. Their touchstones – respectively, collection that is "limited to what is necessary in relation to" the stated purpose and further processing that is "compatible" with the original stated purpose[3] – seem to invite continual erosion. In particular, they have been continually undermined by prevailing design practices that create repositories of data seemingly begging to be repurposed for new uses. Nissenbaum's (2009) theory of privacy as contextual integrity represents an attempt to situate the construct of purpose limitation within a more dynamic frame; sometimes, changes in data flow threaten important moral values, but not always. Exactly for that reason, however, the theory of contextual integrity does not adequately safeguard the public against moral hazard and self-dealing by those who implement and benefit from surveillance systems.

Together, the constraints of sectoral fidelity and data parsimony offer a more reliable pathway to maintaining prosocial surveillance implementations while resisting certain predictable and predictably harmful forms of mission creep. To begin, a sectoral fidelity constraint enshrined in law (and reaffirmed with adequate and effective public oversight) would represent a much stronger public commitment to limiting surveillance in the interest of social sustainability. So, for example, such a constraint would allow reuse of data collected for public health purposes for new or evolving public health purposes, but it would forbid mission creep from one sector to another – for example, from health to security – even when data are repurposed for a security-related use that otherwise would fall inside the doughnut. Instances of mission creep in which data collected for public health purposes flow out the back door to be used for national security purposes jeopardize the public trust on which public health surveillance needs to rely. Systems of national security surveillance are necessary in complex societies, but they require separate justification and separate forms of process.

Absent reinforcement by a corresponding design constraint, however, a commitment to sectoral fidelity that is expressed purely as a legal prohibition, seems predestined to fail. Because surveillance implementations express, and cannot ever

[3] Regulation 2016/679 of the European Parliament and of the Council of April 27, 2016 on the protection of natural persons with regard to the processing of personal data and on the free movement of such data, and repealing Directive 95/46/EC (General Data Protection Regulation), O.J. (L 119) 1, art. 5(1)(b)–(c).

fully avoid expressing, power differentials, they inevitably present temptations to abuse. Where surveillance is necessary for social sustainability, a requirement of design for data parsimony can work to limit mission creep in ways that legal restrictions alone cannot. So, for example, large-grain surveillance proxies that use hashed, locally stored data for credentialing and authentication might facilitate essential governance functions in privacy protective ways, ensuring access to public services and facilitating access to transit systems without persistent behavioural tracking.

Neither the sectoral fidelity principle nor the data parsimony principle, however, speaks directly to surveillance-based practices that have powerful differential impacts on privileged and unprivileged groups of people living in the digital age. A legitimacy constraint capable of counteracting the extractive drift of such systems needs to be framed in terms of equity and anti-subordination (cf. Viljoen 2021). Some kinds of scoring are inequitable because they entrench patterns of lesser-than treatment, and some kinds of goods ought to be distributed in ways that do not involve scoring at all. For example, as Foohey and Greene (2022) document, tweaks designed to make the consumer credit scoring system more accurate simply entrench its systemic role as a mechanism for perpetuating distributional inequity. Piecemeal prohibitions targeting particular types or uses of data are overwhelmingly likely to inspire workarounds that violate the spirit of the prohibitions and reinforce existing practices – for example, "ban the box" laws prohibiting inquiry about employment applicants' criminal records have engendered other profiling efforts that disparately burden young men of color (Strahilevitz 2008). Under such circumstances, the question for policymakers should be how to restrict both the nature and the overall extent of reliance on scoring and sorting as mechanisms for allocation and pricing. The background presumption of inherent rationality that has attached to credit scoring should give way to comprehensive oversight designed to restore and widen semantic gaps; mandate use of data-parsimonious certifications of eligibility; and encourage creation of alternative allocation mechanisms. Where state-driven surveillance implementations must be deployed to address problems of inclusion, equity should be understood as a non-negotiable first principle constraining every aspect of their design.

The fourth and fifth legitimacy constraints – openness to revision and design for countervailing power – follow from the principle of equity. Training surveillance implementations away from the path of least resistance – that is, away from policies and practices that reinforce historic patterns of injustice and inequity – demands institutional and technical design to resist epistemic closure. Too often, proposed regulatory oversight models for surveillance implementations amount to little more than minor tweaks that, implicitly, take the general contours of those implementations as givens. That sort of epistemic closure is both unwarranted (because it cedes the opportunity to contest the validity of data-driven decisions) and self-defeating (because it disables public-regarding governance from achieving (what ought to be) its purposes). More specifically, since failure modes for surveillance are likely to have data-extractive, racialized, and carceral orientations, accountability mechanisms directed toward rejection of epistemic closure need to be designed with those failure modes in mind.

Like strategies for avoiding surveillance mission creep, strategies for embedding a revisionist and equity-regarding ethic of public accountability within surveillance implementations are both legal and technological. On one hand, honoring the principle of openness to revision requires major reforms to legal regimes that privilege trade secrecy and expert capture of policy processes (Kapczynski 2022; Morten 2023). But surveillance power benefits from technical opacity as well as from secrecy (Burrell 2016), and merely rolling back legal protections for entities that create and operate surveillance implementations still risks naturalizing opaque practices of algorithmic manipulation that ought themselves to be open to question and challenge. An oversight regime designed to resist epistemic closure should mobilize technological capability to create countervailing power wherever surveillance implementations are used. As a relatively simple example, algorithmic processes (that also satisfy the other legitimacy constraints) might be designed to incorporate tamper-proof audit mechanisms designed to open their operation to public oversight. A more complicated example is Mireille Hildebrandt's (2019) proposal for agonistic machine learning – that is, machine learning processes that are designed to interrogate their own assumptions and test alternate scenarios.

12.4 CONCLUSION

The doughnut model for privacy suggests important questions about the appropriate boundaries between surveillance and privacy and about the forms and modalities of legitimate data-driven governance that should inform future research and prescriptive work. Living within the doughnut requires appropriate safeguards against forms of data-driven surveillance that cross the outer perimeter, and it also requires data-driven governance implementations necessary to attain the minimum requirements for human wellbeing. In particular, automated, data-driven processes have important roles to play in the governance of large, complex societies. Ensuring that any particular surveillance implementation remains within the space defined by the doughnut rather than drifting inexorably across the outer perimeter requires subjecting it to additional legitimacy constraints, of which I have offered five – sectoral fidelity, data parsimony, equity, openness to revision, and design for countervailing power. Strategies for bending the arc of surveillance toward the safe and just space for human wellbeing must include both legal and technical components – such as, for example, reliance on surveillance proxies such as credentialing and authentication to facilitate essential governance and allocation functions in data-parsimonious ways. Ultimately, governing complex societies in ways that are sustainable, democratically accountable, and appropriately respectful of human rights and human dignity requires techniques that are appropriately cabined in their scope and ambition, equitable in their impacts, and subject to critical, iterative interrogation and revision by the publics whose futures they influence.

REFERENCES

Ada Lovelace Institute. "International Monitor: Vaccine Passports and COVID Status Apps." *Ada Lovelace Institute*. May 1, 2020. www.adalovelaceinstitute.org/project/international-monitor-vaccine-passports-covid-status-apps/.

Ajunwa, Ifeoma, Kate Crawford, and Jason Schultz. "Limitless Worker Surveillance." *California Law Review* 105 (2017): 735–776.

Allen, Anita. *Why Privacy Isn't Everything: Feminist Reflections on Personal Accountability*. Lanham, MD: Rowman & Littlefield, 2003.

Alstadsaeter, Annette, Niels Johannesen, and Gabriel Zucman. "Tax Evasion and Inequality." *American Economic Review* 109, no. 6 (2019): 2073–2103.

Americans for Financial Reform, Anti-Corruption Data Collective and Public Citizen. "Report: Public Money for Private Equity: Pandemic Relief Went to Companies Backed by Private Equity Titans." *Americans for Financial Reform*, September 15, 2021. https://ourfinancialsecurity.org/2021/09/report-public-money-for-private-equity-cares-act.

Anderssen, Pernille Tangaard, Natasa Loncarevic, Maria B. Damgaard, Mette W. Jacobsen, Farida Bassioni-Stamenic, and Leena E. Karlsson. "Public Health, Surveillance Policies and Actions to Prevent Community Spread of COVID-19 in Denmark, Serbia, and Sweden." *Scandinavian Journal of Public Health* 50, no. 6 (2021): 711–729. https://doi.org/10.1177%2F14034948211056215.

Arendt, Hannah. *The Human Condition*. Chicago: University of Chicago Press, 1958.

Bannon, Alicia, Mitali Nagrecha, and Rebekah Diller. *Criminal Justice Debt: A Barrier to Reentry*. New York: Brennan Center for Justice at New York University School of Law, 2010.

Benjamin, Ruha. *Race after Technology: Abolitionist Tools for the New Jim Code*. New York: Polity Press, 2019.

Bridges, Khiara. *The Poverty of Privacy Rights*. Redwood City, CA: Stanford University Press, 2017.

Browne, Simone. *Dark Matters: On the Surveillance of Blackness*. Durham, NC: Duke University Press, 2017.

Buolamwini, Joy, and Timnit Gebru. "Gender Shades: Intersectional Accuracy Disparities in Commercial Gender Classification." *Proceedings of Machine Learning Research* 81 (2018): 1–15.

Burrell, Jenna. "How the Machine 'Thinks': Understanding Opacity in Machine Learning Algorithms." *Big Data & Society* 3, no. 1 (2016): 1–12.

Chang, Agnes, Amy Qin, Isabelle Qian, and Amy C. Chien. "Under Lockdown in China." *The New York Times*, April 29, 2022. www.nytimes.com/interactive/2022/04/29/world/asia/shanghai-lockdown.html.

Citron, Danielle Keats. *The Fight for Privacy: Protecting Dignity, Identity, and Love in the Digital Age*. New York: W. W. Norton, 2022.

Cohen, Julie E. *Between Truth and Power: The Legal Constructions of Informational Capitalism*. New York: Oxford University Press, 2019a.

Configuring the Networked Self: Law, Code, and the Play of Everyday Practice. New Haven, CT: Yale University Press, 2012.

"Turning Privacy Inside Out." *Theoretical Inquiries in Law* 20, no. 1 (2019b): 1–21.

"What Privacy Is For." *Harvard Law Review* 126 (2013): 1904–1933.

Corvallec, Herve, Alison F. Stowell, and Nils Johansson. "Critiques of the Circular Economy." *Journal of Industrial Ecology* 26, no. 3 (2022): 421–432.

Couldry, Nick, and Ulises A. Mejias. "Data Colonialism: Rethinking Big Data's Relation to the Contemporary Subject." *Television & New Media* 20, no. 4 (2019): 336–349.

"The Decolonial Turn in Data and Technology Research: What Is at Stake and Where Is It Heading?" *Information, Communication & Society* 26, no. 3 (2023): 786–802.

Crawford, Kate. *Atlas of AI: Power, Politics, and the Planetary Costs of Artificial Intelligence*. New Haven, CT: Yale University Press, 2021.

Crootof, Rebecca, Margot E. Kaminski, and W. Nicholson Price. "Humans in the Loop." *Vanderbilt Law Review* 76 (2023): 429–510.

Etzioni, Amitai. *The Limits of Privacy*. New York: Basic Books, 2000.

Eubanks, Virginia. *Automating Inequality: How High-Tech Tools Profile, Police, and Punish the Poor*. New York: Macmillan, 2018.

Farrell, Henry, and Bruce Schneier. "Research Publication No. 2018-7: Common-Knowledge Attacks on Democracy." Berkman Klein Center for Internet & Society at Harvard University. November 17, 2018. https://papers.ssrn.com/sol3/papers.cfm?abstract_id=3273111.

Foohey, Pamela, and Sara S. Greene. "Credit Scoring Duality." *Law and Contemporary Problems* 85, no. 3 (2022): 101–122.

Fourcade, Marian, and Kieran Healy. "Seeing Like a Market." *Socio-Economic Review* 15 (2017): 9–29.

Friant, Martin Callisto, Walter J. V. Vermeulen, and Roberta Salomone. "A Typology of Circular Economy Discourses: Navigating the Diverse Versions of a Contested Paradigm." *Resources, Conservation and Recycling* 161 (2020): 1–19.

Garvie, Clare, Alvaro Bedoya, and Jonathan Frankle. "The Perpetual Lineup: Unregulated Police Face Recognition in America." *Georgetown Center on Privacy & Technology*, 2016. www.perpetuallineup.org/.

Gilliard, Chris. "The Rise of 'Luxury Surveillance.'" *The Atlantic*, October 18, 2022. www.theatlantic.com/technology/archive/2022/10/amazon-tracking-devices-surveillance-state/671772/.

"The Two Faces of the Smart City." *Fast Company*, January 20, 2020. www.fastcompany.com/90453305/the-two-faces-of-the-smart-city.

Gilliom, John. *Overseers of the Poor: Surveillance, Resistance, and the Limits of Privacy*. Chicago: University of Chicago Press, 2001.

Gilman, Michele E. "The Class Differential in Privacy Law." *Brooklyn Law Review* 77, no. 4 (2012): 1389–1445.

Gilman, Michele E., and Rebecca Green. "The Surveillance Gap: The Harms of Extreme Privacy and Data Marginalization." *New York University Review of Law & Social Change* 42 (2018): 253–307.

Global Alliance for Tax Justice. "The State of Tax Justice 2021." *Tax Justice Network*. November 16, 2021. https://taxjustice.net/reports/the-state-of-tax-justice-2021/.

Green, Ben. "The Flaws of Policies Requiring Human Oversight of Government Algorithms." *Computer & Security Review* 45 (2022): 1–22. https://doi.org/10.1016/j.clsr.2022.105681.

Grubaugh, Nathan D., Emma B. Hodcroft, Joseph R. Fauver, Alexandra L. Phelan, and Muge Cevik. "Public Health Actions to Control New SARS-CoV-2 variants." *Cell* 184, no. 5 (2021): 1127–1132.

Guyton, John, Patrick Langetieg, Daniel Reck, Max Risch, and Gabriel Zucman. "Tax Evasion at the Top of the Income Distribution: Theory and Evidence." *National Bureau of Economic Research*, December 2021. www.nber.org/papers/w28542.

Hendl, Tereza, Ryoa Chung, and Verina Wild. "Pandemic Surveillance and Racialized Subpopulations: Mitigating Vulnerabilities in COVID-19 Apps." *Journal of Bioethical Inquiry* 17 (2020): 928–934.

Hicks, Jacqueline. "Digital ID Capitalism: How Emerging Economies Are Reinventing Digital Capitalism." *Contemporary Politics* 26, no. 3 (2020): 330–350.

Hildebrandt, Mireille. "Privacy as Protection of the Incomputable Self: From Agnostic to Agonistic Machine Learning." *Theoretical Inquiries in Law* 20, no. 1 (2019): 83–121.

Hill, Kashmir. "The Secretive Company That Might End Privacy as We Know It." *The New York Times*, January 18, 2020. www.nytimes.com/2020/01/18/technology/clearview-privacy-facial-recognition.html.

Hoffman, Tamar. "Debt and Policing: The Case to Abolish Credit Surveillance." *Georgetown Journal of Poverty Law and Policy* 29, no. 1 (2021): 93–119.

van Hulst, Merlijn, and Dvora Yanow. "From Policy 'Frames' to 'Framing': Theorizing a More Dynamic Approach." *American Review of Public Administration* 46, no. 1 (2016): 92–112.

International Consortium of Investigative Journalists (ICIJ). "Offshore Havens and Hidden Riches of World Leaders and Billionaires Exposed in Unprecedented Leak." *International Consortium of Investigative Journalists*, October 3, 2021. www.icij.org/investigations/pandora-papers/global-investigation-tax-havens-offshore/.

Jackson, Jason, and Aziza Ahmed. "The Public/Private Distinction in Public Health: The Case of COVID-19." *Fordham Law Review* 90, no. 6 (2022): 2541–2559.

Kapczynski, Amy. "The Public History of Trade Secrets." *U.C. Davis Law Review* 55 (2022): 1367–1443.

Kendzior, Sarah. *Hiding in Plain Sight: The Invention of Donald Trump and the Erosion of America*. New York: Flatiron Books, 2020.

Kiel, Paul. "It's Getting Worse: The IRS Now Audits Poor Americans at About the Same Rate as the Top 1%." *ProPublica*, 2019. www.propublica.org/article/irs-now-audits-poor-americans-at-about-the-same-rate-as-the-top-1-percent.

Kumar, Lakshmi, and Kaisa de Bel. "Acres of Money Laundering: Why US Real Estate Is a Kleptocrat's Dream." *Global Financial Integrity*, August 2021. https://gfintegrity.org/acres-of-money-laundering-2021/.

Leiwant, Matthew Harold. "Locked Out: How Algorithmic Tenant Screening Exacerbates the Housing Crisis in the United States." *Georgetown Law Technology Review* 6 (2022): 276–299.

Luukkanen, Jyrki, Jarmo Vehmas, and Jari Kaivo-oja. "Quantification of Doughnut Economy with the Sustainability Window Method: Analysis of Development in Thailand." *Sustainability* 13 (2021): 1–18. https://doi.org/10.3390/su13020847.

McLeod, Allegra. "Envisioning Abolition Democracy." *Harvard Law Review* 132 (2019): 1613–1649.

Milner, Yeshimabeit, and Amy Traub. *Data Capitalism + Algorithmic Racism*. Demos, 2021. www.demos.org/research/data-capitalism-and-algorithmic-racism.

Morgan, Jamelia. "Responding to Abolition Anxieties: A Roadmap for Legal Analysis." *Michigan Law Review* 120 (2022): 1199–1224.

Morten, Christopher J. "Publicizing Corporate Secrets." *University of Pennsylvania Law Review* 170 (2023): 1319–1404.

Murakami Wood, David, ed. *A Report on the Surveillance Society for the Information Commissioner by the Surveillance Studies Network*. London: Mark Siddoway/ Knowledge House, 2006. https://ico.org.uk/media/about-the-ico/documents/1042390/surveillance-society-full-report-2006.pdf.

Nadler, Anthony, Matthew Crain, and Joan Donovan. "Weaponizing the Digital Influence Machine: The Political Perils of Online Ad Tech." *Data & Society*, October 17, 2018. https://datasociety.net/library/weaponizing-the-digital-influence-machine/.

Nissenbaum, Helen. *Privacy in Context*. Stanford: Stanford University Press, 2009.

No Tech for Tyrants and Privacy International. "All Roads Lead to Palantir: A Review of How the Data Analytics Company Has Embedded Itself Throughout the UK." *Privacy International*, October 29, 2020. https://privacyinternational.org/report/4271/all-roads-lead-palantir.

Podkul, Cezary. "How Unemployment Insurance Fraud Exploded during the Pandemic." *ProPublica*, 2021. www.propublica.org/article/how-unemployment-insurance-fraud-exploded-during-the-pandemic.

Poon, Martha. "From New Deal Institutions to Capital Markets: Commercial Consumer Risk Scores and the Making of Subprime Mortgage Finance." *Accounting, Organizations & Society* 34, no. 5 (2009): 654–674.

Post, Robert. "The Social Foundations of Privacy: Community and Self in the Common Law Tort." *California Law Review* 77 (1989): 957–1010.

Raworth, Kate. *Doughnut Economics: 7 Ways to Think Like a 21st Century Economist*. White River Junction, VT: Chelsea Green Publishing, 2017.

Richards, Neil. *Why Privacy Matters*. New York: Oxford University Press, 2021.

Richardson, Rashida, and Amba Kak. "Suspect Development Systems: Databasing Marginality and Enforcing Discipline." *University of Michigan Journal of Law Reform* 55, no. 4 (2022): 813–883.

Rogers, Brishen. *Rethinking the Future of Work: Law, Technology and Economic Citizenship*. Cambridge, MA: MIT Press, 2023.

Roessler, Beate. *The Value of Privacy*. Cambridge, MA: Polity Press, 2005.

Rowe, Elizabeth A. "Regulating Facial Recognition Technology in the Private Sector." *Stanford Technology Law Review* 24 (2020): 1–54.

Rozenshtein, Alan Z. "Digital Disease Surveillance." *American University Law Review* 70 (2021): 1511.

Singh, Ranjit, and Steven J. Jackson. "From Margins to Seams: Imbrication, Inclusion, and Torque in the Aadhaar Identification Project." In *Proceedings of the 2017 Conference on Human Factors in Computing Systems*, 4776–4824. New York: ACM, 2017. https://doi.org/10.1145/3025453.3025910.

Smith, Erin, and Heather Vogell. "How Your Shadow Credit Score Could Decide Whether You Get an Apartment." *ProPublica*, 2022. www.propublica.org/article/how-your-shadow-credit-score-could-decide-whether-you-get-an-apartment.

Solove, Daniel. *Understanding Privacy*. Cambridge, MA: Harvard University Press, 2008.

Steeves, Valerie. "Reclaiming the Social Value of Privacy." In *Lessons from the Identity Trail: Anonymity, Privacy and Identity in a Networked Society*, edited by Ian Kerr, Valerie Steeves, and Carole Lucock, 191–208. New York: Oxford University Press, 2009.

Strahilevitz, Lior J. "Privacy Versus Antidiscrimination." *University of Chicago Law Review* 75, no. 1 (2008): 363–381.

Swire, Peter P. "Financial Privacy and the Theory of High-Tech Government Surveillance." *Washington University Law Quarterly* 77 (1999): 461–512.

Thierer, Adam. *Permissionless Innovation: The Continuing Case for Comprehensive Technological Freedom.* Arlington County, VA: Mercatus Center at George Mason University, 2014.

Traub, Amy. *Discredited: How Employment Credit Checks Keep Qualified Workers out of a Job*. Demos, 2014. www.demos.org/research/discredited-how-employment-credit-checks-keep-qualified-workers-out-job.

Viljoen, Salome. "A Relational Theory of Data Governance." *Yale Law Journal* 131 (2021): 573–654.

Wang, Yuliang, Xiaobo Chen, Feng Wang, Jie Geng, Bingxu Liu, and Feng Han. "Value of Anal Swabs for SARS-COV-2 Detection: A Literature Review." *International Journal of Medical Sciences* 18 (2021): 2389–2393.

Zuboff, Shoshana. *The Age of Surveillance Capitalism: The Fight for a Human Future at the New Frontier of Power*. New York: PublicAffairs, 2019.

Index

www.ingramcontent.com/pod-product-compliance
Lightning Source LLC
LaVergne TN
LVHW091530200926
848483LV00002B/349

* 9 7 8 1 0 0 9 3 8 3 8 7 5 *